The Smallest *of* Miracles

DOUGLAS CARPENTER

The Smallest of Miracles

Printed in the United States of America.
ISBN: 979-8-9941574-0-4

To all who find answers within this book.

TABLE OF CONTENTS

Preface

Life can be likened to a grand symphony. It is most beautiful when each individual instrument plays together in unison. When one or more are out of tune, we cannot reach our full potential.

Self-improvement books can be beneficial, but many tend to focus on tuning one instrument only. Perfecting an orchestra requires taking to heart many overlayed life lessons. Capturing everything in a single book is not possible, but the attempt herein is to tune many of the more important instruments within one's most played sections.

It is easy to look back upon our lives and define them by major milestones. While the day you married might be the significant milestone you remember, it was the decision to go on that first date that holds true importance. The decision by an alcoholic to drive past the bar rather than go in is what makes a difference. The decision to take up smoking, steal, accept a bribe, cheat on taxes, or to not do these things, all become long forgotten and underappreciated moments. It is the path we take when confronted with the small everyday fork in the road choices that result in life altering implications.

It is said truth is stranger than fiction. The story that follows is rooted in many true events. Irrespective, if I have done my job as an author, you will be entertained. If I have done my job as a fellow human being, this book will cause you to reflect, fine-tune your instruments, and bring to the world a more fulfilled you.

AMBUSH

Whether a person is good or evil is determined by what at the time may be believed to be insignificant decisions, and Ted Carrington's path had been determined on a day when he was barely 12 years old. The ultimate result was a man who now, along with Devon, his attorney, drove toward the elementary school he attended as a youth in the 1970s. It was a mistake to presume his sole or even primary purpose was to make a donation that would secure this bankrupt institution's financial future. Ironic how such a beautiful, warm, cloudless day in May could be contrasted so sharply against the storm heading toward that school.

While fiscal salvation was the supposed reason people waited to meet him in the school's office, those sent to precede his arrival knew it to be more complicated. To this forty-nine-year-old man, money had ceased to carry meaning. It was power, influence, and the expression of his unique talents that were his focus.

Playing on words and messing in the lives of people was a habit from his youth he never outgrew. Rather, it was perfected as he increased in wealth and power, morphing over the years into a most favored preoccupation.

Hannibal displayed power through the war elephant. Rommel struck fear with his panzer divisions. This wolf's tack was different, preferring to employ an innocent smile, gentle manners, and a Toyota Corolla as sheep's clothing.

If he'd wanted to be famous, it was easily within reach. But notoriety was a poison he refused to drink, a disease he wanted no part of. There was an art, and he had mastered it, in remaining unseen, unknown, and underappreciated. A snake best lies camouflaged in wait.

He had been asked on more than one occasion which was more important: what you know or who you know? He answered both were important to success, but if you wanted power, real power, then it came down to what you know *about* who you know. Following his own advice, he made it his business to learn as much of the personal information of anyone he was to meet, and today, as evidenced by the three thick folders readied for the meeting, was no exception.

A half hour prior to his arrival, his most trusted assistant, Karen, a middle-aged woman who had served by his side for more than twenty years, back when it was only state senators and governors who stiffened when he entered the room, arrived at the school's office. She warmly greeted those present, making the excuse she had the meeting time wrong. That was unthinkable. Her purpose was to ensure all was to plan and to usher out all except those allowed to be present, a selection from the school of just three.

Robert Wayward was a fit, middle-aged man, six years Ted's senior, with gray hair and black-rimmed glasses that made him seem as though deliberately dressing the part of principal. That morning, wearing his best suit, he discussed the upcoming day with his wife, Linda, over their usual morning cup of coffee.

"Bob, I hate to see you this tense," she commented as she rubbed his shoulders from behind his chair at the breakfast table.

"Once today is over, I'll feel much better. It'll be nice being able to go to work from now on and not have to worry if we still have electricity in the building."

"Is it really that bad?"

"Worse. People know St. Augustine is struggling, but only Sister Margaret, the trustees, and maybe a few others are aware of the whole story. You would think the bill collectors would catch on and stop wasting their stamps sending us notices. I didn't even think we'd be able to graduate the senior class."

"Well, it ends today. You can be nothing but proud. Because of you, the school is back to its number one ranking. Think about that, Bob. The highest-ranked private elementary school, grades K-8, in the entire state of New York. Just like it was forty years ago, and you did it as principal in just seven years. Number one, and it's because of my bear," she said, giving him a hug.

"I should be celebrating all this, but I'm just not feeling it."

"You know what we need? We should go away somewhere. We haven't been away in forever," Linda suggested, looking off, imagining some place she always wanted to go but couldn't name.

"Yeah, and when we got back there wouldn't be a roof over our heads. We're already two mortgage payments behind."

"I could get a second job."

"You already doubled your physical therapist shifts. I wish I earned more."

"Maybe you could charge students for the tutoring you do after school. Couldn't they give you something extra for all that coaching you do on the weekend?"

"No, it doesn't work that way. And I love working with the kids. It's the best part of my job, and it's not even in the description."

"These Catholic schools just don't pay well. We talked about you switching."

"And I decided not to," Bob said as he finished his coffee, glad it was time to leave for work. Any new employer would require a background check, and there are some things people don't want anyone, including their spouses, to know.

Working with Robert was Sister Margaret, the school's treasurer, a nun of the Sisters of Mercy for twenty-three years. Earlier in her life, she had earned a degree in accounting and taken a position with a small construction company after college. It was the collapse of that side of her life that drove her to becoming a nun. Now a soul of fifty-two, she enjoyed her position with the school, allowing her to break from the rigorous routine that comes when one dedicates one's life to Jesus.

There were many things her colleagues didn't know about her. It would have left them shocked if they knew she had given birth to a child who she gave up for adoption. She carried a wound, one that tore a hole in her heart and that remained to this very day. It was that she never got to hold her daughter. All she remembered was a small dollop of black hair on an otherwise bald head as they whisked her away while she was still woozy in the delivery room.

Other much darker secrets dated back to that time, and she'd hoped her misdeeds would be remembered only by and forgiven by God. As anyone who had dealt with Ted knew, he made it his business to know such things too.

Given the meeting's purpose, the presence of the principal and treasurer were understood. The last and only other person requested was the school's guidance counselor, Theresa McDowell. A voluptuous, long-haired blonde of thirty-four who, no matter how conservatively dressed, always turned heads. Although none of the kids listened to a word she said, she usually had the full attention of the male faculty. Neither Robert nor Margaret could understand why on earth she had been invited.

Her presence at such an important meeting made them both nervous as she tended to be unrefined. They also suspected, but could not prove, that she drank. She had surprisingly good credentials for someone who would take a position such as hers. Even with that, they never would have hired her had they been aware of her questionable background—a past that did not fit well with a conservative Catholic school.

She had lived with a much older man during college, he having paid for her education and her, well, providing other things. She had made it standard practice through much of her adult life to use men as suited her needs; it seemed only fair. They had been using her to satisfy themselves from when she had been a much younger age.

After earning her master's in psychology, she turned a new leaf. Marrying a man she genuinely loved, she remained committed to her work and excelled in her personal life and career. She was promoted twice in three years at her social services job and volunteered her time whenever someone was in need. She had authored a book entitled *Deficiencies within the Educational System in Addressing the Emotional Development and Coping Skills of Young People.*

Quite a mouthful, Ted thought as he reviewed the text before the meeting, finding it, in his words, "A most insightful work from a brilliant professional." Things had changed.

It had been five years since the last of any of her accomplishments. The wounds from her early life opened with her younger sister's passing from an overdose, one she tried to prevent but could not help. Heavy drinking preceded numerous terminations from jobs, each one a bounce lower on the pay scale. Withdrawing into a world of liquid coping, she neglected the needs of her husband Ron and two daughters. She promised many times she would change, but it had remained unfulfilled.

"Do you think you could help with the kids this morning, put them on the bus?" Ron asked.

"I have an important meeting I have to get ready for," Theresa replied, applying makeup without turning away from the mirror.

"It's always something. Bad enough you pay no attention to me, but can't you give some to the kids?"

"Don't do this now. I have to get ready."

"Then when? You act like they aren't here. You used to do so much with them. Jeannie asked me last night if you were ever going to take her back to the summer home. She still remembers the time you used to spend with her. What am I supposed to say? They miss you. They want you back in their lives more than anything."

"I'll take them tomorrow."

"You say that every day. There never is a tomorrow. I don't know if I can do this anymore. Maybe I won't be here when you come home."

"Maybe I won't either. I can do a lot better than you."

"You may have to," Ron replied as he went down the stairs.

"Come on. Mommy says she's not feeling well. I'll take you," he said as he closed the front door.

"Mommy never feels well," she heard Jeannie respond through the window from outside.

Theresa breathed a sigh of relief and then put her face into her hands, careful not to smear the makeup she had been applying for the past half hour. Her hands were trembling, not from the conversation or the upcoming meeting, but because she hadn't had a drink yet this morning.

Listening for a sound that might give away her husband had returned, she reached behind the credenza, pulled out a three-ounce bottle of Smirnoff and drank the remaining half. Grabbing her keys, she blew a kiss to herself in the mirror and headed out the door.

The opportunity to gain the attention of a man like Ted appealed to her like a flame to a moth. She could not help but fantasize about her life if she were to wrap a man like him around her finger. Today she selected a short skirt and tight blouse, conveniently leaving the top three buttons open.

On sight, Robert's reaction was disgust, yet a part of him refused to look away.

Sister Margaret stopped midsentence to comment. "Do you really think that's appropriate?"

"It's hot out today. I didn't have anything else ready."

One can only imagine the comment Sister Margaret would have made had she known there was nothing on under the skirt. Theresa sometimes dressed in this manner to give herself a feeling of power and figured no one would know if she kept her legs crossed and didn't have to pick anything off the floor.

Before the meeting, all three had made their own attempts to look up information about Ted online, ever since the donation had been divulged discretely two weeks before. They found it surprising that a man of such supposed power and wealth could exist without a trace of who he was or, perhaps, pretended to be.

The only other place to go were his school records, which were in a box that had to be pulled from archives. Theresa and Robert had reviewed what little was available the previous day, and it raised more concerns than answers. He had maintained his grades around a C average throughout, except for an unexplained rise to straight As at the end of seventh grade. Comments from his teachers were sparse but the common theme was that he had not been working to his potential. The words *belligerent*, *inattentive*, *lazy*, and *genius* appeared liberally, sometimes all within the same sentence.

His fifth-grade teacher had commented that he appeared to be "an adult trapped in a child." He had been in the principal's office for disciplinary reasons an extraordinary number of times but only the number of detentions were given rather than the reasons. He had served as an altar boy beginning in the sixth grade, and some incident almost resulted in his expulsion. If there existed an explanation, it could not be found as they sorted through the material.

Theresa speculated. "He's probably one of those undisciplined, spoiled, rich brats."

Robert added, "Not true. When it was suggested I call him about our situation—"

At that moment, they stumbled upon the results of an IQ test administered in fifth grade. This was the kind of information Theresa found most interesting, and she pulled it from Robert's hands to review by herself.

"What does it say?" Robert asked as she scanned the page.

She lightly shook her head and replied with one word. "Wow."

In the twenty minutes after Karen arrived, through hints, facial expressions, innuendoes, and finally the direct approach, she whittled those present down to just the three and herself. As soon as the last of the uninvited left, she took it upon herself to hang a preprinted Private Meeting sign on the office door and closed it.

Curious, Robert asked, "What do you think we can expect?"

"I assure you this is a day you will never forget," she said and took a seat as though a member of an audience waiting for a show to begin. The only thing that seemed missing was a bucket of popcorn.

"Any advice?" Robert asked, hoping to get just a bit of color from Karen.

"Listen carefully and see what you can learn."

At ten minutes till, all eyes except Karen's fixed to the door as they heard the knob turn. A man in his early twenties, looking as though he were in high school instead of a college graduate, walked through.

"John, you're late," Karen snapped at the new arrival.

"He's not even here yet," John retorted.

Karen shook her head.

John countered, "Besides, what is there for me to do? I'm here to observe."

"It's called training, and you're supposed to be helping me."

"I see you hung a sign on the door. Got it. Hi, I'm John," he said, holding his hand out to Robert.

John, a recent hire, just out of college and barely six months into employment, was nothing like Karen. Ted liked to groom new graduates before they became tainted by the regimented thinking of the world and usually did an excellent job of it. Karen and Devon were examples. John, however, had been a disappointment. Unpolished, unprofessional and like so many, he talked too much and accomplished too little.

Devon recommended his termination, but Ted wanted to see him in action. Today was to be the first time he would attend such a meeting. Like rumors of Bigfoot, John had only heard of the things Ted, a man who could make or destroy a person with little more than a phone call, would do in these type meetings.

Ted had one chief rival, an archenemy, a man named Ben Arlington. The two continually countered and sabotaged each other's business deals. Word was they could not comment about the weather without arguing. John had pictured Ben as a hulking figure, but when they'd met two weeks prior, at the end of an arduous job-interview process, John found Ben to be surprisingly smaller than Ted's six-foot, two-inch height.

Ted was generous with compensation and had even bought John a Mercedes as a sign-on bonus. He liked to believe that it's never lonely at the top if you bring enough people with you. John however, hoping to do better, had approached Ben with a tempting offer.

It is incredible how much damaging information can fit onto a flash drive. Having broken into Ted's servers, he held information priceless to Ben. Texting back and forth all morning with Ben's head of HR, all that was left was to make his hiring official.

Now, if Ted beat Ben's offer, he might be dissuaded. He needed a demonstration of his ruthlessness to ensure Ted understood how serious this situation was. He, too, believed he knew Robert's secrets and was preparing a surprise for him of his own.

As they sat in the office the final minutes before Ted's arrival, Robert tried again to probe Karen for information.

"So, Karen, I couldn't find out much about him. What is he like?"

She wished people would ask easier questions by comparison, like the mathematical formulas for quantum mechanics. How was she to describe the personality and quirks inherent to a super intelligent man afflicted with Asperger's?

"Let's just say he's an experience," she stated, being reasonably accurate.

Rebuffed, Robert changed his approach. "Well, we're quite proud of alumni like that. Do you think the school had anything to do with it?"

John was tempted to take the bait but remained silent, instead scanning Robert with his eyes, wondering what his boss was going to do to this man. A week prior, a single page regarding Robert had been left on the photocopier. John read it and assumed the rest. Believing what Robert had done to children, he had no doubt that Ted would destroy him, but being an artist in such matters, the real question was how. John's own plan against Robert was already in motion, and he hoped to unveil it before Ted's coup de grace.

Theresa, also wanting information, was more direct and fired at Karen. "What does he do? How did he make his money? Was it an inheritance?"

John jumped at the chance to answer this beautiful woman and offered from his limited knowledge. the information he had.

"I don't know about an inheritance. I think in the early days Ted did it all through investing in stocks. I've never seen anything like it. It seems he's always several steps ahead of the market. These days, he buys and sells entire companies. He is an inventor and, as well, funds research."

"John, be quiet" Karen scolded.

"Tell you one thing, whatever the size of his donation here today, he'll still have more money tonight than he did this morning." John added.

"John, shut up!" Karen snapped.

Karen, an expert at diverting topics of conversation, next, did just that.

"Ted has an extraordinary ability to say things that make no sense at the time but do later. He'd deny it, but I believe he is more of a philosopher than anything else. My favorite saying of his is that "a single piece of information can change the understanding of anything."

Staring up at the clock, she observed, "If that time is correct, he should be here in five minutes, thirty seconds. Devon will be with him. He's the attorney. I know he intends to spend time with each of you. We will close out the day with the speech you want him to give the senior class."

"When do you think he'll sign the paperwork? I'm only asking because, quite frankly, I can't guarantee the electricity will stay on," Robert inquired.

"Well, I know he likes a captive audience, so I'm guessing not before end of day."

At precisely two minutes to the hour, Robert glanced out the window to see a car pull up. It was not the kind he had expected.

"That's them," Karen proclaimed.

"Oh, I didn't realize he was..." His voice trailed off as Karen walked up behind him.

"Black?" Karen inquired.

"Well, no, yeah, you know, the students back then, well, they were mostly Irish, Italian, and German."

"Well, that's Devon. Ted was the one driving," Karen stated.

"He owns a Corolla?"

"Owns it? Maybe. I'm not sure if it's paid off," Karen said, fighting to maintain a serious expression. Offering a piece of philosophy, a habit picked up from Ted, she added, "Robert, it's healthy to put aside your preconceived notions now and then."

Knowing they would be in the office momentarily, all stood while Karen moved to the door. Robert wondered what his handshake might be like. Sister Margaret, if he was a man of faith. Theresa, what her life would have been like had she landed a man like him. None of them would be wasting thoughts on any of it had they understood what was really coming through the door.

* * *

Entering the school and turning to the office, Ted hesitated and motioned for Devon to pause.

"Wait a moment. We're forty-five seconds early," Ted noted, looking at his watch, a Citizen Skyhawk, chosen not because of its style but because of its reputation as being one of the most accurate in the world.

Devon had long given up trying to reason with Ted's anal retentiveness.

Standing at attention in his black suit and pressed, white shirt, Ted repeatedly straightened his already perfectly aligned tie. He paused to take a slow breath.

"The last time I walked through this door, there was a dagger in my heart. Now I hold the daggers," Ted commented, slightly elevating the folders in his hand.

"Try to be personable," Devon responded. "Remember your own words. It's easier to manipulate people when they like you. And you might want to smile."

"How's that?" Ted asked, forcing the corner of his lips upward.

"Eh."

"How about now?" he asked again, trying harder to make it seem natural.

"Much better. You ready?"

"Three, two, one." Ted counted down, looking at his watch and wondering if at this time tomorrow in what condition his three targets would be.

With a nod, Devon opened the door, ending the anticipation that had lingered like a fog in the office air since the car pulled up.

Having a look at him, Robert saw someone projecting power, yet within was something gentle. Sister Margaret saw a man of determination with an innocence about him. Theresa, wealth masking vulnerability. Whichever was correct depended upon the angle of view.

Ignoring all, his eyes first darted across the room, instantly evaluating every picture, item, even the placement of furniture. Finally breaking his gaze, he turned to give Karen a hug.

"Armani suit today. Matching tie. Tell your wife she did a nice job," she joked, with only Ted and Devon understanding the inference.

As Ted had no fashion concept, if anything matched, it was only luck or because his wife had picked it out for him. She was often the only reason he would leave the house wearing shoes from the same pair.

"I was asked to speak to the graduating class, so I'm dressing the part," Ted replied. "Now please be so kind as to introduce who's who." Of course, he was only pretending he didn't already know.

Sister Margaret, introduced first, shook his hand and began. "We really appreciate what you are doing for us. You are a good man."

"Let's not jump to conclusions. There is no way you would have enough information to make such a determination. You, Sister, twenty-three years as a devoted nun, and your background, I believe I have enough to reach a conclusion."

Her face went a little pale.

"You know how long I have been a nun?"

"I know much about you."

"How far back do you go? Did you know I grew up in Billings, Montana?"

"Billings, yes. It says that on your Facebook page."

Karen always knew the right moment to interrupt and moved the attention to Theresa.

"My goodness, look at you," Ted stated, pausing for a moment before breaking his uncomfortable gaze. "I read your book."

"Oh that. I think it sold like five copies."

"It is impressive work."

"I think you are the only person to ever say that to me."

"What was it you wrote? Children go to school and are taught facts, learn to think, and yet the most important subject is absent from the curriculum. You then devote three chapters pointing out that lack of emotional development, ignoring how to cope is the greatest flaw in the educational system. You published that book seven years and four months ago. Have you expanded on the concepts at all? Any follow-up?"

"No, that was it."

"Did things get in the way? Or rather did you lose your way?"

Before she could answer he turned to Robert. Ted's face lit up. He reached out, grabbed Robert's hand, and pulled him in. He shook for several seconds before reaching out with his other hand to clutch his forearm, then shook even more.

"So, you are Robert. *You* are Robert," Ted gushed as if he were meeting a celebrity. "Your programs here are incredible. Evolutionary-based learning. This school is the top school in the state again because of him." He turned to the others. "His methods are amazing. He has older students tutor the younger grades. He incorporates the five senses into learning. Diffusers add scents into the classrooms to associate a distinct smell with each subject. He makes learning as hands-on as possible! Your methods can't just stay at this school. You know that, right?"

Robert appeared embarrassed by the extra attention but thankfully Sister Margaret chimed in. "I think I speak for everyone when I say how grateful we all are to you."

"Well, you know the verse: to whom much is given much is expected."

"I realize you are wealthy, but the amount is so generous."

"I wasn't referring to wealth. How one gives is more meaningful than how much."

Sister Margaret missed the hint.

For his own amusement he decided to add another piece to the puzzle. "Besides, my fiftieth birthday is just around the corner, and I have a significant meeting I've been preparing for practically all my life."

Margaret wondered if perhaps he wasn't well. A terminal illness could explain such generosity. Again, she was wrong.

"When do you think you might complete the donation?" Sister Margaret asked, trying not to be too forward but wanting it to end. "Every ring of the phone you are hearing is more than likely a bill collector."

"Well, you can start to take care of it now."

Ted was referring to a $1 million advance he had wired into the school's operating account first thing that morning. He incorrectly assumed she was aware.

"I'll sign the paperwork later, and I'll address the senior class last. In the meantime, I would like us to get to know each other better."

"Yes, I guess that gives us time to kill," Robert noted.

"Time is not what I'm here to kill," Ted replied with cold eyes.

He then eyed the private back room connected to the school office. In his day, parents sometimes met with the principal in that room, but it was strictly off limits as a student. He felt a tinge of victory as he laid claim to it for the day and, just to observe proper etiquette, asked Robert if he could use it. Devon began setting up before he had finished the request.

Curiosity was getting the better of Theresa. Given the car he drove, missing confirmation of his position in the world, and even his grades, she wanted to clarify a few things by formulating a question, she thought cunning.

"What is it like to be Ted Carrington? Were you born into money?"

Robert closed his eyes and made a wish. He saw it wasn't answered when they reopened, and Theresa was still there.

"If you are asking what it's like to be wealthy, in some ways, it's similar to taking a vow of poverty. Not needing to think about money provides freedom. I find it brings out people's true natures. Sometimes that's good, but usually not. Money will never make you a better person, but it can definitely make you worse."

"And born into money? I wasn't even born with a name. I remember it, though. I remember the actual day I became Ted Carrington."

Each ventured a guess.

"Is that when you made your first million?"

"Were you born again?"

"Did you change your name?"

"No," Ted responded. The explanation was more complicated.

A Garden Begins With A Seed

1966

The infant, barely a day old, lay in an incubator in the corner of a neonatal ICU in a hospital in Toronto. He had been found in a church and transferred, arriving in a place considered best at dealing with such cases. Although care of premature births had come a long way in the preceding decades, infants such as this in the 1960s only had a small chance of survival.

"Pray hard for this one," the nurse requested of Sister Kathleen, an elderly nun who had come to complete paperwork regarding the fragile boy clinging to life.

If he was to survive, his adoption would be overseen by Catholic Charities. The nun had been summoned, as she had many times for others, to initiate the process. It hurt to see babies on the ward, knowing she would never experience the joy of motherhood. However, she always went to the nursery to look at the baby she had been assigned.

He was by far the tiniest. He was hooked to tubes and connected to earth by wires, and an IV slowly dripped into his small body. His cry was little more than a raspy yelp.

Each breath took monumental effort. She immediately offered a prayer before asking one of the nurses his prognosis.

"We'll have to see. He's stable now, but we can't be sure he'll make it through the night."

She had many things to tend to back at the parish, but all felt distant and unimportant. She pulled up a chair and sat beside him, first whispering prayers through the walls of the incubator, then softly humming a nursery rhyme.

"God loves you, little...," she said before it dawned on her she didn't know his name. "Let's see who you are." She added as she took hold of the small blue card taped to the side of the incubator.

Where his name should have been it read, "Abandoned."

"Sweet Jesus, you don't even have a name," she murmured as her eyes filled with water, and her heart broke. She quickly composed herself. "We have to get you baptized right away. And you need a name."

She excused herself to make a phone call to the parish rectory, requesting one of the priests come immediately. She returned with a pen in hand. He could not be baptized without a name. She sat thinking, tapping the pen against her palm before it came to her. On the card, she wrote Theodore. In Greek, her native tongue, it meant "Divine Gift."

Amid an array of medical procedures, the priest came, and Theodore was baptized that evening. Without the fanfare typical of such events, the sacrament was brief, with a few drops of water poured onto his incubator rather than his forehead.

"There's no one with him. He can't be alone. Not tonight. Would it be all right if I stay?" Sister Kathleen pleaded.

It was against the rules, but no one was going to refuse the request. She settled into the chair next to his incubator and, for hours, rubbed the glass as though it were his small chest, whispering prayers and encouragement.

"Good. That was a nice breath. Now take another one. Good."

It was sometime around four in the morning that she fell asleep and one of the nurses covered her with a blanket. She awoke with a start just as the shifts were changing and, eyes filled with fear, glanced at the incubator. She would not have been able to forgive herself if something had happened and she had not been there for him.

"Teddy made it through the night. So far so good," the nurse noted, surprising her, very pleasantly, that they had adopted his name.

She went back to the parish to attend morning mass, pray, then ignored her many responsibilities to return to the hospital to be with Ted. She bought a small teddy bear at the gift shop and placed it beside the incubator. She also had with her a stack of children's books.

"If this is his last day, I want to make it as special as I can," she replied to the nurse who questioned why she had brought so many.

For fourteen hours, she lavished attention on him and then went home, only to return a few hours later. As fate and medical science would have it, it was not his last day. There were more that followed and more after that. Sister Kathleen became a fixture in the neonatal ICU, treating him as though he were her own.

She was there when he spiked a fever. She allowed him to wrap his hand around her pinky when he was taken from the incubator to receive injections. She was there when they took the tape off his eyelids on the day he was ready to see the world. She was part of the celebration at each milestone in his development.

"You missed Sunday worship again," one of the nuns noted in surprise after she had spent another full Sunday with Ted.

"My dear, God's work is God's will."

Days passed in a blur, ultimately leading to the inevitable. Ted had been gaining strength, the complications had ceased, and he was moved to the nursery.

"There he is, doing great," the nurse in the infant ward observed. "They told us about you. You are a legend around here. Would you like to feed him?"

"More than anything!" she exclaimed, her excitement unhidden.

"You have the magic touch. He doesn't eat for us like that," the nurse observed as he gulped down a bottle of formula held by Kathleen's hand.

As happy as it made her, she knew this meant their time together was coming to an end. She could not believe three months had passed so swiftly. Just days later, a foster family was arranged. Her heart was heavy as they spent their last hour together but also filled with profound joy that this day had come at all.

Just before turning him over, she asked to be alone for a minute so she could say goodbye.

"I will pray for you every day that I have left, and when the Lord takes me, I will look down on you after that. I bless you Theodore, Divine Gift, you are not like any other. Use it for the goodness of God."

She left the hospital despondent after giving him one final kiss. Returning to the parish, finding the church empty, she knelt directly in front of the altar. There she dropped her head into her clasped hands and openly wept. She questioned the cruelty of a God who would tease her with motherhood in such a way. But as she prayed, she could sense a presence that covered her in the feeling of a warm embrace. Her perception changed.

Had she chosen to live her life in any other way, she would not have been there for Ted. She could not help but believe she had made the critical difference. She served as his mother in his greatest time of need and even had the honor of naming him. She now realized, after years of devotion, this had been God's way of thanking her.

She left the church a bit consoled and returned to the convent. There she was greeted by her fellow nuns with a cake and a round of applause.

Ted would never again be with the person he assumed, as much as an infant can, had been his mother. The only possession taken with him from the hospital was the name she had given him. Now he needed one more.

Baptism

Spring 1968

A pregnancy test usually ushers in news a child is on the way, not a phone call to a home in Queens, New York. Joseph Carrington, a sergeant with the New York City police department, and his wife Annette, a homemaker, had long and eagerly awaited the call. Paperwork moved much slower in the '60s, and Ted was four months past the age of two before the process was completed. Now Joe and Annette needed to get themselves to Toronto to receive their new son.

The transfer from his foster family to his new life took less than an hour.

Dropped off at their hotel room by the social worker, she remained only long enough to ensure all was okay. Nothing was in Ted's world. Curiously, he looked over the two adults before him. Joe well-built, muscular, with black hair and green eyes, and at six two, he looked enormous to Ted's eyes. Annette was a slight woman, a full foot shorter than Joe, with a high voice and long brown hair.

While they gushed over him, the affection was unreturned. He spent much of the drive to New York toward his new life either sleeping or gazing out the window, not comprehending the permanency of the day's event.

Annette flipped through the paperwork as they drove. It mentioned he had a condition commonly known as pigeon toe, which made him a little unsteady on his feet. They suspected he also was slightly asthmatic, a likely leftover from his premature birth.

Annette was concerned, if not horrified. She had expected a perfect child.

"I wanted a healthy child, not some freak they couldn't get rid of!" she screamed at Joe. Joe eventually succeeded in convincing her it likely wasn't serious. A pediatrician confirmed it the next day.

Before the adoption, Joe and Annette had planned a trip to Florida. The agency thought it a great opportunity to bond and encouraged them not to cancel it. All had it wrong. On the long drive down, Ted went on a hunger strike. The entire thirty-hour trip, not a single morsel. Once there, they went to an amusement park, and he refused to go on any of the rides. They visited a zoo, and he refused to walk. At a puppet show, he hid his eyes. Hugs were met with a struggle to get free. Every attempted kiss resulted in him pushing at their face.

"You dirty dishrags!" he screamed, using a two-year-old's equivalent of the F bomb when they told him they would be spending a long time in the car as they packed for the return trip. Annette had been frustrated, but Joe was devastated.

"I don't know what to do," he said to Annette. "I can't make him love me. What if he never accepts me?"

At the halfway point to New York, they checked into a motel in South Carolina. Joe brought Ted to the motel's pool and settled on a chair a few feet from the diving board. A man was getting ready to jump, and Ted seemed interested. Joe picked him up so he could get a better view.

It was at this moment that events came crashing down, and something inside snapped. Ted began hysterically screaming to be put down, and when it didn't happen, he revolted. As his terrified panicked mind searched for a way out, he decided to do something taught to him in his foster home. It was a thing they had told him to do only in a most desperate situation. He began to scream, "Help me! Help me! This is not my father! This is not my father!"

How understandable the words were to a stranger was debatable, but to Ted, they were unquestionably clear. For Joe, who had spent the entirety of the week doing everything he could to form a bond with Ted, it was enough to cause his heart to fall to the pavement.

In a panic, Ted began swinging his arms and legs wildly in every direction, contacting whatever was in reach. His mind disconnected from reality, and his response became as though he were in death throes while being stabbed.

This large man had many times wrestled hardened criminals to the ground. He had been trained in martial arts. He fought out of trenches in two wars. None of that provided any ability to control the full-blown tantrum of a two-year-old. All he could do was maintain his grip and descend toward the cushion covering the chair to carefully place his new son into the middle. This left him to deal with the embarrassment that a man of his size could not control a child and nurse the deep wounds caused by the rejection he had once again received.

Ted, realizing his freedom, jumped from the chair to the opposite side. As if chased by a lion, he ran for what he viewed as the safety of the pool. Joe was just a half step behind when his foot hit the water. He never expected to disappear beneath the surface.

He dropped deep enough for every hair on his head to go under. A large hand grabbed his arm, and an instant later, he was above the surface choking on water that had already invaded his lungs. He was greeted by the softest and most loving embrace.

A basic instinct took hold. The one that tells us when we are truly loved. It triggers an emotional response from the heart so powerful it overrides everything in the brain. It was right then that Ted understood this man loved him.

Why he would love him, he had not the slightest clue, but realization of this new fact changed everything. He looked up at the man holding him so differently now than just a minute before. No longer just a recognizable stranger, this man was his father.

It did not matter what documents said or how any judge ruled. Bathed in the rays of a warm July sun, poolside at an ordinary motel, in the arms of a man who loved him, Ted transformed from "Abandoned" into Theodore Carrington. Wrapping his arms around his father's chest as far as they would reach, Ted buried his face into his broad shoulder and cried as furiously hard as his lungs would permit.

SUNFLOWERS

Present Day

Sitting in a chair in the office, an expression like that of a wounded child enveloped his face. Few could have been more surprised than Devon and Karen. Working with him for more than a decade, they could never recall a display of any emotion beyond an insincere smile or, very occasionally, a genuine one.

"My first two years were in foster care. Then I was adopted." He looked to the floor, his mind in a different time and place. "The sun was shining. I was in my father's arms. It was at that moment I became Ted Carrington."

A silence fell across the office until Sister Margaret, driven by curiosity spurred by her own circumstances, broke it.

"Did you find it difficult being adopted? I mean, did it bother you at all?"

"Traumatic events can be tough on kids. I'll tell you, though, the best tonic, the magic cure-all, is simply for parents to spend time with them. Lots of time."

* * *

Anyone who knew Ted's mom might disagree with that. They argued constantly and mostly because his mother's straw didn't quite reach the bottom of the glass. She had several, shall we call them, quirks, intertwined into obsessive-compulsive tendencies. She loved him dearly and would have done anything for him. The problem was she had some odd traits beyond her control.

Following the adoption, Ted suffered recurring nightmares. All revolved around the theme of being taken away. The worst found him sitting in his room. The lights would go out suddenly, then illuminated by flashes of lightning. There standing at the window, visible in one of those flashes, was a man in a ski mask. Next the glass would shatter, and he'd be grabbed and pulled out.

The image would be interrupted by a bloodcurdling scream as he awoke. His mother had a visceral reaction to his midnight ruckus and would spank him each time. "You'll wake up the whole neighborhood!" In time he adapted by covering his mouth with his hand the instant he was consciously aware it was happening. By the time he was five, the nightmares had ceased.

His new home could have been the envy of any museum curator, everything always obsessively neat and clean. Christmas morning, his mother would stand behind him waiting for him to hand her all the pieces of wrapping paper. They were immediately placed into a trash bag to avoid the creation of a momentary mess.

Dinner was served at 6:00 p.m. Heaven forbid Ted was not sitting and ready at the table as whatever it was came out of the oven. If not, a lecture on how dinner was ruined followed, sometimes capped off with the entire meal being tossed into the garbage.

Anything from Ted's past had to be disposed of, lest it attract dirt and bugs. He'd stop playing with a toy for a few weeks only to find it missing, his mother trying to convince him he must have somehow thrown it out. Books once read, school records, arts and crafts, everything, all gone. It was as though there were gremlins following him around, doing all they could, and succeeding, in erasing all traces of his existence.

Her behavior outside the home could be downright bizarre. Ted thought the worst was when she ran into someone handicapped at a store.

"Oh my God, look at them! They have to live like that!" she'd shout.

Even from a young age, Ted would try his best to divert her away or get her to stop.

"They can hear you," he'd loudly whisper.

"No, they can't. And even if they can, they can't understand me."

"I sit on more brains than you have in your head, lady," a man in a wheelchair once responded. Six-year-old Ted laughed for an hour despite his mom screaming at him for finding it amusing.

Most kids learn dirty words from their peers. Ted picked up his from his mother behind the wheel of the car.

"You stupid moron! Go s—t in your hat!" Whatever that was supposed to mean.

She'd scream with the windows closed, usually with a cigarette hanging from her mouth. The smoke exacerbated Ted's asthmatic condition and would cause him to choke. This was concluded with a pounding of the horn at whichever driver had cut her off.

Receiving the finger, she would respond, "Go to hell you son of a bitch!"

"Mom, I'm the only one who can hear you," a surprisingly relaxed seven-year-old Ted would call out from the back seat.

Such was the everyday of Ted's life. Something would happen, his mother would fly off the handle, and he'd be the one to calm her down.

By the age of eight, he had become a master at hiding emotions. Painted on his face, never leaving, was a dull smile. His answer to any question about how he was feeling was always the same. "Fine." Ted was always smiling and fine. At least on the surface.

There was only one thing, and it might be considered silly, but it truly got under his skin. Oddly, it was his love of mammoth sunflowers.

Large and bright, these beauties stood tall above everything. They provided shelter and food for insects and squirrels. The seeds could be a snack. Sunflowers were like having a party in the garden. Ted loved sunflowers.

Oversized and ugly, they took over the garden. They attracted bugs and rodents. The shells from the seeds made a mess. Sunflowers were an imposter in the garden. His mother hated sunflowers.

Every spring the battle was on. He'd manage to get his hands on some seeds and plant them throughout the yard. While Ted was at school his mother would hunt for them and rip every last one from the ground. She'd blame squirrels, drought, neighborhood cats, anything to shift the blame. Year after year, Ted tried in vain to grow even one.

* * *

"I meant do you ever think about your mother? Your birth mother?" Margaret continued.

"Are you sure that is really what you wanted to ask?"

"How do you mean?"

"The answer is yes or no. How much is that telling you? I think what you meant to ask is how do I feel about her?"

"Yes, I suppose that was it."

"But you camouflage the question. Curious. I have always found what people say vastly less interesting than why. I will be happy to answer but now is not the time."

"I just thought of something," Theresa interrupted. "The yearbooks. We have every year, all the way back. We should get yours."

"That's a great idea. You have it here?"

"No, they are in my office. I don't know why I didn't think of it before."

"We'll get it later. I need to review the contract, so let's not worry about it right now."

"By the way, Ted," Robert interjected, "I have something for you. Would it be okay to give it to you now?"

"I thought it was made clear I do not accept gifts."

"This isn't a gift. This is a message."

CHAINS

Robert disappeared into his office and emerged with a small white square box. Tied around it was a white satin ribbon.

Ted's mouth fell open. "No way. That can't possibly be."

"It's not to keep. She wants it back, but she wanted you to know she still has it. She even kept the box and ribbon you gave it to her in. She said that day you changed her life. She happened to recommend me for the job here. She is the reason I contacted you. When she found out the school was in desperate trouble, she said call Ted Carrington. If anyone made it big it would be him."

Ted took the box from his hand. He looked to Karen, then Devon, without words trying to offer some explanation that he could not grasp. He took hold of one end of the bow, gave it a tug, and then took off the lid.

Reaching in, he pulled from it a beautiful gold necklace with a red rose pendant and held it up high to observe. Amazed at the sight but horrified at what it implied, he had a question for Robert.

"How is it that you know her?"

Robert shuddered. Why would that be important? Unless he suspected the worst. Despite the risk, he clarified.

"She was my younger foster sister for a couple of years. We lived with other foster children. There were a bunch of us."

Ted possessed a superhuman ability to hold his emotions. Karen wondered what it could be when his face turned alabaster, and it appeared he was having difficulty breathing.

"How old was she at the time? How old were you when she was your sister?" Ted struggled to ask.

"Foster sister, you mean. I don't know. I was there first. She came later. When she was around five. I was maybe nine or ten, until I was twelve. We were split very abruptly."

The answer Ted most feared had been given, and he collapsed into the chair behind him. His face went blank, eyes turning to the ceiling, staring off as though it were a hundred miles away.

Then came the unthinkable. Tears began to roll down Ted's face. He buried his head in his hands. Karen would not have been more surprised had the four horsemen of the apocalypse strode past the window.

Devon quickly disappeared into the private office. The others just looked away uncomfortably. Karen, the master she was, suggested Ted show her around the school. Ted readily agreed.

Robert had not expected the exchange to go this way. Knowing now what he was sure Ted must know, life as he knew may have just ended.

REFLECTIONS

"You want to talk about it?" Karen asked as soon as they left.

"Thought I was showing you around."

"We can do that too. I wouldn't mind seeing the cathedral if you want a place to start."

"I'm so ashamed of my behavior. How I treated her. There are times I hate that God made me a snake."

"I assume you are talking about when you were here?"

"Yeah, there are things you don't know. And now I wish I didn't know."

"You're making the mistake you point out to others. You are measuring the behavior of a child using the standards of an adult."

"I know you're right, but it doesn't make it any easier," he responded just as they completed the short walk to a side door that opened to the church.

"Wow, this is enormous," she commented.

One of the largest in the state, the cathedral's inverted V-shaped ceiling and ornate chandeliers were suspended on fifty-foot-long chains ending twenty feet over the long rows of tan pews. Statues of saints larger than life adorned the length of the wall on one side. On the other wall, stained glass windows ten feet wide by twenty-five feet tall depicted such biblical scenes as Mary's ascension to heaven and St. Paul speaking to followers. In the daytime, the windows bathed the inside of the cathedral in a reddish-orange hue.

"It can seat about nine hundred uncomfortable worshipers. Those pews are murder. Looks like they added air conditioning since I served here."

"You were an altar server here?"

"Yeah. Back then it was just boys, though. I'll be giving a speech to the senior class here later. That's why the seats are set up beside the altar. It's for our friends in the office. Although after I am through with them, I doubt they'll be attending."

With that, they left and the tour continued. A school is a school, and there isn't much to see other than classrooms and hallways. The school never had a formal auditorium and used a large open room in the basement for everything. With long rows of tables, it was the cafeteria. Set chairs in rows, it became an auditorium. Projects affixed to the walls, it was an exhibition hall. Keep it wide open, a dance floor. Add an altar, it became a makeshift church. Just like people, what it was perceived to be depended upon how it was presented.

He looked over students sitting there and thought of the speech he was to give at the end of the day to the graduating class. They wanted him to speak to them of success, and at this moment, he had no idea what to say. As he headed back to the office, he stumbled upon a sight he had nearly forgotten.

"The mirror! It's still here!" Ted shouted, referring to a six-foot-wide floor-to-ceiling mirror on a wall facing the front entrance. Back in his day, the kids would give themselves a quick glance to see that shirts or skirts, and in Ted's case, his tie, were all in order as they came in from the schoolyard.

"I don't believe it. It's the same one. When I was in first grade, our teacher lined us up right here. She had each of us in turn stand in front of this mirror, point to ourselves, and say, 'I am the most special person in the world.'"

"I was the only one. I was the only one who refused to say it. Just stood in silence staring at my reflection. She got so mad at me. I never behaved the way other kids did, and she thought it was just more belligerence. She didn't understand. I didn't want to say it because I was convinced all the other kids would laugh at me. That refusal earned me a week of having to wash the chalkboards. The truth she didn't comprehend is that I could not think of anything more preposterous than saying those words about myself."

"I bet you would have no trouble now," Karen chided.

"Well, let's see," Ted said, accepting the challenge but immediately regretting it the moment his eyes fell upon his reflection.

That began an obsessive effort to straighten his tie. He moved it the tiniest bit one way, then another trying to fix imperfections only he could see. Time seemed to warp as he waited for the words to come. He was there. He was back as a six-year-old. So vivid in his mind he could feel the presence of his classmates lined up on both sides, just waiting for the moment to laugh at him.

"You want to know something, Karen" he began. "One of the most difficult things about growing up is discovering all the things you cannot do. Realizing all the ways other people are better. You see a champion on TV. They are the best at whatever it is they do. You don't see the thousands of people who tried to be as good as them and aren't. Nobody interviews them, and yet they represent the vastness that comprises everyone else. Growing up, I felt so strongly I couldn't measure up. It was one thing after another I wasn't good at. But greatness, Karen? Greatness isn't about being great. Greatness is about becoming yourself."

He snapped from his trance, raised an arm, and extended a finger toward his reflection.

"I am a unique person, and that makes me special." The pride in his face was evident. "Did you see that, Karen? I finally did it. Now let's move on."

SECRETS

"So, you selected our three friends in the office carefully. What did they do?" Karen inquired as they walked.

Ted nodded. "I can start with Theresa. Such a shame. So talented. Do you realize if she pulled herself together how many people, how many children, she could help?"

"That bombshell? Did you get a look at her? At what she's wearing?" Karen noted.

"I love her subtle attempt to seduce me. She won't go all the way, you know. She's just doing it to see if she could."

"And could she?"

"I'm going to turn the tables on her, and she will give me anything I want."

"And if she doesn't?"

"I will burn the life she has today to the ground, and her with it. But she will get to choose her fate."

"And what about the esteemed treasurer, Sister Margaret?"

"Margaret might be responsible for bankrupting the school. Haven't had enough time to dig into the financial records."

"Incompetence?"

"Embezzlement. Wouldn't be her first time. Decades ago, before becoming a nun, she put an eighty-two-year-old company with thirty employees out of business. Robbed them blind. Most of the money went up her nose. She got convicted, then served thirty-four months of a sixty-eight-month sentence. Had a baby she gave up for adoption while she was incarcerated."

"So that's why you brought up your adoption."

"Yes, forge the connection. Margaret's real name is Harriet Norwich. After prison, she became a caretaker. When one of the women she was caring for died, she jumped parole and stole everything the woman had, and I mean everything, including her identity. She is a fugitive. There is a two-decade-old warrant under her old name out for her arrest. And Billings, Montana, my ass. Did you catch that shallow attempt she made to see if I had bought into it? She grew up in a suburb near Allentown, Pennsylvania."

Karen was shocked. "So how are you going to find out if she stole the money?"

"I've already freaked her out a little by indicating I may know her past. All I have to do now is wait for her to make a mistake."

"And then what?"

"Either way her fate is sealed. I just don't know which one of the two it will be."

"If she's guilty, are you going to show her any mercy?"

"Isn't mercy wonderful in theory? Forgive and let things go. Unfortunately, mercy is the antithesis of justice. So, no, we can't have any of that."

"And Robert?"

"If I do one thing today, it will be to put Robert in a place where he needs to be. Honestly, Karen, I was up half the night trying to decide how to bite and what venom to use. Dealing with him scares the hell out of me."

"The world's most powerful people climb out windows to get away from you, and you're scared of Robert?"

"Especially now, knowing what I know. You don't understand."

RESPONSIBILITY

They arrived at the main office, but Ted first ducked into Theresa's to get the yearbook as Karen took her place standing watch.

Good, he thought. *The door is unlocked.*

Theresa was inside.

"Oh!" she said startled. "Don't you knock? What are *you* doing here?"

Ted was surprised too but showed no indication. "I think the question is what are you doing in here?"

"I work here."

"Is that what you call it?"

He swung the door open wide as a class of third graders was moving past. At random, he pointed to one of the girls. "What's her name? The blond-haired girl?"

"I don't know."

"How about that boy next to her?"

Theresa stared blankly. Ted looked down for a moment, then quietly closed the door.

"I suppose you are too busy prancing around here without underwear on to learn their names."

Shocked, she grabbed at the skirt in a feeble attempt to pull it lower. "How do you know that?"

"You've been pulling at your skirt all morning. It was a guess, but your reaction confirms it."

"Well, it's not true!"

"Okay then, pull it up."

"Excuse me!"

"Just pull up the side. Show me I'm wrong."

"What kind of nerve you have!"

"Oh please, don't give me a righteous attitude. You'll sleep with anyone with a pulse. Provided they have enough money, that is. That would certainly make me your type."

She didn't know quite how to answer that. She suddenly realized this man must know way more about her past than she wished. "Listen, I've done things I'm not proud of, but I'm married now. I would never do anything to hurt my husband."

"Really! Is that so?" Ted's reaction could only be described as wildly amused.

"Well, I'd like to discuss a few other things. I can't wait to see the look on your face from my next question. Might you be able to tell me what happened to that thirteen-year-old boy you ran over two years ago? I assume you were sober enough at the time to remember hitting him. Even the police don't know how long he lay on the side of the road unconscious."

Theresa's face turned pale, her head taking on a light feeling as if it might float off her shoulders. She closed her mouth and eyes, swallowed hard, and hoped this was a nightmare from which, in a moment, she would wake.

"I suppose with two DWIs you couldn't stick around to find out if he was dead or alive. They don't know who did it, but they will if I want it out."

The defiance that had filled her face moments before was replaced by the whimpering eyes of a beaten puppy.

"I got help, and I'm better now. Please, Ted," she whispered as though the room were running out of oxygen.

"You treat your husband like dirt. Your kids are neglected. All the money you can get your hands on goes to your liquid love affair. You blew through your kid's college funds. You are a therapist, and you buy booze for underage kids. Does it bother you when you steal from your own mother? What? You thought only your husband knew all this?"

"I haven't had a drink in years!" she insisted, desperate to change the momentum.

"I bet I can prove you a liar on that too. What I can't decide is if I want to stay a little late tonight so I can watch you lose your job and the police take you away. Has it ever occurred to you that what you had here was the most important job in the school, had you done it right?"

"I know how important it is," she replied, unable to hide the fear written on her face.

"I'll bet those three boxes of mint tea on your desk you don't. And that brings up a question. What kind of person drinks mint tea and keeps two boxes at the ready?"

"You don't approve of tea?"

"You leave too many clues," he stated as his eyes combed over the room. "I'll find the answer."

He looked about as if trying to pinpoint some mysterious sound. Carefully scanning, he fixed on a thick dictionary on the top shelf of her bookcase. Walking over, his eyes skimmed the books lined alongside it. His right hand hovered high in the air to build anticipation.

"What are you doing?" she asked in a whisper.

"Proving you a liar. The truth is always hidden behind things that are out of place. No one uses a dictionary anymore. So then why is it here? Look at the books on this shelf. There's dust in front of all, curiously, except this giant dictionary."

Her eyelids blinked repeatedly, her mind searching for the way out. Every instinct in her body screamed run, but she stood frozen in place. Ted pulled at the book, and there behind it was a one-third full bottle of vodka.

"Oh yes!" he gushed, pumping his fist down toward the floor, lost in self-satisfaction. "You drank just before I came in, didn't you!" He gleamed.

"Well, I would end your career right now, but I believe the natural order is for a cat to play with a mouse before killing it."

Theresa might have collapsed if not for her heart's hard pounding, which forced her to remain conscious and upright.

"Please, please, Ted, Mr. Carrington. I'm begging you."

"Let's see. How should we do this? I think I want to set things up and reveal it to everyone at just the right moment," he said, looking off as though dreaming about some fantasy.

He placed the bottle on the center of her desk, then looked around the room. "That's it!" he exclaimed while snapping his fingers, grabbing her wastebasket, scattering the small bit of garbage within across the floor, turning it upside down, and placing it over the bottle.

The first thought that went through her mind, of all those that could have been, was she now needed a different place to vomit.

"We'll leave it like that and go back to the office. You go first. I need to tidy up around here. Don't ruin my surprise and try to look happy to the others."

She shook her head in disbelief. "Please, you don't have to do this. You have everything you could want. What could this possibly do for you?"

"Let's just call all this a hobby of mine," he responded with a grin the devil himself could not have replicated.

"You can't possibly be this evil," Theresa pleaded.

"Get to know me better. Listen closely to what I have to say today and let's see if you can figure out what the cat is going to do with the mouse."

Her image of Ted was replaced from one of a classy gentleman to that of a sadistic bully. Had others witnessed the exchange, they might judge Ted as a snake simply being a snake. Others still might regard him as a talented surgeon making precise incisions. Given limited information and varying points of view, perception will differ. The only certainty is that people are rarely what they seem.

PRISM

"Sorry for the delay," Ted said confidently as they entered the office one by one. "I was looking for that yearbook in Theresa's office. It's not there."

"Oh, it's in the stack on the shelf above the filing cabinets," Theresa responded, doing well, having years of being drunk on the job, of appearing as though nothing were wrong.

"No, it isn't there. That is for certain," Ted scoffed with annoyance. "Theresa, you look like you could use a drink. Karen, why don't you get her some water?"

Taking the hint, Theresa dropped the subject. She figured her only hope at this point was to try to find her way onto Ted's good side if he had one.

Following his initial impression, Robert had convinced himself Ted's display of emotion was likely just sentimental. Margaret believed the truth of her past was still safe.

Ted was, at this point, fishing for a way to bring up the topic of youth. There was so much to teach. Eight years of knowledge garnered in this school crammed into a lesson of just a few hours.

Robert beat him to it. "As long as we have some time, maybe we can talk about some of your experiences in this school."

Robert already knew Ted's grades were lackluster, so he started elsewhere. "Did you play sports? Were you in any of the leagues?"

"Baseball. In the lower grades, I played baseball each year in the spring."

"Were you a good ball player?"

"Indescribable. You would not have believed your eyes."

"You were that good?"

"No. I hated the game. If you took me today as an adult and put me on that same team with the little kids, I'd still be the worst player. The only reason I joined is because my father loved baseball so much. He went to every game. I was awful, but that gleam in his eye said, *Yeah, son, I know you suck, but maybe if you give it just one more season.* Perhaps if I was in a wheelchair, I at least would have garnered some sympathy. It wasn't just baseball, though. I was never like the other kids."

"What makes you say that?" Theresa inquired, now desperate to learn as much about him as she could.

"Because of the way my mind works. I've always interpreted the world using a prism it seems no one else has. It ultimately became a great strength. I've made fortunes in the stock market by being able to see opportunities before others. Sometimes I misinterpret completely, but the successes, the times I get it right, like everything in life, more than make up for the failures."

"Seeing the world differently made me quite the fortune, but back then, it was a horrible affliction. Quite the curse."

"How is that a curse?" Theresa asked. "Wouldn't having all those insights put you ahead?"

Ted paused for a moment, then walked over to the desk where a glass of water was sitting. "Half empty or half full?" When they hesitated, he asked again, "Is the glass half empty or half full?"

"Half full, half empty," his three targets each ventured an opinion.

"It's neither," Ted concluded. "The glass is completely full, one half with water, the other with air. When I gave that answer in the fifth grade, they looked at me as though I were from outer space. When I answered it in high school, I got hit in the head with a pencil eraser. At university, though, I wrote a paper on it for a philosophy class and received an A."

"So you *are* brilliant" Theresa chimed in.

"Not at all. Now Karen here, she's the brilliant one. She has two doctorates—psychology and social science. See, Theresa, you aren't the only one in the room walking around with double Ds."

Karen buried her face in one hand and groaned. She'd try to explain to him later why what he said was wrong, but there were always so many inappropriate things he'd said by the end of any day. He'd listen patiently and nod that he understood, but as brilliant as he was, he could never grasp the concept. He wondered how can something be offensive when he didn't mean it to be so?

"Being different, Ted, did that make school difficult?" Robert inquired.

"It was tough not being accepted, but I have no regrets. It shaped me into the person I am. The problem is people, society too, make it as though being different is something bad. I realized much later in life that being different is a gift from God. Unfortunately, those lucky enough to be afflicted with it find it's a gift that takes a very long time to unwrap."

With that Ted looked at his watch, then up to the clock on the wall.

"Karen, you need to fix that clock. It's twenty-three seconds slow." It was bothering him.

Acceptance

Ted went on to those in the office about how he got into the school back in 1972. It was, at the time, the number one, top-rated elementary school in the entire state. In addition to its being very expensive for a working-class family to afford, there were somewhere near fifteen applicants for every available seat. Children of alumni and those who already had a child in attendance received automatic placement, and although unsaid, those of large donors were first in line as well.

Despite the odds, Ted seemed like a shoo-in. Although there were a few noted behavioral issues from earlier schools, he showed superior academic promise. By kindergarten, he could perform multiplication and division and was absorbing fifth-grade-level science books.

Ted and his family had to go to the school for a test, a tour, and an interview. His parents put Ted in a jacket and tie for the occasion. All went well until one of the nuns, a sourpuss named Sister Howard, whom Ted believed was so old she might have met George Washington, and in complete sincerity asked her if she did, when referencing his adoption referred to him as a bastard. Ted didn't know how the meaning related to himself but knew it was a bad word because of the number of times he heard his mother shout it while driving. Calling him that didn't sit well with his father, and the entire affair became rather uncomfortable. Regardless, obviously, he got in.

Once Ted had been accepted, his parents had to figure out how to pay for it all. There was the possibility of his grandfather, who had owned a grocery store for years and accumulated modest wealth, and would have given the shirt off his back along with a kidney to help his family, but they determined that wasn't an option. Instead, Joe took additional shifts while Annette cut spending to the bone.

For the occasion, they decided upon a modest splurge—a furniture set for his room. It wasn't anything elaborate, but grand to Ted's eyes. It had drawers, a bookcase, and a desk to do homework. Ted insisted the top shelf of the credenza remain empty. That was reserved for all the trophies he would one day win. He wondered if one shelf would be enough.

Third

Anyone believing children in a schoolyard are having fun has forgotten what it is to be young. The dynamics are fierce—a daily struggle for dominance, if not just survival. Ted spoke to those in the office of the social order beginning in third grade.

"By the time I reached grade three, I was pretty much universally detested. I did have two friends, Itch and Upchuck. They were high academic achievers. I, on the other hand, helped keep our combined grade-point average from getting too out of control.

"Itch was the most abrasive kid you might ever encounter. He got his nickname when his first-grade teacher said he was as annoying as having a rash.

"Chuck, on the other hand, had the misfortune of throwing up in the cafeteria in second grade. It only took once to brand him Upchuck for life. Unlike Itch, who was a troll, Chuck was good looking and had a pleasant personality. He could have been well liked, but he was his own worst enemy. He would applaud, actually applaud, when teachers gave homework. He'd whine that he was failing if a grade ever fell below ninety-five."

Speculation by the administrators in the office that Ted may have been a popular superstar when he attended was quickly eroding. From what they were hearing it was hard to connect the boy Ted was describing from the man before them. They wondered what it was that had been the catalyst driving what was obviously his success. That link would take place three grades past the time he was describing.

"What really did Chuck in was how he used to tattle on everybody. One time he got beat up for being the jailhouse snitch. There was this kid, a tough, muscular, oversized bully named Ciro Gatalatano. His father was some bigshot capo in the Mob. They used to call the guy 'Vinny No Show' because he'd set up meetings with people and they would never be seen again. They'd ask him what happened, and he'd say, 'The guy didn't show.'

"Anyway, Ciro had been stealing money from his teacher's purse. Chuck ratted him out. Ciro got suspended and, the day he returned, hit Chuck in the head with a metal lunch tray. I mean blood and everything. It resulted in some big hush-hush principal's meeting with their parents. From the bits I heard, the only thing Vinny No Show was upset about was that Ciro had admitted to it. The rumor was he told the principal that with all the money he donated, she'd be expelled before his son.

"Ciro was a classic bully. I don't recall one time he failed to take the opportunity to give me a shoulder bump in the hallway. It wasn't just me, though. He was a jackass to everyone. If you were holding something like a stack of books, he'd slam his hand down so you'd drop them. He'd spit in your lunch bag. You'd open it up, and there would be a lump of spit sitting on top.

"And he was the biggest phony. He and his partner in crime, Steve, put on a big show whenever adults were around. Yes, sir, and, no, ma'am, with every sentence. A real con artist. He played Mr. Wonderful, and they ate it up.

"One of their favorite things was to go into the bathroom and push kids into the urinal just as they flushed. He got more sophisticated as he got older. He would splash water on a person's crotch to make it look like they peed themselves.

"Ciro grew up and followed in his father's footsteps. He isn't with us anymore. He met his fate about ten years ago."

"Was he killed by the Mob?" Sister Margaret asked.

"He was murdered, with the leading suspect being cheeseburgers. He ballooned to 480 pounds and dropped dead. Bad as Ciro could be, though, it was Tom Chenko you had to watch out for. Ciro was mean, but Tom was dangerous. I think they accepted him in the school because his brother was a student three grades ahead. That had to be it because Tom was dumber than a stop sign.

"There was something wrong with him. I'm sure if he was in school these days he'd be medicated. In ancient times, it would have been natural selection that determined his fate. Back in the '70s, he was just considered difficult, and we were left to deal with him. It wasn't easy. He threw me down a flight of stairs once."

"Did you get hurt?" asked Sister Margaret.

"Yes. He was a tremendous kid and incredibly strong. Every school has at least one mutant that is so large you just can't believe they belong there. His father was from the Ukraine, that place where the Russian bear comes from. He was something like seven one and worked as a corrections officer at Riker's Island. My dad said he was the only person he knew that large not working for the circus. Tom took after him."

"Do you know what happened to him?" Robert inquired.

"Yes actually. We had lunch a few years ago so I could thank him. He became a Franciscan brother, of all things. You wouldn't believe how nice he was to me when we met. Go figure."

"You were thanking him? Whatever were you thanking him for?" Sister Margaret asked.

How to explain himself? He assumed they were about to give him that you-got-three-heads look he so often received when sharing his perspective.

"I thanked him because he was one of the architects who made me into who I am today. I would have thanked Ciro too if I had the chance. Bullies try to tear you down, but ultimately, quite unintentionally, they do the opposite. They are like coaches. They attack your weak spots, and you learn to reinforce them. They make you miserable and you learn how to cope. They point out anything socially unacceptable about yourself and you make changes. They provide the motivation, reason, and instruction for how to improve yourself. Your friends don't do that for you. It is the bullies who do. If you don't have adversity, you won't change.

"There was another kid named Rob. He was one of the many kids who fall in middle ground for so many of us. He never bullied me, and he never seemed great at anything, but he was always better than me at everything and usually rubbed my face in that fact.

"So let me see who you might know. How about the Pisora family? They own Sunshine Bakery."

Robert recognized the place. "Sunshine Bakery! Yeah, they're world famous. Aren't they the bakery to the—"

"Yes, bakery to the stars." Ted interrupted. "Most amazing stuff. They would get orders from across the country—sports figures, politicians, movie stars. They make cakes for Hollywood."

"I assume one of the owners had a student here?" Robert confirmed.

"Yes, David Pisora. A popular kid. Great baseball player too. Whenever he'd bring in something from the store, there was pandemonium in the schoolyard. Everyone would rush him. Sometimes what he brought wouldn't even make it inside. My favorite, not that I successfully fought the crowd very often, were brownies filled with bits of fudge. Those were amazing."

Just then, Ted snapped his fingers. "I have a name you'll recognize, Walter Burke."

"Why does that ring a bell? I know that name," Robert responded.

"I remember him," Sister Margaret recalled. "Big donor. He put a new roof on the church."

"That's him," Ted confirmed. "His son Ashton was in my grade. His family weren't even members of the parish. They lived about thirty miles from here on the North Shore. I'm sure it was their status and the fortunes he used to donate that got him in.

"Ashton used to get dropped off every day in a big black Town Car. We all thought the man running around to open the door for him was his father. It took a while before we found out that person was Vince, the family driver."

"They had a chauffeur take him to school?" Robert clarified.

"Family driver. Not a chauffeur. I was corrected on that more than once. Walter was one of the wealthiest men on Long Island and a power broker on Wall Street."

"Bet his son was spoiled," Theresa interjected.

"You would think that, but no. He was a friendly kid. I was envious of Ashton because he was so popular. The girls were crazy for him too. When I was a teen, I couldn't get a second look in a whorehouse if I went in waving a thousand dollars. He was ruggedly handsome. Rusted curly blond hair. He looked like some kid you would see on a movie poster. He'd always come in whistling a catchy tune from a Broadway play or opera he had seen."

The envy from Ted was obvious, even all these years later. The school had always had a fair share of such kids, but even the most privileged among them were not in the same league as the wealth possessed by Ashton's family.

"Me, I had the same dirty-blond hair as he, and I was taller, but thin as a rail. I didn't go to any Broadway plays. Instead, my mother was always taking me to different doctors because I was so thin. She thought something was wrong with me. There was, but it wasn't my weight."

Power

1972/1973

What angels, one of the nuns thought, looking at the rows of third and fourth graders gathered in the church for their weekly attendance of 9:00 a.m. mass.

Kneeling, hands clasped, leaning forward against the pews of the next row, it was easy to believe they were all praying for world peace. Reality was in sharp contrast. Those brats not asking God to give them things or complaining were simply catatonically bored.

Like sand at the beach, in a Catholic school, prayer works its way into everything. Mornings and after recess, the PA system in all the classrooms would come alive for an honored student to say the Pledge of Allegiance, then lead the school in prayer. Grace was recited before every meal as if God had put it on the plate Himself.

Priests were of the highest order, living representatives of Jesus Christ, only surpassed in importance by bishops, who in turn were surpassed by cardinals, who in turn were surpassed by the pope, who in turn was surpassed by the saints, who sat with God, and that was as high as you could get. Nuns were somewhere at the bottom of the pile but still more important than anyone who had not committed their life to Jesus.

Ted envied the respect given the priests. He jumped from his seat, along with everyone else, and shouted a melodic greeting, "Good morning, Father!" whenever a priest would enter their classroom. "That will be me someday," he assured himself every time it happened.

Priesthood was only to be the beginning. He would quickly ascend past bishop to become a cardinal, then impatiently await the reigning pope's death. Once anointed successor, he would rule the world and wield the power of God, using it to smite his enemies. In due time, he would become a saint and his bedroom turned into a shrine.

Looking up at his empty trophy shelf, he wondered what the tourists streaming through his room would one day admire.

Unforeseen

Fall 1974
Several Years Prior To His Fateful Decision

Grades three and four had a few notable events. Having been born in Canada, he became a naturalized citizen of the United States in September 1974. He didn't see it as such a big deal, being sworn in with thirty-five others, and he couldn't understand why a Vietnamese lady next to him became so emotional during the oath she could hardly complete it.

This year he had his first crush on a girl—a bossy, opinionated eight-year-old named Elle who sat behind him in class and captured his attention in a way boys never could. Elle was the only reason Ted knew the difference physically between boys and girls. It was she who encouraged him one day to get a bathroom pass and wait for her. She did the same. Next thing he knew she had shoved him into the girls' room to play a fast but complete game of doctor. He never told anyone, and they never got caught.

The most significant event involved his father, who suddenly became ill and was immediately admitted to the hospital. When it happened, they told him very little other than it had something to do with an infection in his abdomen.

Later that night, he went to sleep to the sound of his mother crying.

In the same way a shark can respond to a drop of blood from great distances, Ciro had a keen ability to sense vulnerability. An easy target, he took great pleasure in asking Ted each morning how much longer Ted thought his father would live.

With his father in the hospital and on disability, even the mortgage, let alone the tuition of a private school, became overdue. Two weeks into December, his mother informed him he would have to transfer to public school after Christmas recess. First met with denial, he swore he'd improve his grades. Then reality sunk in.

For two weeks, he was quiet, avoiding everyone, even Elle, despite her persistent conversation attempts. The morning of the final day began with his teacher announcing it as his last, something most of them already knew. She told them life was an adventure, and the more places you go and people you meet, the more exciting it becomes.

Ted was buying none of it. As ostracized as he was in this school, he lamented a new one would be far worse. He moved his eyes across the room, burning in his mind those things around him. The Christmas decorations, faces of friends, and especially Elle, who never seemed as cute as she was today.

The teacher made the classroom holiday party half Christmas, half farewell for Ted. While the intention was to provide a happy send-off, all it did was magnify the agony. Ciro told everyone he didn't belong there anyway. It was that comment that put him into hysterics.

Deeply upset by Ted's emotional outburst, Ashton walked up to the teacher's desk, emptied every cent from his pockets, and offered it all as payment for Ted's tuition.

Wailing uncontrollably, Ted was escorted to the principal's office to wait for his mom, who had been called to take him home. He stopped the moment his mother appeared. "I'm fine," he said from his moisture-covered mess of a face reflexively, convincing no one.

Unable to say anything, he waved goodbye to those in the office while holding his mother's hand as they left.

"Why? Why does this have to happen?" he said with his voice pitching.

"We don't have the money to send you here. I'm sorry. We just can't do this."

Ironically, multiples of the money needed sat in cash, in his pocket that day he visited the school as an adult. But on this day, it was as far out of reach as the moon.

Christmas Eve found Ted on his knees in what could be better described as begging than prayer as he spoke with God or any entity that might be listening. If the devil were interested, an opportunity existed for the purchase of an eight-year-old soul. The price? Bring his father home and allow him to return to school.

He awoke Christmas morning filled with hopeful anticipation Santa, whom he no longer believed in, or God, whom he still did, had delivered a miracle. Creeping down the hall, fear with each step but needing to look, he reached the Christmas tree in the living room. Under it was a stack of wrapped gifts. He rubbed his eyes to be sure he wasn't missing anything and looked over to the emptiness of his father's favorite chair.

He returned to bed and wept with his face buried into his pillow to keep from waking his mother, believing his prayers went unheard.

Anonymous

Christmas, 1974

Ted fretted all Christmas break, trying to ignore the thought of a new school. He lay on the floor of his room, staring at the ceiling two days before he would have to deal with the inevitable when his mom called him to the phone to talk with his father from the hospital. His dad started right in.

"Hey, buddy, I've got good news and bad news. I'll give you the bad news first."

He stared blankly at the wall with the phone to his ear, his mind bracing for something.

"The bad news is you won't be going to public school on Monday, and the good news is you'll be going back to St. Augustine."

The whole thing had been a joke. A crazy sick joke. At least, that's what Ted considered. But joke or not, he didn't know if he should believe it.

"How?" he asked.

"We're not sure, but I think you owe your grandfather a great big hug next time you see him."

"How long can I go?"

"Well, they told us it has been paid through the end of the school year. We'll see what happens after that."

"So, Monday I go back?"

"Yeah, merry Christmas, Ted."

So excited, forgetting to hand the phone back to his mother and without saying goodbye, he tossed it back onto the receiver.

"Let's call your grandfather next," his mom said in a tone attempting to temper Ted's enthusiasm while dialing his dad back to finish their conversation.

Ted sat on his parent's bed rocking back and forth, anxious to blow a kiss into the phone to the man who had saved him.

"Don't get too excited," she said as she picked up the phone to make the call to her own father.

The conversation began differently than Ted had expected. It was more like a witch trial's opening monologue than a call of gratitude, his mother not buying his grandfather's apparent confusion. It soon erupted into a loud argument, ending with her cursing words Ted should not have known but did, because of all his time with her in the car, then her slamming the phone. She knew this eighty-year-old man who couldn't drive or write English must have had help, and she was about to prove it by calling the person she was sure was the mastermind.

"You did this reckless thing!" she screamed at Ted's bewildered aunt after opening with a short list of accusations.

"What are you talking about? Anne, I didn't know you were having money problems!" she replied.

"You're jeopardizing his retirement! Do you want him on the street?"

This time it was his aunt who slammed the phone on her, leaving his mom muttering.

"Okay, so if it wasn't him then who was it?"

He would never voice it, but his heart told him. Ted knew. It was his mother, his birthmother. She must have found him and, from behind a curtain of invisibility, been secretly watching over him. All the pieces fit. Tightly clutching the sheets of the bed, he believed, if he let go, he would float off into space.

Cocooned in a blanket of the unique love a mother has for her child, he was more excited about that than returning to school. He would remember this as the happiest moment of his adolescent life.

A week later, another surprise awaited. Walking in from school there he was, the sight of his father sitting in his favorite chair. Ted leaped for him with such force the chair pushed back an entire inch. His dad was recovering, and there was talk of him returning to work in a few weeks.

Contrasting the cold weather, everything seemed warm otherwise as he blended back within his class as if nothing had happened. Whoever had made the generous donation, the person Ted alone was sure he knew, had gone as far to include money for every expense. Field trips, lunches, bake sales, not a penny was required for the remainder of the year. Each time his teacher said, "No money from you, it's been covered," he could feel the uniquely warm press of his mother's lips against his cheek.

Etiquette

Spring 1975

Three Years Prior To His Fateful Decision

Springtime ushered in the dreaded start of baseball season. Ted committed plenty of errors, but a real disaster occurred during their sixth game. Three runs behind, bases loaded, the last out of the final inning, David Pisora stepped up to the plate. The grand slam he hit cleared the bench. All ran out to celebrate as he jogged to home plate. Ted, among the crowd, fought his way into the closed circle to get a piece of David. Finally making it to the center of the tight ball of kids, he grabbed David's face and gave him a kiss.

It was as though he had pulled the pin on a live hand grenade. Boys scrambled to put distance between themselves and this leper as David gave him a shove. Ted had violated one of the most sacred rules governing male adolescent behavior. He showed a gesture of affection toward another boy.

"Ted is gay! Get away!" they began to shout.

"It wasn't me!" Ted shouted back, the only excuse he could come up with.

Tom reached from behind and put his arm across his neck, forcefully throwing him to the ground. He was lifting his foot to stomp when the coach broke it up.

Pride battered but otherwise unhurt, Ted sat in humiliated silence for the car ride home. He was despondent that he had allowed himself to do something so careless. It was just that he got lost in the moment. The ridicule on Monday back at school would be unimaginable.

Luck was on Ted's side. To have one controversial story go away, all that is needed is a bigger one to replace it. Over the weekend, Ciro's dad made the front cover of the paper. He was pictured with four of his cohorts, all in handcuffs, being walked by men in jackets emblazoned with the letters F-B-I.

Talk of that overtook all else for days as Ciro remained absent. When he finally returned, he was greeted by a horrid chant:

Ciro's dad
Did something bad.
Now he's in jail
'Cause he can't make bail.
His family fears
He'll be gone for years.
But the judge don't care
If he gets the chair.

Ted wished he'd created it, but this Rembrandt was from one of the older brothers of some other kid. First in the schoolyard, then continued at a whisper as he entered the classroom, Ciro walked past his assigned desk and buried his head onto his folded arms.

Ted had prayed many times for Ciro's demise. He'd wished him to be eaten by a lion, slip into quicksand, hit by a meteor, and his favored and most frequent request, fall into a volcano. Today though, he felt badly for him.

However, it was not enough to keep from joining in when others made fun and played with Itch a warped version of hangman. Itch drew the stick figure to resemble Ciro's dad being strapped into an electric chair.

It took a week, but Ciro snapped out of his funk, officially heralding in his return with a hard slap to the back of Rob's head when he started chanting the overheard rhyme. Witnessed by many, the taunting little song was silenced.

As third grade ended the big attraction was an invite to bakery boy David Pisora's birthday party. Held in late May, rather than June, his actual birthday due to an enormous swimming pool set to be installed in their backyard, the invites were almost all that was talked about.

This year they decided to celebrate their heritage with a colossal piñata made to resemble a decorated horse. Half the size of the real thing and packed with enough candy to bury a few children, it took twenty minutes of whacking with a Louisville Slugger to break open. It took even longer for the eighteen guests to gather it all into bags. Uninvited, the closest Ted came to the action was hearing other kids boast about it.

Ted's relationship with Elle ended abruptly on the last day of the school year when she expressed an interest in Tom, and Ted told her Tom was a jerk. That didn't sit well with her, and she broke his heart for the first time in his life as she told him off.

Ted spent much of grade four wondering if his birth-mother would emerge from the shadows. Sometimes he'd gaze across the attendees in church, seeing if maybe one of the women there was her taking the opportunity to get a glimpse of him. Ever since the breakup with Elle, he wanted someone he could talk to about such things. It seemed embarrassing to discuss with his father, and his mother—*adopted* mother, that was—would be the last person he would turn to.

Not good at sports, not good at music, not good at studies, not good at art, unpopular, oddly, Ted found his niche within the field of stocks. At a backyard BBQ at the house of one of his father's friends, Ted watched with envy the attention given to a man, a colleague of his father, who talked about investments. Apparently, he'd done well in the market and imparted investment tips like the pope giving out blessings. He watched from afar, captivated as they looked upon a spread-out *Wall Street Journal* as though generals reviewing a war map. Ted hungered to be like this man.

The next day he used his lunch money to buy a *Wall Street Journal* on his way home from school. Soon, he could be found at the library studying books on the markets and investing.

He followed stocks, read countless articles, suspicious, believing in a conspiracy that it was the paper's overall intention to mislead investors away from the right choices. He repeatedly came across the name Walter Burke and soon confirmed it was Ashton's father. Interviewed many times on all different topics, it was apparent this man was quite special on Wall Street.

Learning everything he could about the markets effectively replaced his other studies. He barely passed fourth grade, and that was only because he buckled down at the last minute and aced his finals.

While he would have preferred to spend all his free time on his new hobby, his mother, wanting to diversify his interests, signed him up with the school orchestra. Drums, that is where they placed him. He hated everything about it from the lame rubber pad used for practice, to the twice weekly group lessons. Tom was right next to him and would tap his skull with the sticks when the instructor wasn't looking. Pleading with his mom to quit, she insisted he hadn't given it a fair chance, forcing its continuation into the next year.

Initiation

Fall 1976

One- and One-Half Years Prior To His Fateful Decision

If a new male student was joining Ted's grade, odds were high he'd be having his first day's lunch in the cafeteria with geeks. Ted's group of three played the role of new-student welcoming committee. They went all-out in their attempt to recruit more people into their sparsely attended reject group. Efforts usually failed miserably. It didn't take long for whomever it was to realize they were associating with the school nerds and flee elsewhere. After such a friendly initial greeting, the added insult was how many would be leading the charge to bully them just a few days later.

With the appearance of someone new on day one of fifth grade, their recruitment drive was on. The new kid was hard to miss, a notably dark-skinned Hispanic in a sea of ivory soap. His name was Ricky Ramirez. Short black hair, brown eyes, he maintained a look on his face as though plotting the murder of everyone in sight, including them. Tied with Tom for tallest, it turned out he was two years older. He admitted to being held back once. The other missing year, they never did get out of him.

He refused to say where he came from, sizing up his company and deciding they weren't worth the effort he'd have to put in answering their questions. All he offered was that his father used to say their neighborhood was so run down that they could move up to the ghetto when they hit it big. He insisted on being called Rip, short for Rest in Peace, his street gang's name. He told them it was in recognition of all the people he killed.

With a passion for working out, from the shape of his physique it looked as though he never missed a day. So different from what they hoped, every time he looked away his three hosts would bulge their eyes and shake their heads at each other. They knew this kid was going to be a nightmare once he realized their low social standing.

"What do you think?" Upchuck asked nervously to Itch as they got up to head for the schoolyard.

No words necessary, Itch clenched his teeth and drew his finger across his throat.

Ted wondered how on earth he got into the school, but there was nothing special about it. As the grades went higher and normal attrition reduced the class's size, seats opened, and entrance standards all but disappeared. The only barrier was the high tuition.

For the Ramirez family, it had almost been insurmountable. There were people with low incomes in the neighborhood, but the Ramirez family was different. The kind of poor where luxuries like air conditioning or a color TV were fantasy. Luxury to them was three meals a day. His father had always worked menial jobs but finally landed a good opportunity as a baggage handler at Kennedy airport and tried to get ahead by putting in as many hours as possible.

The one dream he and his wife held was to move into the lowest-priced house in a neighborhood like this and get Ricky and his sister Isabel, younger by four years, out of the drug-infested school system where they had been living and into a place like St. Augustine. A visit to the church to deliver prayers of gratitude accompanied the day his two children, the joys of his life, were accepted.

Ted's prayers were in direct opposition, begging God to remove this new kid. He never imagined an incident after school on the first day almost brought it about. An exchange happened between Rip and Tom during a basketball game at recess that resulted in the two meeting after school for a fight.

Ted might have been the only one who didn't know beforehand and missed seeing it. According to Itch, Rip got his clock cleaned as was evidenced by the black eye he sported when he arrived, accompanied by his father, at school the next day. Both boys were suspended before the morning bell rang.

Rip now faced a different set of circumstances, returning to school two days later, more turtle than tiger. Most kids hated Tom, but he was a familiar jerk. Rip was an outsider and different. Becoming as accepted as poison he had a choice—sit alone or join the nerds.

While the trio were surprised to see him plop down next to them, Ted, having missed the fight, seized the opportunity to get more details.

"You got a black eye," he said, moving his head close to Rip's face to inspect the still-visible damage.

"Lucky shot, that's all. No matter what you do they can always slip in one good shot."

"Or ten good shots," Itch added derisively.

"You going to go at him again?" Ted asked, hoping not to miss the next one.

"No. We declared friends and shook hands when we were alone in the office."

"Really! He offered you that?" Itch exclaimed in surprise.

When faced with the school's harsh punishment, often after two boys had it out, they would declare "friends." It didn't mean they were actually friends, but it did mean the fight was over and they would try to be civil.

After threatening horrible consequences, the school would often leave the two perpetrators alone for a few minutes to make peace. It worked like a charm.

"So, what happened? Everyone keeps me in the dark."

"We had it out. That's what happened."

"Well, duh. I mean what did he do to tick you off? I want to know that kind of what happened."

"He called me a word no one gets away with, ever."

Ted begged to tell him the word. "Oh please, please, please tell me what it is. This way I know never to call you it."

Rip refused to share. It would be months before Ted found it out.

Itch saw this as the perfect opportunity to torture Ted, something he just loved to do.

"I'll tell you something Ted. How about I tell you about summer camp?"

Ted both loved and hated to hear the stories about the sleepaway Boy Scout summer camp Itch attended. It was six weeks of pure unadulterated bliss—endless stories of catching fish, campfires, ghost stories, archery, BB guns, pitching tents, hunting rabbits, tracking deer, and more. It made Ted miserable. He wished he had joined the Boy Scouts but, a few years before, had decided against it. Now all he could do was hear about it. The stories went on for days.

Meanwhile, unlikely as it might have seemed, a friendship began to form between Ted and Rip. In those first days, Ted showed him how to fix a tie and helped him with some of the assignments. Rip offered to teach him Spanish, but all Ted wanted to know was the swear words. Rejected, Rip offered the highest honor he could, an offer to come over to his house after school and work out. Ted always responded with unappreciated laughter, thinking no crazier image than himself lifting weights.

Itch and Upchuck barely tolerated Rip in their group, but there wasn't much they could do about it. Pushing his way in, he was crude, did poor academically, seemed to dislike most, and never lacked a derogatory comeback. These were the very traits Ted liked most about him.

Upchuck was obsessed with becoming a doctor and already had his sights on attending Johns Hopkins. Itch was less specific but wanted to run an international business empire. Ted's ambitions went no further than keeping out of summer school. No longer the only dummy of the group, he finally had a companion on his comparative trip to nowhere.

The other two did enjoy some of Rip's antics. A favorite was when he'd call over one of the nuns to their lunch table, paint an angelic expression on his face, and sweetly say something like, "Sister, Dios puso un pájaro en tu cabeza en lugar de un cerebro."

Charmed, she would reply, sometimes even placing a hand gently onto his cheek, "How sweet. What does that mean?"

"God has given you many blessings."

"Thank you. God blesses you too."

They'd wait expressionless until she was out of sight, then lean in to find out what he'd really said. Rip would translate. "God put a bird in your head instead of a brain."

They'd laugh like a pack of hyenas.

Debutante

Two weeks following the start of the year, a new girl entered the school. While boys in Ted's grade had an invitation to dine with nerds, a girl's first day went differently. Typically, she'd be gushed over by groups of girls with warm introductions, hugs, and greetings, only to be ripped apart from shoes to hair as soon as she was out of earshot.

Like that of her life, Anna's introduction to the school was an unhappy one. Unkempt, enormously overweight, she received no greetings and hugs, and no one pretended to like her. She had entered this world addicted to drugs due to her mother's use. Her parents divorced when she was an infant. At the age of three, her mother died suddenly from an overdose, and she moved to California to live with her father.

By this time, he was clean, but soon after was diagnosed with terminal cancer. Spending much time being babysat by friends while her father received treatment, she hardly saw him.

There was a day, nearing the end, that her father gathered himself together and skipped chemo so they could have one last outing. She was four, and his dying wish was this would be the one memory of him she would keep forever.

The choice he gave was a day at Disney or the Sequoia National Forest. To his surprise she picked the forest. A long drive followed but was worth it. The day was spent exploring nooks, walking, albeit slowly, along paths and marveling at the enormous trees. At her tender age, she had no understanding why he told her as she went to bed that night, eye to eye, that she had been the best thing that ever happened in his life. It was the last time she would see him outside a coffin.

With no living relatives other than her grandmother, too sick at the time to care for her, she entered the foster system. She was placed in a home for almost a year and enjoyed her time there, but unfortunately, it could not be forever. Her foster father lost his job and found another in a new city. Anna would not be going with them. It broke her heart when she had to leave.

It was then that the nightmare began. Placed with a new family that was already fostering several other children, she soon discovered humanity's darkest side. Were a detailed description of the abuse she suffered written as a work of fiction, it would be banned in most countries.

Set upon by not just the adults, but also siblings forced on each other, the only thing that kept her sanity was the memory of that last day with her father. She clung to it like a teddy bear when her body and mind became too overwhelmed with pain. She prayed he somehow would come back and rescue her.

The hellish torture continued for three years, until one morning when she was awoken by a social worker and two police officers. As suddenly as it had begun it was over, but the damage was horrific.

When she entered that home, she was beautiful, considerably thin with crystal-blue eyes and a spontaneous curiosity. What was pulled from that home could barely be called a child. Introverted and sullen, she no longer spoke. It had been so long since she had smiled that if she tried, it would have hurt her facial muscles. During the experience, she had ballooned to better than twice the weight of a girl of similar height.

While the law dealt with those involved, she was moved to a new foster home, one especially selected to help her deal with the trauma she had been through. Her foster mother there was wonderful. Even so, it took three months before Anna spoke her first word again when she referred to the woman as "Mom." The event was celebrated with a cake.

Patient and loving, over time, she painstakingly coaxed Anna partly out of her self-contained exile. By day, the woman was a beautician, something that piqued Anna's interest, and she spent much time with Anna sharing her skills.

"Anna, you have a most wonderful gift of bringing out the beauty in others," her foster mom would frequently say.

Meanwhile, her grandmother had recovered, and with Anna getting older, she was now able to care for her. While the woman was poor, living on social security and a small amount of savings, she loved Anna deeply. A judge made it official, and Anna now had a home in the school district of St. Augustine. Years of volunteer work for the church enabled her to successfully beg for Anna's tuition-free attendance.

Now Anna lay awake the night before her first day in the new school, her new life, a jumbled mix of mostly apprehension but also a touch of excitement. She naively thought the children in a prestigious private Catholic school would treat her differently than all other kids the world over. Worse, one of those kids was Ted Carrington. If God were one of mercy, he never would have allowed that to happen.

Wrecked

It was her first day, and she packed in her schoolbag a small doll, her favorite, both for good luck and maybe to use as a way to start a conversation.

Arriving at the schoolyard, she stood by herself, with no one wanting to be seen talking with this new enormously obese enigma.

When the teacher asked if she preferred Anna or Annabelle, she froze and stared catatonically at the board. Ted, although of drastically limited talent, had a knack for nicknames.

"Ani-mul, that's what we'll call her. Ani-mul. Call her Ani-mul," he spread to whomever he could get to listen. It stuck, and after that, her new peers referred to her as nothing but. A sickening lump filled her empty stomach in the cafeteria at lunch as reality took hold.

She had packed two extra cupcakes, hoping to share them with new friends. Now not wanting anyone to see her eating, although famished, she touched nothing she had brought. In the cafeteria, surrounded by others, she was alone with no student wanting to be seen speaking with her.

Painfully shy, she did little to help her own cause, scowling at the few who attempted to reach out.

Ted had his group zero in on her from across the room and challenged themselves to guess her weight. Itch said two hundred pounds, so Ted had to go right for three hundred. Upchuck bid five hundred before Rip asked if they thought her hair could be pumped for oil. Among themselves, they began to suggest alternate things her clothes could be used for—a tent for a family of six, a car cover, a trampoline.

Ted circulated a rumor that she smelled, and the boys dared each other in the schoolyard to get close enough to take a whiff. Itch went first and then returned.

"It's true, man. It's true. She's a human garbage truck."

"I'm going in," said Rip as he made a sign of the cross, then returned with his report. "She's like a farm with manure spread all over. Your turn, Ted."

This new girl, Ani-mul, as she had already been christened, who, for the record, did not smell, remained frozen like a statue with a flock of pigeons dirtying it. She heard it all.

"She smells like the bathroom after Ciro used it," Ted observed while the others chuckled.

As school let out, all fifth graders but one went home accompanied by friends to their parents' anticipation. Anna dragged herself home, dreams of a new beginning in shambles. When she arrived, as usual for the afternoon, her grandmother, made tired from her medication, lay sleeping. In the quiet house, Anna wanted to awaken her to beg her never to send her back. She knew somehow, though, impossible as it seemed, she would have to return the next day.

She needed to get started on her first homework assignment and would soon have to get dinner on for both of them. She probably should have washed the dark pencil smudges off the one and only white shirt she owned, but for a while, all she could do was stand paralyzed in the doorway. Finally, she could hold back no more. She pulled her lucky doll out of her book bag, threw it across the room, and staggered to the couch. There she buried her face into a pillow so that her wailing would not wake and upset her precious nana.

Phantoms

Suspicious of everyone, afraid of being hurt even more, time passed slowly for Ani-mul. Two months in, she had still made not a single friend, unless one were to include the phantom clutch she hung with at lunchtime. Sitting at the base end of one of the lunch table rows, she ensured the two seats to her immediate left and right always remain unoccupied. It created a buffer from her relentless tormentors and a place for her four imaginary friends to join her.

To her right were Penelope and Darlene; to her left were Charlotte and Casey. They were always happy and engaged Anna in lively conversation. All held secrets similar to Anna's and never spoke of them. Penelope, just like Anna, had small scars that dotted her back from cigarette burns, a legacy from when she'd misbehaved. Darlene, just like Anna, had been locked in the same closet for days on end.

She was closest to Charlotte, the two having endured the same insidious tortures. Hair pulled out, head held underwater, forced to stand outside naked in the freezing cold. She understood what Anna had been through.

Anna's favorite was Casey. Several years younger than the other girls, Anna had gone out of her way to protect her in the foster home. Now Casey worshipped the ground Anna walked on. While Casey was too young to be having lunch with the fifth graders, this was Anna's daydream, and she didn't have to justify it.

Anna was not insane. She knew none of them were real. But imagining them there talking with her was the only chance she'd have all day for conversation. Once lunch was over, she ditched her ghostly peeps and sat alone on a half wall at the far end of the schoolyard, as far away from everyone as could be had. She exiled herself the entirety of the period in silence each day, scribbling into a notebook that never left her hands.

Muzak

In this part of New York, when most of the leaves had fallen from the trees and the temperature began changing from cool to cold, it was a sure sign of the upcoming holiday season. Each school seemed to herald in the upcoming holidays with a concert. This was when all orchestra members gathered in front of their parents to musically massacre a few holiday classics. Ted was only technically part of the ensemble. After almost a year of drum lessons, forced upon him by his mother, he remained not skilled enough to produce anything resembling a beat. The school needed to include him somewhere, so Ted was assigned the job of turning the pages for the piano player during his big solo.

The person running the music program, a man named Peter Rodan, came from a place of high goals and big dreams. Proficient in three instruments, all through his school years his violin solos placed him front and center in concert halls, taking the breath from those in attendance. The highlight of his life was being accepted to the Juilliard School of Music. He graduated and, like many, was led to believe a bright future awaited.

Flash-forward twenty-two years to a reality that, as good as he was, there was always someone just a bit better. The furthest he got was music director at this elementary school, teaching a bunch of unappreciative, talentless kids who made fun of his stammer.

By this age, he'd shaken the terrible stutter he'd had as a child, but it would return when he became flustered. Not unnoticed, the kids referred to him as the "muh-muh-music teacher."

Despite looking incredibly overdressed, he insisted on wearing a tuxedo when conducting these concerts and took his place in front of the orchestra standing tall, as though about to lead a grand symphony. He closed his eyes and dreamed there was an audience of five thousand people behind him. In front was the Boston Symphony Orchestra; he'd always dreamed of playing with them. Tapping his baton three times bringing all to order, he was just a moment away from the first glorious note of Beethoven's Ninth.

The fantasy was rudely chased off by the first screeching sounds of "Jingle Bells," many of the notes played off key. He looked over the kids trying to comprehend the reason, whether he had done something terrible in this life or some other, God had chosen to make him king of this part of music hell.

Ted's only moment of the night was to turn the pages for a piano player named Brian during his solo. Refusing to take it seriously, after turning the first few, he decided it would be more fun to mess the kid up and turned several together. Two notes into the new page, the kid stopped, wholly lost, and with panic in his eyes, shook his head toward Mr. Rodan. Ted only made it worse by mocking him behind his back, contorting his face and waving his hands with his fingers bent as though they were broken.

In the audience, his father wanted to strangle him while his mother held her head in one hand whispering to all in earshot, "I'm so embarrassed." He was pulled from the stage and brought by one of the nuns to an empty classroom to await whatever they intended to do to him. He listened to the torturous attempt at music while he waited, but once it stopped, he knew it would be his turn to face the music. He braced himself.

Appearing at the door were his parents and Mr. Rodan, who would have looked like a fine gentleman in his tux had his face not been so filled with rage.

"The pages got stuck together. It wasn't my fault," he pleaded before the yelling started.

"But you were making fun of him too!" Mr. Rodan snapped.

Ted answered purely on impulse. "It was just Brian. You can't tell me it didn't sound better after he stopped."

Any chance of mercy evaporated. "You are out of the orchestra!" Mr. Rodan declared, as if it were the comment that brought about the decision, which had already been made during the quick chat with his parents.

Ted hated orchestra but didn't want to be thrown out just like that. He'd much rather have quit moments before they needed him to do something important.

"I can do better," he blurted, his mouth acting separately from a brain surprised he was even trying to stay in.

"You have no talent at all!" Mr. Rodan shouted now flustered, face turning red, his big night ruined by this impish child. "You can't even t-t-t-t turn a p-p-p-p-page!"

"I'm s-s-s-s-sorry!" Ted retorted.

Ted accepted his fate. His mom would scream at him for a few hours, maybe teach him a new curse word he didn't know and, by tomorrow, forget she was mad at him. His dad concerned him much more. The well-trained policeman would bide his time and unleash a meaningful punishment.

Privileges, grounding, oh no! Christmas presents, Ted thought, suddenly realizing all the options available.

Everyone was still milling about after the concert grabbing the desserts that were being served. His father, knowing his son quite well settled on the worst punishment possible, public apology. First, he had to apologize to his teacher. Then it was off to Brian, whose parents reiterated he should be ashamed of himself. Finally, he was brought to the podium.

"You want to be the center of attention, here you go," his father stated as he stood waiting for Mr. Rodan to get everyone to look. Now it was Ted who stammered as he stumbled through a minute-long rambling insincere apology. His father finally grabbed the mic and finished him off.

"My son wants to be funny, so anyone who wants to laugh at him, please go ahead."

Ted and his folks left after that, causing him to miss the best reason for wasting a night there—one of the special chocolate fudge brownies David's family had donated for the event.

Candle

Fortunately, there were two boxes of Ted's favorite brownies left over, and the next day were passed out to his class. He'd almost missed those too, on account of being in the principal's office getting assigned detention for his antics the night before. Caught by surprise, he was under the impression detentions could only be given for things done during school hours. He returned to class just as they completed the distribution and had Itch to thank for making sure one had been placed on his unoccupied desk.

Although no one knew it, and no one would have cared if they did, it was Anna's birthday. Most girls in the school on their birthdays could expect cards, hugs, and gifts, and, if they were especially popular, find their desks covered in gift wrap.

Guys, too, celebrated each other's birthdays although their ritual was more barbaric. Usually administered first thing in the morning, the guy's friends would gang up on him in the schoolyard, each punching him once in the shoulder to give him a dead arm. The more people who hit, the greater the prestige. It was practiced primarily by the popular boys, which meant Ted never had to worry about a sore arm on his birthday.

The only thing Anna had to look forward to was the modest cake later that night with her grandmother, adorned with a single candle. Anna would tell her stories about her special day, how they sang "Happy Birthday" to her in class, how she received so many hugs she wanted them to stop.

She'd make wishes, but they weren't the type made by most eleven-year-olds. She desperately wished for a friend. Anyone would do. She wanted to have one lone day without ridicule. She wished she could forget all the horrible memories that haunted her from when she was younger. Mostly, she wished she'd never had a birthday at all.

In the classroom, she held her brownie up and took a bite. Its deliciously sweet chocolate flavor burst inside her mouth. She closed her eyes and pretended all of this was for her. The sounds of the others were an imaginary party, and everyone was getting ready to sing. Just then she heard her name, or at least what she was called.

"Watch Ani-mul suck down that cupcake without chewing it," one girl snickered.

"She could eat both boxes all by herself," the other replied.

She put down the remaining half, not wanting to be seen eating anymore. Despite her watering mouth, she touched it no further.

Birthdays for her were terrible. The day returning from Christmas break was worse.

Favorites

The day back from Christmas break found Anna assaulted by what the gods had favored on all the other kids. There were bicycles, makeup kits, concert tickets, games, gingerbread houses, stockings stuffed with candy. The list went on and on.

Anna's best gift was new shoes that replaced ones that were starting to hurt her feet. She would have given a piece of her soul to have been any one of those other kids on Christmas morning.

She returned home that day defeated, her spoon just swirled around the soup her nana prepared for her, not one drop raised to her lips. Nana leaned over to place a kiss on her forehead.

"What's wrong?" she asked.

She had not spoken a single word that day, unless the conversation she had with her four imaginary friends during lunch was to count. After a long pause, a tear rolled across her cheek.

"Nana, why does God hate me?"

"Why would you say that?"

"God loves the other kids, but not me."

"God does not play favorites."

"What! Come on, Nana! God does nothing but play favorites. And it's obvious his least favorite is fat girls like me."

"What happened at school today?"

"Nana, you should hear what the other kids got for Christmas."

"Oh, Anna, if we had money—"

"It doesn't matter," Anna interrupted. "Friends aren't for sale. Nana, why was I even born?"

Her nana's eyes filled with water. What could she possibly say to that?

"Anna, you were born so that I could love you as much as I do."

Insufferable

The teacher posed a question one day after they had watched *The Sound of Music.*

"Share one of your favorite things and tell us something about yourself we don't know."

Questions like this were common. The miracle today was that Anna, that girl who never responded to anything, a girl so quiet and seldom heard that some thought she could not speak, raised her hand. Upon seeing it, her teacher's heart leaped.

"Oh yes, Anna! Please share with us. Tell us one of your favorite things."

It had taken a level of courage few would understand for her to raise her hand. The room was silent enough to almost hear the poor girl's heart pounding in self-created terror.

She wanted to share with the class that she had seen the trees of the Sequoia National Forest. That glorious day with her father was one of the happiest of her childhood. First, though, she had to address her favorite thing. Love in her world could be defined as a simple eight-by-ten marble notebook she always kept with her. Everyone assumed she was studying, but the pages contained nothing short of her soul. She would offer something less intimate instead. She cleared her throat.

"I like flowers. Red roses are my favorite," she whispered with her eyes aimed at the floor.

"I wonder what other kinds of flowers she likes to eat," Ted quietly derided to all within earshot.

The teacher hadn't heard, but Anna did.

"That's wonderful, Anna. Now tell us something you would like us to know that we don't know about you."

Ted's comment made her uneasy and unsure if she should share that beautiful memory. The hesitation turned into a long pause. Ted gleefully filled the gap.

"Sheeeeeeeeee's fat!" Ted screeched.

"Theodore Carrington!" the teacher exploded.

"Wait, all of us already know that," he retorted.

Furious, she needed him to leave before she did something that would get her fired, if not arrested. She waved her arm and pointed to the door. Ted, quite familiar with the gesture, knew to head for the principal's office. Without a word, he rose and smiled toward everyone as though he'd been called to accept an Academy Award. Once outside, he defiantly walked the entire length of the hall holding up his middle finger back toward the class.

"I'm so sorry about that, Anna. Please go ahead."

She had already returned to her catatonic state.

"Please, Anna. We all want to hear whatever you want to say," she pleaded.

"Just leave me alone," Anna replied from deep inside her shell with her head buried in her hands.

That afternoon as it was on his route home, Ted disappeared into his favorite place, although few would have guessed—it was the library. The smell of books, the knowledge that filled the building, the enforced peacefulness, all comingled to make this his happy place. On many days, he'd stop in. Years before his mother used to take him to get books from the children's area. These days he frequented the science and business sections. He was also developing an interest in self-improvement books. However, to anyone's observation he never put any of that to use.

Inclusion

During one's youth, getting anything in the mail with your name on it, even if junk, was nothing short of an event. Ted loved the occasional letter that would be for him. This one was not like any before. Thick, canary yellow, the envelope had a grain he could run his fingers across. Whatever it contained was something special.

He was lucky it came on a Saturday, and he just happened to catch the postman delivering it. Otherwise, his mother would have opened it and blabbed the contents, removing all pleasure from the surprise of what could be inside.

He dashed to his room before she noticed to open it in private and sat on his bed holding it as though it were a magic lamp. Once the initial excitement subsided, he carefully ripped open the top to reveal its assumed wonderous message. Resembling something more appropriate to announce a wedding, he was in disbelief. Ashton Burke had invited him to his tenth birthday party!

The exclusivity of a Burke party was legendary. Usually limited to ten fortunate guests, the attendees would return to school with descriptions of how incredible his house was. There were claims it was larger than the school.

Ted was thrilled to be attending a party that wasn't limited to the company of just Itch and Chuck. He would get to see the colossal mansion for himself. Best of all, the thing that made all else irrelevant was a chance to meet Ashton's father, the megawealthy, famous, incredible Walter Burke.

Gaming

The beginning of baseball season coincided with the turn of Ted's stomach. For him, it signified another season having to play the reviled game. For those three months, his dad always dutifully sat in the bleachers watching over all the action trying to overlook the disasters Ted would cause. Each year Ted couldn't wait for summer to usher it all away. This year there was added stress. The coach was Tom's father, Mr. Chenko. The seven-one, 290-pound corrections officer was too large and inflexible to play but he made up for it by driving the kids hard.

Mr. Chenko carried into the season a problem. He loved to bet, and more often than not was in over his head. This money-draining habit was exacerbated by his high-stress job and miserable home life. Married to a woman who could empty the shelves of a liquor cabinet in a single day, he could always count on one thing—coming home after a long tiring day to find her passed out on the floor, usually in a cocktail of her own bodily excretions.

While most of his wagers were on sports, there were no restrictions. One of his more lucrative scores occurred when he won $3,000 correctly guessing the hour Hurricane Camille made landfall.

He had met his current bookmaker at his job. The man had been an inmate for a brief stint, and the two talked sports whenever the opportunity presented. Just after release, he became his full-time go to bookie. On a cold, early-spring morning as they conducted business, he mentioned his son's playing on a ball team. With the season yet to begin, and without performing one stitch of due diligence, he was offered three-to-one odds on his son's team just making the playoffs.

Mr. Chenko snapped at the opportunity and placed $1,500 against a total bet of $5,000. He had big plans for the winnings. Most of it would go toward a brand-new Chevy Malibu he had become enamored of. A beauty. Gold with a black top, tan interior, and all the amenities. Air conditioning, auto transmission, power steering, AM/FM radio, the works.

If the team lost, the consequences would be dire. Unable to cover the full bet, he could wind up with his legs broken or some equivalent. Instead, he focused on the positive. His son was a powerhouse hitter, and David Pisora could hold his own in any position.

He should have considered the other players. Standing right at the fork in the road that could make the difference between driving a creampuff or sitting in a wheelchair, was a kid who couldn't even keep a glove on straight, Theodore Carrington.

Malibu

Mr. Chenko delivered an impassioned speech but had the Malibu on his mind as they gathered for their first baseball practice of the season.

"Looking at you, kids, I can't help but think what a privilege it is to have this opportunity to be your coach. It's a privilege I take very seriously. I expect each of you to play this game just as seriously. You may not always be happy with what I demand of you, but I want you to win. I can be hard sometimes. Gentlemen, life is hard all the time. You need to know something. How hard you play on that field and how well you do doesn't only determine who wins the game. It determines who wins at life. Ask yourselves: Do you want to be champions?"

"Yes, Coach!" They all screamed as if in basic training.

"I am not going to make you champions. Instead, I am going to bring out the champion in each of you. We are going to win, win all season, and win the playoffs. You want a trophy?"

Suddenly, he had Ted's attention as Ted imagined getting one so big it wouldn't fit on that barren trophy shelf in his bedroom.

Mr. Chenko concluded, "You'll have it when we win the series. Believe it and believe in yourselves. This year's champions! Now let's show everyone how to play ball!"

The enthusiasm waned quickly. Mr. Chenko realized he had a severe problem when he saw Ted stop an easy grounder with his face. So awful that it was unlikely he'd even make a good mascot. Yet there he was and, according to league rules, had to be played at least half of every game.

Ted was watching a butterfly when a high pop up landed ten feet in front of him. When he did get to it, he hurled it, theoretically, in the direction of the second baseman. What should have been an easy out turned into a home run that drove in two runners.

Trailing the last inning by three runs with bases loaded, Tom smashed the ball over the fence, winning the game with a grand slam.

Despite Ted's continued error filled performance over the next two games, the team went into its fourth undefeated. Mr. Chenko went to the dealer after each win to look over his dream car. Then they had their first loss, and Ted's fingerprints were all over it.

When Ted struck out twice at bat before letting a grounder pass through his legs, Mr. Chenko had had enough.

"We got to talk," he barked at Ted at the end of the game. "Good God, Ted, really? What are you doing out there? You have no reason to be here."

Unexpectedly, Ted was a deer in the headlights. Speechless. Stunned. Fearful of the man yelling at him who stood more than two feet higher and two hundred pounds heavier.

"This must end. You got to stop playing."

"Why?"

He had to ask? Mr. Chenko pondered in disbelief. He struggled to find a way to call Ted a clueless moron without using the actual words. He believed he had a diplomatic way to convey his dismay but only proved he was not good with children.

"Your friends are winners. You are going to make them lose. Do you want your friends to be losers because of you?"

"No."

"Good, then we are settled."

"Yes, sir," Ted stated in an affirmation that meant nothing. He wanted to quit but couldn't do that to his dad.

Despite the speech Mr. Chenko had delivered about baseball determining success, Ted had defined it differently later in life.

SUCCESS

Present Day

Ted faced a dilemma. He was to deliver a speech to the graduating class at the end of the day, directing them on how to become successful. Therein lay the difficulty as he tried to suppress an old devil from his past that would not stop its interference. *These kids are virgins*, he thought, but not meaning it in the physical sense.

Ted had lost his real virginity to this world in his mid-thirties. It began with sending one of his vice presidents to Moscow to investigate a company Ted was looking to buy. The man was named Steven Reece. He was a bright, promising, newly hired executive, a graduate of Harvard Business School, and a devoted family man. Hours after his arrival at the airport, a call was received by his office demanding a half-million dollars for his safe return. Any hint of police and Reece would be sent back in pieces.

Following intense negotiations, the authorities were kept out, and all parties agreed that he would be released safe for a payment of $100,000 wired to a Swiss account. Within two hours, the money was wired. Two more hours followed before they received word the police had found Steven's badly beaten, dead body dumped in a park some fifteen miles from the airport.

There may be no darker day when a man has to tell another man's wife and children that their husband, their father, is never coming home, and it was because of something you had asked him to do. Ted returned from this task, which he did in person, deeply shaken. He sat in a recliner in the almost entirely dark den of his home, sipping a single glass of scotch for more than three hours. He raised the phone, deciding to do something he knew he would regret, call Ben Arlington.

Among the many things that annoyed Ted about Ben was the way Ben would lecture Ted. Ben was one month younger but always treated Ted as though he were twice Ted's age, three times his intelligence, and four times as wise. However, it was a sacrifice he would make to get access to the strong connections and power he knew that man to have in Russia.

He began the conversation, contrite, holding his emotions in check with the words. "Ben, I need your help." It was the first conversation in years where Ben did not argue about anything.

Golf courses and graveyards are places where two people can talk without worry of electronic eavesdropping. It is why US Presidents often play golf during some significant national crisis. It was the same reason Ben flew in on a red eye from California to meet Ted the next day at the sprawling Calvary Cemetery in Queens.

Both men, wearing fine business suits, arrived alone and, at sight, began walking apart from each other up a hill before them. On this cold, overcast, late autumn day, the cemetery was empty, parts of the ground covered in leaves that crunched as they briskly walked past the many headstones.

Descending the hill on the other side, out of the easy sight of anyone, they closed the distance between them and warmly greeted, shaking hands, and embracing. Pleasantries complete, they turned and began walking at a pace that barely moved them from one headstone to the next, conversing without looking at one another. Ben began.

"You know Ted, I haven't forgotten what you did."

"I wish you would."

"Well, that's not going to happen. I am sorry about your circumstances, but your call to me was a pleasant surprise. You are well familiar down the road I travel. Nice of you to finally join me in darkness."

"Let's not go overboard. The consensus on the street is you have become the devil."

"Flattery will get you nowhere. But your opinion means a lot to me. So, tell me: What do you think?"

"I know your methods."

"But do you understand them? Ted, being the devil isn't such a bad thing. You know how the myth goes. Satan was an angel, God's most powerful. Second only to God Himself. They had a falling out, and good and evil have fought ever since. But you know Ted, Satan is misunderstood. Ask anyone and they will tell you the devil's end game is pain and suffering, destruction, and chaos. That is just propaganda spread by those who benefit by manipulating the truth. God and the devil want the same thing. Peace on earth, prosperity, all of us to live in harmony. What sets them apart, what has caused the fight to rage since the beginning of time is that they differ in the methods they use to achieve it.

"But I digress. You are in way more trouble than you realize. The word on the street about you is that you are an easy target. Now everyone is going to go after you and your people. I just hope you're not looking for lawful justice or worse, get soft in the end and offer forgiveness."

"This is something I can't forgive."

That brought a smile to Ben's face.

"Good. Forgiveness is what people offer when they have no better options. I always offer better options."

"And what are these options."

"I worked on this after your call. The man responsible is Sergey Youmenkoff. He is a midlevel thug. Extortion, kidnapping, theft, he's been known to prey on tourists coming from the airport. I was told it went wrong immediately, but when he realized the connection to your company, well, he saw a big fish and went forward anyway."

"How do you know all this?"

"This comes straight from the KGB. He's been under surveillance, and they all but witnessed it."

"I assume, if they knew this, they would have arrested him already, if they intended to."

"Yes, they are aiming at much higher-ups than him. This is one we'll have to take care of ourselves. If you want to that is."

"Ben, I had to tell a woman her husband was not coming home, ever. I had to look into his five children's eyes and explain why they did not have a father, and I was the one who put him in harm's way. I don't want a bullet in the back of his head. That's too quick. I want it slow. I want him to know it is happening, and I want him to suffer. Revenge times twenty is what I want."

"I love this side of you. Do you know Vladimir Ruskin?"

"Dracula! You wouldn't be crazy enough to be doing business with Dracula?" Ted exclaimed.

Vladimir was a wealthy Russian oligarch widely regarded as a sadistic psychopath. Vlad's first name and his insanely enthusiastic use of medieval torture devices on those who crossed him had thoroughly earned the nickname.

"I have better than that. I own people in his network. I have access to every bank account. I know every phone call he makes, every conversation that takes place. The KGB pays me a fortune for this information, not to mention the favors I can ask.

"So, Ted, Vlad has a bank account I can access with $8 million. We'll wire it here and there as if we were trying to cover our tracks, but in the end, it will land in the same account you sent the $100,000. When Vlad traces it, I don't think you'll have to worry about Sergey's death being too fast."

Ted stopped walking. Suddenly, the air seemed much colder, the wind more substantial, and the sky a darker shade of gray than he noticed before. He looked for guidance from a sun hidden by clouds.

"Justice, Ben. I'll take justice instead."

"You don't get it. Justice needs to be in your hands. That is why you are who you are and I am who I am. He's killed before, and I'm sure he'll kill again. Maybe another five children will be without a father. Then you can blame it on yourself for your own spinelessness. Do it my way, and no one is going to know about the stolen money. All they will know is that Sergey crossed you and then was stretched to the breaking point on a medieval rack and torn apart one piece at a time."

"Okay, Ben. Do it your way."

Ben smiled. "As you wish."

They shook hands. Ted stood in place, contemplating while Ben left first.

Reaching almost fifty yards, Ted yelled, "Wait!" then ran up to him. "I can't do it."

Disgusted, Ben threw his hands into the air. "Just go home. Call me once you've dealt with the marshmallow you have for guts."

Ted had fitful sleep that night and many that followed. Checking in with Steven's widow more than a month later his emotions overcame morality. He picked up the phone to let Ben know he had changed his mind.

"Ben, I know you are going to be furious."

"It's done." Ben said the moment he heard Ted's voice. "I took care of it. It's all over."

A stunned Ted struggled to speak. "What happened?"

"What happened is no one over there is ever going to mess with you again, but your stomach is far too delicate for me to tell you the details. Revenge times twenty I assure you."

"I didn't want you to do it, Ben."

"Of course, you did. That's why you were calling me. You can't lie to me. Remember how long I've known you. I'm such a hell of a guy that when I knew you couldn't pull the trigger, I did it for you. Now because of me your misguided sense of morality allows you to have a clear conscience. But I know you believe sin is all about intention and how much you like puzzles, so I'll let you roll this around. Does the fact that you were calling to tell me to go ahead now make you just as guilty of his murder?"

"Ben, how do you live with this?"

"It's perception, Ted. You can see yourself as an evil monster or a hero who stopped a man from killing again. Had someone taken this approach a year ago five kids would still have a father. You can look at it from whichever angle you want but you know the one I have chosen."

"There are many people who might disagree."

"When the God-fearing, law-abiding sheep you are referring to are violated and they get on their knees to pray, they may offer forgiveness and ask God for all different things, but do you know what they truly want? Deep in their hearts, buried under heaps of denial, they hope God will ignore it all and answer their prayers by delivering to them a man like me."

Ted was speechless.

"You're welcome," Ben said, then laughed. "And you always thought it had been a girl who took your virginity. I'll see you from the opposite side of the corporate battlefield."

The line went dead.

Ted contemplated this dilemma. How was he to explain the world's actual workings to the fourteen-year-old students he was to later address?

Tycoon

Spring 1975

Three Years Prior To His Fateful Decision

Ted jumped out of bed and onto his knees to pray the morning of Ashton's party. Perhaps he had taken a page from one too many Disney movies, but in his mind, it was clear. Some circumstance would put him and the magnificent Mr. Burke in a conversation, they would hit it off, go into business together, and he would become rich. There were many unaddressed details, but he figured God would use his magic to fill in the rest.

He held a gift in one hand and a card in the other as his mother drove.

Anticipation built, then doubled as they entered his exclusive neighborhood some thirty miles away. No row houses here. Every dwelling, at least those that could be seen from the street, seemed ever grander than the previous as they moved closer to Long Island Sound. Large properties, finely manicured lawns; the only thing that seemed missing were people.

Attempting to follow the directions, his mother first went past the driveway, mistaking it for a separate street. Beyond iron gates left open on account of the gathering, the view of the house was blocked by thick rows of tall pine trees beside the driveway. At the end, there was a sharp turn that brought into view a mansion as stunning as its appearance was sudden. It was several hundred feet further to get to the carport beside the main entrance. There was supposed to be a man at the door to greet them but one of the guard dogs had gotten out and retrieving the beast was priority.

"Oh wow. You think this is it?" his mother questioned as she stopped in front. There was no house number to be found anywhere.

"Yeah, that's Ciro." Ted noted of the boy getting out of a car that had just pulled up behind them.

"You part of the hired help?" Ciro chirped upon seeing Ted.

No response from Ted was offered as they walked up the stairs together. Ted looked straight up at the three-story structure resembling some British castle from the Middle Ages. Ciro stood behind, firmly grabbed the back of Ted's neck, and banged his head into the door twice, enjoying that more than using the door knocker.

Ted broke free and was still rubbing his head when a man answered. Ciro thought it was Ashton's father, but Ted, having seen his picture in the paper and figuring he wouldn't be dressed in a tux, knew otherwise. It was Keith, the family's butler. Stiff and stuffy, the vibe he exuded made the two boys feel as though they had just entered the White House. The first room immediately inside only enhanced the setting.

"This is half the size of my house," Ciro marveled as they stood in what could best be described as an entrance rotunda, the floor covered in white marble, the walls decorated with numerous oil paintings.

"I didn't realize people lived in museums. This is crazy," Ted observed as they were led through several large richly decorated rooms and out to the back yard.

"Those have got to be the ugliest paintings I've ever seen," Ciro shot off as they walked past works of modern art on the wall, loud enough to worry Ted someone in the house might take offense.

"And I bet the most expensive too," Ted shot back. "Now that's fine art," he added as they passed a painting from the 1800s of a topless woman lying on a sofa, his eyes admiring it longer than the others.

Ashton was in the backyard sitting at a table under an umbrella by himself next to a swimming pool that was precisely one-half in length, but otherwise, all other dimensions of an Olympic. He was reading the latest copy of *Mad Magazine* waiting for his guests to arrive, of which Ciro and Ted were the first.

"Best magazine ever!" Ciro shouted as he walked up, and Ashton rose to greet him with a high five.

"Where's your dad?" Ted asked before saying happy birthday, not able to contain himself.

"Nice to see you too, Ted," Ashton responded sarcastically, simultaneously with Ted realizing he'd left his card and gift in the car. "My dad? He's flying in from a business trip. Hope he gets here in time. He hasn't been at one of my birthdays since I can't remember when. But he helped plan this one, so I think he'll be here."

Ted's heart sank. What if he didn't come? Additional members of the obnoxious popular crowd began to arrive. Other than seeing the house, meeting Mr. Burke was the only reason he wanted to attend.

To avoid becoming the party's verbal piñata, he slowly distanced himself from the group before walking off onto the grounds. The exploration beat anything the party could offer. Beyond the pool were tennis courts and a putting green. There were a pair of guest homes off to one side and a greenhouse the size of a barn on the other. The thirty-five-acre parcel stretched to the shoreline and offered views of Connecticut, twelve miles away on the opposite shore.

There was a trail he followed that led to a small but intriguing maze made from tall hedges. It offered a secluded oasis in the middle of an already secluded oasis. He ventured inside and, after a few turns, arrived in the middle. It was a beautifully peaceful spot, the ground covered with small white pebbles, surrounded by twenty-foot arborvitaes. In the center was a large decorative fountain fifteen feet high. Placed at points exactly north, south, east, and west were four benches.

One of the grounds people saw Ted enter and thought he might like to see the fountain running. It magically sprang to life just as he sat on the north bench. If he lived here, he would do all his homework, eat all his meals, and even sleep there if he could get away with it. No noise from anywhere outside, tucked away and in solitude, Ted might have just found his favorite place on earth.

He sat, lost in his own thoughts, only waking from them when the fountain, set on a ninety-minute timer, shut off. He returned to the party where they were just finishing relay races and beginning preparations to serve the cake. His long absence had gone unnoticed.

He scanned all doors and windows hoping to catch sight of his idol. There was no sign until they readied themselves to sing "Happy Birthday." Then, like a phoenix, there he was!

Ashton jumped up, leaving candles burning and delaying the start of the song, to run over and give his father a hug in front of Ted's jealous eyes.

"Dad, you made it!"

"Of course. Wouldn't miss it for anything!" he stated as he returned the hug. "Looks like I got here for the best part."

Just as they finished the birthday song, one of the servants took the cake to be cut. A line formed with David beating Ted for a place behind Mr. Burke.

Undeterred, he grabbed David by the shoulders and pushed so he could squeeze in between the two.

"I owe you, okay. Besides, you get great cake all the time." Feeling some jostling behind, Walter casually glanced over and offered a forced smile.

Ted's heart skipped a beat from the mere act of the man looking in his direction. Tongue-tied, he managed to get words out of his throat anyway.

"Your home is truly magnificent, at least the tiny bit I saw."

"Thank you," he responded while awaiting his plate of cake.

"I'm Ted," he blurted, throwing out his hand and not knowing what else to say.

"Oh, you're Ted. Ted Carrington, right?" Walter replied, accepting the offered handshake.

Ted's heart leaped with a joy that almost sent it out of his chest. Heavens! Somehow the man knew his name!

The next words left him lightheaded. "Would you like me to give you a tour of the house?"

"Oh yeah!" Ted exclaimed, realizing after he said it his level of enthusiasm was embarrassing.

Ted didn't bother getting any cake. He just hung by Walter's side waiting, obsessively, for him to finish. Seeing the eagerness Walter hurried, wiped his mouth, and led Ted inside. Away from the party Ted now had this man all to himself. He was close to fainting.

Walter for his part, took him from room to room giving details on the antiques, artwork, and features of the house. He was never brought to the upper floors. The first was impressive enough with its den, office, two large kitchens, maid's quarters, library, and billiard room with four fantastically large ornate bathrooms. The basement, as large as the first floor, had several sections including a weight room, game room including an air hockey table, a music room, full bar, and a room with carefully placed bean bag chairs just for meditation. Ted enjoyed the tour, but most of his attention was focused on finding some way to impress his host.

"Any questions?" Walter asked as the generous twenty-five-minute tour ended with them in the living room in front of a stone fireplace big enough to stand in.

"Do you do any investing?" Ted responded.

Surprised, not the kind of question he was expecting, Walter answered, "Yes, quite a bit, is that something you are interested in?"

The stage was all set. Lights, camera, action! This was his moment and he pounced. There was a medical company he had been following for months. They had been denied FDA approval on a drug they developed, and the press proclaimed them hopeless. The stock had fallen from ten dollars to $1.25, then bounced back to two dollars. That wasn't the story.

From what he gleaned from various articles, they had enough cash and no debt. They recently reapplied for FDA approval. Most significantly, they just hired a CEO who, according to the paper, specialized in turn-around situations. Ted was convinced it was ready to jump and sat on the couch across from Mr. Burke sharing with him every piece of information he knew. Walter could see his enthusiasm and sat with his hand on his chin lightly shaking his head for most of the time, as amused as he was amazed by this boy.

"I'll have to look into it," he said as Ted finished. "How do you know all this?"

"Read it in the *Journal*," he answered, trying to sound sophisticated with his casual delivery of the explanation. "I've got over a million dollars invested in it." He was surprised by his own words and held in abeyance a cringe.

"Really? A million dollars?" Walter countered. "I had no idea I was sharing my time with a tycoon. If you don't mind my asking, how did you acquire such wealth? Corporate bonuses? Horses maybe? Blackjack table?"

Ted recognized his position and tried to wiggle out of it. "No, I grew it from other investments. Probably shouldn't talk about it."

Walter rubbed his forehead, "Ted, be honest with me and be honest with yourself. You don't have a million dollars in it."

"No, I swear I do, a full million."

"You don't have a million in it," he said with a tone of definitiveness that Ted could not counter.

Ted looked to the floor, stood up from the couch and admitted, "No. I wish I had a million dollars, but the truth is I don't have a dime to my name."

"So why did you attempt to mislead me?"

"Can I go now?"

"I just asked you a question and leaving without answering is rude. You can leave after you tell me why you said what you did."

"Well, I said that"—he paused as sweat began to seep from every pore—"because I wanted to impress you."

"As if you needed more than just being yourself. Well, I was very impressed, that is, up to the point when you lied to me. Now why don't you go back to the party and get a piece of cake before it's all gone?"

Ted's eyes scanned the floor as he left wishing for a trap door to allow him to exit faster. Humiliated, he spun back anyway to face Mr. Burke one last time.

"That stock. I didn't lie about it. It really is a good investment."

"And I said I would look into it," Mr. Burke replied.

Returning, Ted found the party over and himself the last guest. Despite servants the rule was Ashton had to clean up after himself and was busy doing it. Ted called his mom to pick him up, then walked out to the yard to wait. He looked at the pool longingly, scanning for a rock he could tie around his neck before throwing himself in. Needing a distraction, he offered to help clean and joined in anyway after being turned down.

"Something wrong?" Ashton asked, noting the long expression.

"I'm fine," he replied with a complete lie. Abysmally disappointed in himself, he had reached a reckoning as to why nobody should invite him to their parties.

Loser

Ted's baseball team had its ups and downs, and two-thirds of the way through the season, it looked as though making the playoffs might come down to them and one other team. This left Ted an extreme risk playing in a single game that would determine who made the playoffs. Mr. Chenko had to get rid of him. He believed he had found the way.

As Ted stepped up at bat, Tom and a few others stood pressed against the dugout's chain-link fence. Then it began. A chant. Slowly at first but becoming louder and picking up pace.

"You suck. You suck. You suck! You suck! You suck! You suck! You suck! You suck!"

Half panicked, half mortified, he threw down the bat following his strikeout and ran to his coach.

"Coach! Why are they doing that? Please make them stop."

"What am I supposed to do?" he replied with an air of complete disinterest.

"Please, my dad's here! Please tell them not to do that."

"Maybe you should have quit when I told you to."

Ted couldn't get the words out fast enough. "I'll quit. You'll never see me again. Just don't let them do it. Not in front of my dad."

"I'll think about it," was the cold reply.

If Ted thought his first time at bat was bad, the next was worse. This time the entire bench cleared to call out the chant. All except Itch. He was the only one, despite overwhelming peer pressure, who refused to inflict this humiliation on his friend.

"You suck! You suck! You suck!" It continued through all three pitches, all three strikes.

Mr. Carrington came down from the bleachers to talk with the oversized coach. There was a discussion, somewhat heated, with Ted only hearing Mr. Chenko's last sentence.

"I don't control the kids."

The team lost soon enough, only their third defeat of the season. Everyone cleared out while Ted remained sitting slumped on the bench. He was filled with a sense of dread but unsure from which of the many potential sources it was coming. His father approached and put his hand lightly on his shoulder.

"I don't think baseball is for you," he offered.

With that, Ted rose and staggered back to the car desperate to hold off feeling anything. Once in the passenger seat, he burst into tears.

Badly hurt, it wasn't what the kids had done. The only reason he played was to please his father. What tore him apart had nothing to do with giving up baseball, but rather the sense that his father had just given up on him.

Joe let him go long enough to get his seat belt on and start the car. It was probably the police force environment he was immersed in every day that brought about a most unsympathetic reaction.

"Oh, come on, that's enough," he snapped. "Grow up, will you? Act like a man. Crying is for girls and babies!"

It took a couple of minutes and an Olympic feat of strength, but Ted managed to pull himself together. There were no words when he got home. He went to his room, locked the door, and allowed the pieces of himself that remained to fall onto his bed.

He shed every stitch of clothing. As long as he was naked, he reasoned, he wouldn't leave his room. He never wanted to face the world again. Obviously, eventually, he had to and did so hours later, begrudgingly with two conditions. He vowed he would quit baseball and no matter the circumstance, never again allow himself the disgrace of acquiescing to his emotions.

As determined as he was to keep those vows, inevitably, he would come to break both.

Playoffs

It was true Ted had quit baseball. He stopped going to any practices and missed the next two games. The team was one game away from making the playoffs. It was down to a single sudden death game. This game could be the difference between a wheelchair or a Malibu for Mr. Chenko. Itch, sensing the significance began to badger Ted to rejoin. It wasn't that he wanted him in the game, his motive was more sinister. He hated Mr. Chenko almost as much as Ted and knew the best revenge would be to bring him out of mothballs for this most important game.

It took three solid days of nonstop annoyance to finally get Ted to agree. Itch had it all figured out. Ted brought his baseball uniform to school the next day so Itch could stash it at his house. Ted went over to his place Saturday morning to get changed, then go with Itch to the game. Ted's parents were none the wiser.

Itch wished he had brought a camera. The look on Mr. Chenko's face when he saw Ted approaching was as unforgettable as it was indescribable. So infuriated, he ripped the cap off his bald head and threw it to the ground, shouting the F-word as it hit.

The first three innings didn't go well, errors stacked, and the opposing team drove in runs. Having been kept out, Ted couldn't be blamed. They were down 7-0 by the fourth inning when, reluctantly, Mr. Chenko had to put Ted in. He took the batter's box. The bench cleared, again, all except Itch, and the chant started again. Hoping Ted would walk off the field right then and there, Mr. Chenko even instigated them.

"You suck! You suck! You suck! You suck! You suck!"

"Hold up! Hold up! Time!" the coach from the other team shouted while making a T sign with his hands. Ted glanced over to see a man who could not have been a hair over four feet tall, a raging ball of fury, double-time it to their dugout and stick his finger into the giant man's face.

The first few shouts were loud and clear. "What the hell is this? This is how you let your players treat a member of their own team, and you encourage it!"

A neutron star is one of the densest objects in the universe. A single teaspoon contains the weight of an entire mountain. By comparison, one of the densest concentrations of swear words ever gathered on the surface of this planet is what followed that day on that baseball field. The man's shouting degraded into a high-decibel rant, individual words hardly intelligible but the meaning obvious. All the while, Tom's father, backed up against the chain-link fence, appeared as if he were trying to squeeze through one of its two-inch squares. It was like watching a bear being nipped senselessly by a Chihuahua.

Returning to his dugout, the coach shouted as he passed home plate, "What's your name, son?"

"Ted."

"Come on, Ted! Hit the ball! Knock it out of the park!"

His own shouts not enough, within moments, the man had five kids in the dugout from his own team on their feet, cheering as well. The first pitch was a strike. The shouts of encouragement only became louder and, with more prompting, were joined by players on the field. Ted's own team, now silenced, stood like zombies as the spectacle washed over them.

It had become clear. One by one, they hung their heads in shame as each realized what this implied. They were losers, and it had nothing to do with the score.

After his strikeout, the dugout he returned to was very different. Even Tom tapped him lightly on the shoulder to say, "Nice try."

In the final inning, Ted took his place at bat with one out and no one on base. First pitch, strike! "No, no," the opposing coach called out along with "Time!" He then walked up to Ted.

"You are doing this all wrong. Your feet are supposed to be here and here," he said, pointing.

The umpire interrupted; it was against the rules for a coach to assist a player in the batter's box.

"I'm not *his* coach," he barked, "and I don't think that half-ton lump of s—t over there has a problem with it, so back off."

He corrected Ted's posture and some other things.

"Keep your eye on the ball, follow it into the catcher's mitt. Ted, you are going to hit this."

There was another strike, but he got a piece of the next one. It wasn't a great hit, but it did skip past the third baseman, putting him on first. He was one of four from his team to get on base that day but the only one to get a high five from the baseman when he did. The season ended with the strikeouts of the next two batters. If looks could kill, the one his coach gave him as they departed would have done the trick.

Arriving at Itch's house, he changed back into regular clothes. Before leaving, his mother made lunch for the two boys and Itch's sister Jessica. One thing about Jessica—she loved animals and was begging her mom to buy her a snake. It was still on Ted's mind when he arrived home. When asked by his father what he had been doing that morning, he diverted.

"Dad, can I get a pet snake?" he asked, not really thinking his father would take him seriously.

His father held unexpressed concerns regarding his son's lack of interest and ability in sports. In fact, ever since his colleagues witnessed an attempt by Ted to play in a game of touch football at a police-sponsored picnic, they would sometimes joke by asking, "How's your little girl at home doing?" Not wanting to squander what he saw as a rare sign of masculinity, Ted's father threw him into the car before Ted could change his mind.

They wandered through the pet store, first looking at some other pets before gravitating to a tank with about a dozen garter snakes. As an employee approached, Ted noticed two three-foot corn snakes in a different tank and, pressing his luck, asked, "Can I get these?" now aiming to get two snakes.

"Sure," his dad called back, barely glancing at what the tank contained.

"Them snakes," the store employee chimed in, in a dialect from somewhere Ted didn't know but which was not

New York. “You can give ’em the frozen food, but to be best off, you got to feed them live mice.”

Ted paused a moment to figure out what the man had said before his father interrupted. “Would you be okay with that, having to feed them mice that are alive?”

“I get to have mice too!” Ted blurted excitedly.

“They are not pets. They’re food. You can’t get attached to them. Will it bother you to have to feed them to the snakes?”

“Why would it? I’m not the one eating them.”

“You own snakes before?” the employee interrupted.

“No,” they both responded together.

“Before you set on it, let’s see how you do,” he replied as he picked one snake from the tank to put on Ted’s outstretched hands.

No sooner had he placed it, the snake coiled back and bit Ted firmly on the wrist.

“It bit me!” Ted exclaimed, unsure if he should be upset before realizing it barely hurt and was more amused than anything else.

He gently placed a finger under the snake’s nose and coaxed him off, then offered his hand to allow it to slither part way up his arm.

“He’s a natural. Everyone jerks away once they’re on ’em. Your boy, it’s like he was born one of ’em.”

Ted and his dad left the store with two corn snakes, six white mice, and all the necessary paraphernalia to take care of them. He set it up in their small basement and decided to give them a welcome lunch by dropping two mice into the cage. One ate immediately. The other took its time but there were just four left when it was over.

He went outside to gather twigs and leaves to give them as natural an environment as possible amidst the sounds coming from the heated argument his dad was having with his mom over the snakes. Ultimately, Ted got to keep them.

After a few weeks, he became a master at their care and tended to them each day after school. He liked that his friends thought they were cool but the thing he loved most is how terrified some people are of snakes.

Tiring quickly of just shoving them in people's faces, he devised a unique trick whereby he'd hide one in the back of his shirt and let it come popping out his collar as a surprise. It was a sight that sent many, including a policeman friend of his father with a particular fear of snakes, one who had previously ridiculed Ted's masculinity, fleeing the house. His father, just a little proud, gave him a minimal scolding even though he deserved a lot more. Realizing the fear some have of mice, others of snakes, Ted reveled in the homemade horror kit available in his basement.

Sexuality

In fifth grade, kids are on the verge of becoming young adults. That signaled an awkward evening of sex education, delivered, of course, with a Catholic spin. Each child came with a parent who was relegated to the back of the church while the soon to be educated, and copiously embarrassed, sat up front.

For girls, it was administered by a nun named Sister Anne. She was among the youngest of the order, a woman in her mid-thirties, and a favorite of the children. Slightly over six feet tall and filled with energy, it was hard not to see her likeness to Julie Andrews in *The Sound of Music*.

The girls took the instruction seriously, but it was challenging to get the boys, who received it two nights later, to do the same. Theirs was administered by a priest named Father Tom.

"He never uses his! I should be teaching this class," Ciro bellowed as Father Tom took the podium.

Father Tom picked up on it fast. "It seems I have a test dummy who wants to demonstrate. Thank you, Ciro. Come on up and remove your clothing."

The room became silent faster than Ciro's face could turn beet red.

This was no ordinary priest. Athletic, forty-two years old, tall, head shaven, and whenever outside, regardless of the weather or time of day, wore dark-shaded glasses with his priest's collar. He looked more like an international spy than a man of religion. His approach to implementing church doctrine was far too practical for him to be going anywhere within its hierarchy. Wildly popular, the phone at the rectory would ring off the hook starting on Friday evening with parishioners calling to find out which mass he was scheduled for on Sunday.

Known to keep his homilies short, he began each with the same opening line.

"Let me get right to the point of what this Gospel means in your life."

What could be an hour in church on Sunday with another priest, Father Tom usually had done, over, and finished, in twenty-five minutes, twenty during football season! He'd sometimes end the mass with a special request.

"Please pray for the Broncos. I've got money on them."

The Catholic version of the evening went against his grain, but he stuck to the party line that everything about sex is wrong until married. Once joined in holy matrimony, it should be done as frequently as possible but only to produce babies. That was the first half of the simplistic lesson.

The rest of it, laid out in rudimentary sketch pictures, was mostly new to Ted. All of it had him either horrified, embarrassed, or baffled. After hearing the details, he turned to look at his father and clung to a sliver of hope that, since he had been adopted, it was at least possible his parents had never done what they were describing.

When question-and-answer time came, his mind was jammed. Plucking one from many he raised his hand believing, naively, that the warning they had been given not to make fun of anyone would protect him.

"After doing what you told us, you know, the man and the woman—"

"You mean sexual intercourse between a married man and woman?" Father Tom clarified.

"Yeah," Ted replied, not entirely sure what Father Tom said and already unhappy he'd raised his hand. "How long are you supposed to do it for?"

"Do you mean until how old?"

There were already giggles.

"What I'm asking is, when you are doing that thing to make babies, how do you know it's time to stop? When is it over?"

The answer, Catholic and chauvinistic, but unfortunately correct, was given.

"Sex is over as soon as the male achieves orgasm."

"Sadly, I would have to agree with that," one of the moms quipped to another in the back.

Solitude

Summer 1976

Summer vacation always passed too quickly, and in a flash, the two months became a memory. Their new sixth-grade teacher employed a reliable time waster so she could prepare a lesson on the chalkboard. "Tell us about your summer." They went around the room. Ted thought Ashton's answer was brilliant.

Embarrassed by his wealth and privilege, many of the kids knew he spent summers in a mansion on the Italian Amalfi Coast, but all he said was, "I got to spend time with my family."

When Ted's turn came, he began by stealing Ashton's line, "I spent time with my family."

He looked around and noticed, as far as he could tell, not one person was listening to anything he was saying. Even the teacher seemed uninterested, back turned while writing on the blackboard.

Ted's family didn't have money to go to Italy or anywhere that year. However, a colleague of his father extended an offer to join him, his wife, and son at a large cabin they were renting in Wisconsin for a week. Free was within their budget. All they had to do was get there. Billy, their only child, was a year older than Ted. The cabin was on a lake in the middle of nowhere, and his parents were thrilled their son would have a companion.

Leaving before dawn, they stopped for breakfast at a roadside diner. Over a plate of pancakes Ted's parents told him a detail about Billy they incredibly didn't think had any significance. Billy, just like himself, had been adopted.

Usually, Ted was less than enthusiastic about meeting the children of his parents' friends. It just meant he was going to be outdone by someone new. With this additional information, his anticipation of meeting Billy increased with each mile of the fourteen-hour journey.

Billy was nowhere near the image Ted had imagined. Given Billy's Irish parents, the fact he was two full shades darker than Rip came as a complete surprise. Billy needed little else to confirm he had been adopted. Tall, built, athletic, fast-tracking toward Eagle Scout, voted MVP in two sports, he was the kind of kid Ted would do his best to avoid had he been at school. Waiting in the driveway for Ted's arrival, the two boys hit it off the moment the car pulled up. It was as though they had been best friends since toddlers.

It turned out to be one solid week of the most fun Ted ever had. They explored trails running through the woods, boated on the large lake in front of the cabin, fished, and caught frogs by the shore. In the evenings, they would sit on the porch and watch bats flying silhouetted against the twilight sky, then sneak off down to the shore and set campfires that were not allowed, busying themselves all seven days from sunrise to way past sunset.

Early one morning, they decided to take a small boat onto the lake. After putting on life jackets and stowing more to use as pillows, they began paddling. They made it their mission to row to the center of the lake, six miles long and a mile wide.

This was not done casually. They were in a fight for their lives, pretending there was a sea monster, like Loch Ness, that could rise from the lake and swallow them at any moment. They determined the only safe place was the exact center and that is where they stopped when they believed they had arrived.

"We're safe now," Billy said jokingly between pants.

Once they regained composure, they arranged the extra life jackets and laid back opposite each other with enough room to separate them.

The sky, a magnificent blue, captured both their imaginations. Ted had been sharing his philosophical thoughts all week, something Billy seemed to enjoy.

"Got something for us to talk about?" Billy inquired.

Ted considered for a while in silence before thinking of something neat.

"Billy, think about this. Imagine if you could meet your future self. Like say when you are fifty. Suppose you could ask yourself one question, what would it be?"

"Well, let's see, maybe I'd ask..."

"Don't tell me. That will make you change it. Just think about it."

Billy remained silent and laid all the way back. Ted did the same. His mind wandered as he closed his eyes and conjured an image. He placed himself in an undecorated room, with just four walls and two chairs facing each other, one of which was empty, while he sat in the other. He then invited himself way in the future to come and sit in the other chair.

When nothing happened, he realized summoning himself from a future that had not happened was impossible. But, he reasoned, nothing was keeping his future self from coming back here. He set in his mind that in forty years, on his fiftieth birthday to be exact, so he would remember, he would return, sit in the opposite chair and answer his question.

He thought hard, fishing for what it should be. *How much money do you have? Did you become pope? Did you destroy your enemies?* All seemed so one dimensional. Then something completely different. He had it!

"Tell me why I should be proud of you?" he demanded of the empty seat.

Satisfied, he opened his eyes. His eyes were filled with visions of the beautiful sky. All he could hear was the sound of small waves licking the side of the boat. Lost in all sorts of wondrous thoughts, he was not in the habit of sitting still. This was something so marvelous it felt he perhaps had reached the pinnacle of life. His only purpose in the world right then was to simply exist.

The two lay in silence long enough for an entire cloud bank to appear on the horizon, cover them in shadows, then move on to disappear over the opposite horizon. So silent Ted began to worry if Billy was still in the boat. There was no way to be sure without looking. Had it been a half hour? Two hours? No idea. Was Billy asleep? Did he fall out unnoticed and Ted, stupidly, was just lying there?

Difficult as it was, he made the decision to do something he had never consciously done before. Let go of the many irrational thoughts and just trust everything will be fine. As the minutes passed, one thing became clear. The best moments of our lives are those where we remain in stillness and absorb the beauty that is ever present around us.

Then way off in the distance—he happened to be looking in just the right place—a bird (it was an eagle) caught his eye. He leaned up slightly to watch it scream down from its heights, splash across the water's surface and pick up a sizable fish in its talons. As it flew off into the trees, he wished Billy had seen it.

"Did you see that?" whispered Billy.

His breath was taken both from the stunning beauty of the eagle and again by the fact Billy had seen it. He never before felt so connected with another human being.

"Yeah, I did," he whispered in reply.

"We have to be getting back," Billy announced as they sat up and stretched.

They had drifted far from the center, further out from the cabin, and it would be a long paddle back. The return trip was relaxed, their oars poking almost teasingly at the water rather than the life-saving row they did going out.

Thinking of the eagle, Ted began to speak the kind of thoughts no one else seemed to understand without worry of laughter from his classmates or the look of bewilderment from his mother.

"Do you think the eagle knows how amazing it is?" he asked.

"How so?" Billy replied.

"It's amazing what it can do. Fly like that, scoop up a fish it would take me all day to catch and then maybe not even. It does it so easily. Do you think it realizes how special it is?"

"Probably not. How would it know something like that?" Billy said.

"I guess it doesn't," Ted surmised but then thought something more profound.

"We don't give much thought about what makes us special either, do we? Maybe we should." He paused to let that sink in but soon offered another thought. "Do you think it's happy?"

"What do you mean, the bird?"

"Yeah, the bird. When it soars, swoops, catches a fish. Do you think all the amazing things it can do makes it happy?"

"Are birds supposed to be happy?"

"Why not? God created us and them too. I would think he'd want them to be happy."

"Does happiness matter to them?"

Ted pondered it, then had a new revelation. "You know what, Billy? *Happiness* isn't the right word. *Satisfied* is better. Catching that fish probably made it satisfied."

Then he burst with excitement!

"That's it. Think about it. Satisfaction equals happiness. One brings the other. We just need to be satisfied with the things in our lives that matter."

"And what would you say are the things that matter?"

"I'm not sure, but I bet that bird knows more about it than we do."

Billy raised his oar out of the water and turned back to look directly at Ted.

"I don't know how you come up with these things."

Suddenly embarrassed, Ted held any further thoughts to himself and paddled a bit faster. The sparkle of the waves, each glint stabbing into his eyes, made him feel as though the entire lake was laughing at him. Nothing else was uttered until they reached the dock. Stepping from the boat, Billy broke the silence.

"You know something, Ted? I would give anything, absolutely anything, to have your head on my shoulders even if it was just for one week."

On the last night of their stay, there was a strong wind outside blowing through the leaves of the innumerable trees surrounding the cabin that made it sound as though there were a titanic waterfall next to the house. It woke Ted in the middle of the night, and he sat up, leaning on his elbows and looking around the darkened room. He could hear nothing but the wind in the trees and the very faint sound of Billy breathing as he slept on a mattress on the floor next to his.

This week had been the first in his life he fully experienced the joy of pretending to be no one other than himself. It was a gift given to him by Billy. He suddenly remembered, thinking it odd, that as much as it secretly bonded them, they never discussed their adoptions.

Grateful for their time together, Ted offered a prayer of thanks, doing so twice to be sure it got through. When finished, he looked around to take in the subtle beauty that darkness can bring to a room and pondered the question Billy had asked. "What is it that matters?"

He took a deep breath of the cool fresh air and looked over at Billy, sleeping so peacefully. To call him a friend would be an insult. He gazed upon him as the brother he never had.

Then it came to him. The answer! He leaned over to whisper to Billy. Very quietly, it flew from his lips into Billy's ear with muted excitement.

"I got it, Billy, I figured it out. I know what matters. It is the effect we have on others. This week, Billy, you did that for me. You mattered so much in my life."

He basked in the glow of his answer for a moment before succumbing to a crushing reality. Because Billy's family was moving to another state, their fathers would no longer be working together. It was most likely they would never see each other again. With Ted leaving before dawn, Billy would still be sleeping when they left. This was it, and tears began to well in his eyes.

He hovered above Billy in the darkness for a while, using the precious little light to see and memorize every detail of his face. Leaning over, he gently placed a kiss on Billy's forehead. He thought of school and how resoundingly he'd be hanged if anyone discovered what he had just done. They would never understand that he needed some way to ensure their last moment together was special.

* * *

"Is that it?" the teacher asked as she continued to write on the blackboard, jolting Ted from his recollection.

Lost in those thoughts, he was barely aware of what was leaving his mouth but believed no one was listening anyway. Following the statement about spending time with his family he continued, but with words now contaminated by sadness.

"I discovered the purpose of life. It's all about the effect you have on others. And...I made plans to meet with someone I hope doesn't disappoint me."

"Anything else?"

"Did you hear me? I said I figured out the meaning of life."

His teacher replied in a way that might be likened to some reader of novel when they have been given such wisdom. "Good for you. Next."

Diversion

September 1977

Seven Months Prior To His Decision

That first day of sixth grade meant Ted once again would have to be subjected to Itch's stories about Boy Scout camp and the fantastic time he had. The evening campfires! Swimming at all hours! Fish eaten just after being caught!

Ted hated hearing about it but couldn't tear himself away. Envy poured from him as he absorbed every word and lamented that it must be just like what he experienced at the cabin, except six weeks long!

Hanging out by the short wall on the playground, they chatted, just a few feet from where Anna was sitting in exile scribbling in her notebook. She strained to overhear their conversation, knowing she would have none of her own with anyone that day. Their topic moved from camp to the movie *Star Wars*, which had enamored everyone over the summer. Most of the boys tried to outdo each other in the number of times they claimed to have seen it. For Itch, it was eight, Rob twelve, Ashton fourteen, and Ted only once.

He may have been the only kid in America who didn't want to see it a second time. He found some of it boring, but worse, he couldn't get past the many scientific inaccuracies. Explosions heard in space, earthlike gravity everywhere, and come on, two robots brimming with gears roaming a planet made of sand. There was something deeper though that disturbed him, and he decided to share it with Itch. The hope was he would react to this innermost thought in the same way Billy had.

"What about the stormtroopers?" he inquired. "I feel bad for them. I bet most of them just got sucked into the evil empire, you know, like the draft. They didn't really want to be there, but they had to. They have families that love them back at home, and yet they just get blown away like its nothing."

Itch looked as though he had ceased breathing, with his mouth open, stunned, waiting for Ted to fully finish.

"It's a movie, dumbass, a galaxy far, far away. Did you miss that part, or maybe you can't read? I've always suspected that." He continued chuckling sarcastically. "Oh no! Shooting at the stormtroopers hurts their feelings. Hey, Rob!"

"Not what I meant. I was just thinking, considering." Ted backpedaled frantically before Rob had a chance to come over. "Just drop it, Itch, okay."

Itch, still laughing, shook his head in amazement. "Ted, they don't have words in the dictionary to describe how weird you are."

Rob, still coming, forced Ted to find a diversion and targeted his favorite victim.

There she sat with the same lonely expression on her face as the year before, writing in the notebook she always had with her.

"What's up, Itch? What did Teddy Bear say this time?" Rob asked, ready to be amused.

"You got to hear this," Itch mused.

Ridicule or be ridiculed? He made his decision.

"I was trying to decide with Itch what Ani-mul over there would look like in a bathing suit. She would probably have to buy it at the aquarium."

Anna wished she hadn't been listening. It was painful being ridiculed by the girls, and they were relentless, but something made her heart especially break when it came from the boys.

"How is it she is always studying in that notebook yet remains so dumb? She's probably getting ready to eat it," he added as though delivering some preplanned comic routine. "At what point, do you think they should stop putting helium in her?"

"Looks like she could pop any second," Rob responded.

"I hope not. I'm still picking at all the joke meat on her enormous carcass."

She allowed each word to pass her ears without response. Inside, her mind was unrestrained, she considered murdering Ted. Poison maybe? Toss gasoline and set him ablaze? Perhaps it was as simple as bashing his skull in with a rock. She awoke from the daydream disappointed in herself. She never wanted to be someone who would hurt another human being no matter what they did to her.

Instead, she furiously scratched her pencil across the page before her, destroying in detail everything she had been writing.

Servers

The call was out for altar boys. Typically, about half the boys in the class made mostly of the popular crowd would sign up for the three-year commitment.

Obligations included four months of training, two days a week after school, and having to serve early masses. Most hated was first mass of the day at 7:00 a.m., which was disproportionally assigned to the new altar boy crop.

Benefits, however, included generous tips when wedding masses were assigned. If assigned a 9:00 a.m. mass, they were allowed to miss first class. The best advantage of all though was the opportunity to get noticed by girls. How dressing in a full-length black robe called a cassock and topping it with what could be best described as an oversized white blouse would achieve that defied logic, but there was no convincing them otherwise.

Coming back from sign up, Ted commented as he passed Anna, sitting at her desk.

"Hey, Itch, Ani-mul should join. Didn't Father Tom say we needed an altar elephant."

"They will have to reinforce the altar first," Itch replied.

As always, Anna sat silent, absorbing it all. Ted took every opportunity, and she hated him for it. She wondered if she'd ever gather enough courage to let him have it.

Stoic

With Ted clearly willing to commit two days after school to this, Rip saw an opportunity to occupy Ted's other free weekday afternoons.

"Come on, Ted. Come over and work out with me."

"Rip, I got so many better things to do."

"It'll be fun. I'll start you slow. You have time for altar training but none for me?"

"Well, you, sir, are not God."

Disappointed, Rip relented. It had been perhaps the hundredth time he had asked, and he wondered why he had bothered yet again.

Later that day, Sister Howard appeared at the door to one of Ted's classes. He was being summoned to the principal's office and braced himself as he began the routine walk to the courthouse. His heart jumped to his throat upon discovering his mother was already in the office, her face was red and eyes puffy.

"Oh God, whatever I've done this is really bad," he feared.

"Ted, it's Grandpa. He was working in the store on a ladder and fell."

"Is he all right?"

"No, he died."

"So, I'm not in trouble?"

Then it hit him.

"Wait. What? Grandpa? What do you mean he died?"

"He fell and hit his head. He's gone."

When Sister Bethany moved to comfort him with a hand on his shoulder, he all but shoved her away. It was such a delicate balance. Anything. Any little disturbance could trigger the flood of emotion he was holding back, he just breathed in and out, expressionless. From the office to home, through the wake and funeral, he held it in. There were no cracks in his facade for weeks. He thought he was past it until Ciro took his shot.

During training one month later, funeral masses were the subject, and Ciro suggested, crossing his arms over his chest with hands on his shoulders.

"Hey, Ted, how about my friends be the pall bearers, and I'll play the part of your grandfather."

Ted ran from training out the side door into the school. Albeit quietly, he could not refrain from doing what he perceived as the most disgraceful thing possible for a male his age. Face in his hands, sitting on the floor hiding behind a statue of the Blessed Mother ascending to heaven, he finally broke down.

It was an all but canceled Thanksgiving and a very subdued Christmas vacation that year. With the New Year's turn, he prayed things would get better, but just how those prayers were answered was a matter of perception.

Judas

January 1978
Three Months Prior To His Fateful Decision

It was no secret Itch and Ashton didn't like each other, but tensions had reached a breaking point a week after the return from Christmas break. It involved a girl.

A cute flirt with black hair named Betsy. Itch mistook her attention as an indication of attraction, but her eyes, along with most of the girls, were sighted on Ashton. That kid had everything, money, popularity, good looks, and now all the girls he could want, including Itch's. Jealousy becoming resentment, Itch refused to stop calling him a "spoiled playboy." It escalated to a fight.

At the end of an altar training, taunts became shoves as they exited to the side of the church. They managed to pause hostilities long enough to take off their coats, Ashton handing his to Ciro, Itch to Ted.

"You got my back, right?" Itch said to Ted, fear in his eyes evident beneath bravado. Ted nodded and gave a thumbs-up just as Itch turned to face off against Ashton, who already had his fists up.

"You are what you eat, which explains why you're such a dick!" Itch shouted.

"I'm going to bust your face!" Ashton countered as he threw the first punch, swinging into air as Itch ducked out of the way.

Itch counterpunched into Ashton's side, hitting him solidly under his ribcage, knocking him off balance. As he began to fall, he grabbed Itch's arm and both tumbled down the stairs, all amidst pandemonium that had broken out among the altar boy trainee spectators with the pull of adolescence far outweighing their dedication to religion.

"Fight! Fight! Fight! Fight! Fight!" joined cheers of "Kick his ass, Ashton! Bust his face! Smash his head in!" Just a sample of the many shouts in the incredibly lopsided support. "Ash-*ton*, Ash-*ton*, Ash-*ton*." Ted could always be counted on to shelve honor and courage whenever it best suited the situation. There was no way he was going to be the only one in Itch's corner.

Abandoning his friend, he shouted, "Punch him good, Ashton! Rearrange his face!"

But Ashton didn't rearrange his face. He barely fought back at all. It became apparent that Itch was good at something Ashton wasn't, which was how to beat someone up.

At the bottom of the stairs, they scrambled to their feet, Itch hurling a punch into Ashton's chin knocking him in one shot back to the ground. Ashton made the mistake of standing upright without being ready for the series of rapid body blows that sent him down again.

This time he wasn't so quick to get up. One of the others helped him to his feet before he turned back and halfheartedly put up his fists, now just hoping he could get out of this with his dignity intact.

"Hey, playboy, had enough?" Itch taunted.

"Come on, Ashton. Take out this dirtbag!" Ted shouted, lost in the moment, and barely audible above the shouts of encouragement from so many others.

Despite the cacophony, Itch distinguished the voice of his friend. The betrayal! What had passed through his ears hurt worse than anything he might have received in the fight. Had there not been so much noise, one might have heard the actual sound of his heart shattering against the ground.

Ashton approached while he was distracted, moving to take a swing, but at the last moment, Itch snapped out of it and landed three knuckles to the side of Ashton's nose. It was a brutal punch that left a quarter of Ashton's face covered with small red droplets. He staggered back, moved his hand to his nose, and pulled it away to find it coated with blood. All knew the fight had been decided. A few of his friends pushed him back, holding him so he could pretend he was trying to break free to continue.

"Let go. I'll kill him!" Ashton yelled.

"Is that the best you got playboy? Pathetic!"

Ciro placed himself between the two and rammed against Ashton, pushing him much farther back with his large body frame to ensure its end.

Itch, standing alone, the church as his backdrop, put his arms up and looked himself over, amazed, especially with the fall down the stairs, to have come out of it without the slightest visible scratch. At least not yet. Given Ashton's popularity, any number of the kids would gladly take a go at him on his behalf.

“Want me to take care of him?” Ciro asked as Ashton leaned against a tree holding his nose while others handed him tissues.

“No, don’t. It was a fair fight,” he insisted in a nasal tone from his fingers pinching his nose attempting to stop the bleeding.

Itch, not sure how the others might react, knowing any moment Ashton’s driver would be pulling up, decided it was time to make a hasty exit. He ran back up the church steps, grabbed his book bag and raced down. Passing Ted, Itch ripped his coat from Ted’s hands. Ted pursued, barely able to catch up.

“Hey, slow down, Itch. That was really something. I didn’t know you could fight like that.”

Itch turned and raised his fist. Flabbergasted, he had trouble getting a single word out before erupting.

“It’s all I can do to keep from punching you out. Even *he’s* better than that! You Judas! You Benedict Arnold!” He paused to capture his breath before continuing. “You are a snake! A lousy, no-good snake! That’s all you will ever be!”

“Itch, I was only kidding around.”

“We tease each other, Ted, but…” Itch had to pause to keep himself from losing it. When he continued it was in a high-pitched voice he struggled to control. Tears welled behind a face reddened with emotion. “In a billion years, I would never have done something like that to you. I don’t ever want to see your lousy face again. You’re dead to me. You understand? Dead.”

“Oh, come on, Itch,” Ted pleaded.

Without turning, he threw up his middle finger as he walked away.

“Fine,” Ted shouted before heading in the other direction. “You just saw how many people wanted to see you get your ass kicked. No one wants to be friends with you anyway!”

Over by Ashton, one kid shouted, “Scram! His ride is coming,” as his black Town Car appeared in the distance.

Like roaches with the light flipped on, boys scurried in all directions, leaving Ashton alone. Multiple inquisitions soon followed, first by his driver, then again by his mom when he arrived home, and finally the school the next day, but Ashton never wavered. Despite all evidence to the contrary, he held fast his injuries were sustained when he accidentally tripped down the church steps.

Ted was used to the way his mom would treat it. They’d have a fight, and it would be over and forgotten minutes later. Things didn’t work that way in the real world. The next day at school, and the ones that followed, Itch acted as though Ted were a ghost he could neither see nor hear. The four misfits now split in two, with Upchuck taking Itch’s side and Rip sticking with Ted. Ted prayed it would all shortly blow over, unaware these were the first snowflakes in a life-altering blizzard.

Friends

The remaining time in altar training dragged on. Having to share the space with Itch, who was actively ignoring him, Ted found it hard to concentrate. Complex Church doctrine and procedures quickly became a jumble, weeks passing with no change. Training ended with a final exam. The narrative in Ted's mind of how he was to become the most outstanding Catholic on earth required a high score. The night after, he waited nervously in a classroom with the others.

"Good news!" Father Tom announced as he hurried in with their exam papers held above his head. "Blessed night. Everyone passed."

Ted positioned himself so he could peek at the other's grades as they were handed out. Many were in the nineties, but there were plenty in the eighties too. In the end Itch's ninety-five, and Upchuck's ninety-nine were considerably more impressive than his own seventy-eight.

In a glum mood over his grade, he wondered why this God of his hadn't intervened to deliver a better score. The look worn on his face sharply contrasted with the others, who were high fiving one another. Then, something unusual, Itch was talking with Ashton! They were actually having a civil conversation, and Ted listened as best he could.

"Thanks for not ratting me out about the fight, *Ashton*," Itch said, stressing the use of his name rather than *playboy*. "I have to show respect to someone like that. Friends?" Itch asked, holding out his hand to shake on it.

"Friends," Ashton returned as he smiled and firmly shook Itch's hand.

Seeing Itch in a forgiving mood, Ted seized the opportunity, moved in, and put his hand up for a high five. A hock and then a warm wet slimy spit landed in his palm, followed by an obscene gesture. His heart crashed. It was officially over between them. He wiped the spit from his hand and exhaled many years' worth of memories, replacing all the happiness they contained with nothing but remorse.

TESTING

Present Day

By the way he told the story of his betrayal of his best friend to those in the office, it seemed to still bother him. Out of coffee and wanting to test if it was time to bite, he held out his empty cup.

"I believe I need a refill," he proclaimed.

"I'll get that for you," Robert offered.

"No, Theresa is going to."

He walked over to where she was sitting and thrust the cup at her face. "Milk, two sugars," he ordered without the slightest hint of politeness.

Karen knew he was seeing if there was resistance. Theresa snapped to attention and filled his cup confirming it was time.

"Theresa, I'd like to speak with you in your office."

The innocent-sounding request sent a chill down her spine. She had dealt with snakes like him her whole life and instinctively knew when one was coiling to strike.

"Sure," she replied, forcing a smile as they left to move next door. Her anxiety doubled when he unexpectedly shut the door behind them.

"Don't sit," he insisted as she moved toward her chair.

As if an actor taking command of a stage, he walked to her desk, placed his hand on the overturned garbage pail, and began rhythmically tapping his fingers. He looked over the room as if each inch held a special memory, pausing long enough for the anticipation to become palpable. Then his words flowed over the office like water from a broken sewage pipe.

"What do you think happens to a person when they have all the things they could ever materially or socially desire? For quite a few pitiful souls, it's never enough. They just keep running the race, assuming that they'll figure out why they began running in the first place. They get lost in this spiral, a never-ending pursuit to obtain what they already have. But that is not me."

"I had to ask myself, *What else is there?* The effect you have on others. That is the true pursuit of happiness. Integrity, compassion, philanthropy, things like that. But I have other interests that address things that are not so nice. That leads me to the real reason we are together today."

Clearly winding up to something, his voice increased in strength.

"I've left in my wake a trail of people far greater than you would be able to count. Corrupt politicians, mobsters, murderers, apropos to today, embezzlers and child molesters. And now I'll add to my list a drunken guidance counselor."

Ted continued. "Do you want to know what is equally bad as evil? The answer is indifference. And the reason is, it facilitates the functioning of immoral people. I would love to be able to sit idle on the sidelines but that is not my nature."

"Why don't you just let me be? I don't know what I could do...." She was going to say. "To show my gratitude if you did." She stopped herself. She knew too well what he might be after.

"Are you going to get me fired?"

"Fired, Theresa? That is the least of your worries. When I destroy people, I like to put some creativity into it. You are going to lose your job, your marriage, your children, your career, your freedom, your future. Everything about you is in the palm of my hand."

Unable to control it, Theresa was shaking. Ted saw it was time to move to the conversation's real purpose.

"Hear me carefully. I'm not without reason. I always offer a way out."

Running his eyes from head to toe, pausing over her skirt and back up, he rested them upon her partly unbuttoned blouse, covering her in lustful desire. It was the same horrible look her uncle used to give when she was a child, just before he would pounce.

"I have a proposal for you. In a little while, a car will pull up to take you to a wonderful Italian restaurant. I like it for the food and excellent service, but best of all, they have a back room that I have reserved. Your way out—let's call it my gift to you—is, if you give me everything I want, all these problems," he said, waving his hand, "will be gone."

Shocked, all his self-righteous talk of integrity only to reveal himself a fraud. In revulsion she jumped back, her hand springing to her chest to fasten the buttons of her blouse.

"I'm a married woman!" she exclaimed, as if for him it would make a difference.

"What, your husband? I'm sure you could do a lot better than him."

The irony took her breath away, those same hurtful words she had cut him with that morning, now used against her. She closed her eyes and emitted a huff of self-disgust as it flowed through her how much she loved him. How precious her life was and how stupid she had been for taking it for granted.

"There is no one better than him," she concluded, wishing he were there and wiping a tear that had emerged from one eye. "Men have been doing this to me my whole life. Please don't do this. Show me there is an ounce of compassion in you."

Ted snapped her out of it.

"I plan to show you as much compassion as girls like you used to show toward me. Let me be clear. I'm insisting on your complete surrender, but in return, you have my word. All these bad things in your life today will be gone. You'll have your job here in September, your family, your freedom, all yours. But you must give me everything I want. If you don't, I will destroy you so thoroughly even the pleasant memories people had of you will be gone. No negotiating, no pleading, no compromise. You will surrender yourself. That's the deal."

She could hardly comprehend the situation. He expected her to be nothing less than a compliant participant in her own rape. Hate replaced the fear she had been feeling moments before. Voice quivering, she knew her next words were risky but could not contain them.

"Your friend was right. You are a snake."

"I cannot change what God made me. I can only work within its confines. But I'm glad to see you have been listening. Now it's time to get back to the others."

"I need a minute to compose myself."

"Sure. Maybe fix your makeup and anything else you think would please me. I think your skirt is already hiked up as far as you can get away with but undo those buttons again. I was enjoying the view.

"Try to remove the hatred from your eyes," he continued. "There may come a time you judge me differently. For now, if the life you have is worth anything to you, when the car comes, I advise you to get in."

She had already made her decision.

REVEALED

Strolling back to the office, a spring in his step, Theresa followed behind with the weight of the world on her shoulders. Those not part of Ted's team were concerned as they entered.

"Is everything all right?" Sister Margaret asked.

"She's fine," Ted answered sharply.

"She just looks, well...Theresa, you look upset."

"Harriett, why don't you go off and pay some bills?"

"That's Margaret, you mean," Robert interjected.

"Sure, whatever she wants us to believe," Ted quipped.

Margaret, or Harriett, depending upon your point of view, stood with the blood leaving her head. All she did was breathe and wish she were dead. The gig was up. For decades, she had been able to hide. The only question that remained was how hard her downfall would be.

She did her best to snap out of it and attempt to recover. As soon as she got this man alone, she would turn in her resignation and beg for his mercy.

"What do you mean, Ted?" she asked meekly, then cleared her throat to sound a bit stronger. "You know we don't have any money to pay them."

Now Ted was the one who looked surprised.

"First thing this morning, I wired a million dollars into your operating account so you could start paying bills."

"Oh!" Sister Margaret exclaimed, bringing her hand to her mouth, embarrassment now joining her other feelings from her apparent display of incompetence. "I didn't know that," she continued sheepishly.

"Obviously," Ted countered with satisfaction written over his face.

He waved his hand for Karen to join him in the private office, and once the door was shut, he burst.

"Well, Karen, did you see that? We have our answer. I knew she would screw up. Now the rest for her is simple. I plan to have us gather in Theresa's office shortly. There is something on her desk I want to show everyone. And those folders, they are Margret's fate. Bring the top two with you at that time. That third one you need to burn, and I mean as in firepit and gasoline. Not a single word contained in that third one is to be left in existence."

"So, what's the verdict?" Karen inquired.

"Come on, you know."

"Yes, of course," she responded, pretending she did.

It truly disturbed her when things unfolded like that. She reviewed every word of the last minute. What was it that gave her away?

Breaking decorum she waited for Ted to leave, then took an unauthorized peek inside the first folder.

Would you look at that? she thought. *Well, I'll be damned.*

BETRAYAL

A month prior, walking a long hallway, John braced for the final interview. It wasn't skills, intelligence, or experience that had brought him to this point but rather what he held in his pocket. It is normal to be apprehensive for an interview, but he was doubly so on account of the warnings he'd been given concerning Ben Arlington. It was time to meet the man, the legend, the mystery.

A 3,500-square-foot guest house set behind his mansion had been converted to serve as an enormous single-room office with stunning Long Island Sound views. Connecting the house to the office was a long hallway. The walls themselves were without windows to protect the fine works of art that liberally adorned the way.

Arriving at what had once been the front door of a separate house, he rang the buzzer and waited. A camera set high in one corner kept watchful eye. Over the door hung an ominous sign:

"Nothing to Hide, Nothing to Fear"

It all seemed to align with his reputation. Rumor had it, although it remained allegations, that Ben's actions led directly to the demise of enough people to fill a sizable graveyard. His preferred method of execution, curiously, was suicide.

His belief, which usually tested correct, was that everyone holds a secret, those in power generally darker than most. Once such secrets were within his possession, he offered a choice among three, full exposure, total submission to his will, or suicide. It bothered him none that so many would choose the latter.

The door chimed and clicked open on its own. John pushed forward into what at first glance might be mistaken for a library. Shelves built on all sides held a great collection of books. A dusty smell of old paper filled the air. To the side was a fireplace, unlit on this warm mid spring day. At the far end was a desk, and behind it sat the myth himself, Ben Arlington.

John had imagined him a towering seven-foot-tall figure but, to his surprise, found him to be short, looking older than his years and rather unattractive.

"Enter," he barked, then sized John up as he traveled the length of the office.

One might expect a hello and a handshake as a greeting, but this was Ben Arlington.

"You're awfully young. I thought a man was interviewing for this job. If I knew they were sending a boy, I would have had some toys set up for you to play with."

His comment was referencing John's youthful appearance, but his real purpose was to set the tone. John said nothing, too stunned to know how to respond, just the way Ben liked it.

"Take that seat," he said, pointing to one of three, redundantly affirming his dominance.

"Tell me what you have heard about me?" he began abruptly.

"Well, Mr. Arlington, quite impressive things. You are successful, powerful, a man who demands respect."

"Hold it," Ben said, holding up his hand. "When I ask you a question, I want the answer, not prefabricated crap to fill the air with something you assume I want to hear. Now I'm going to ask one more time, and if you want this interview to continue, you will tell me. What do people say about me?"

"Well, honestly?"

"I insist."

"All right, hon-honestly, I'm a little afraid to r-repeat it," he stammered.

An upward pull at the corners of Ben's mouth that might have been thought a smile was frustration.

"Please stop treating me as a child you somehow feel the need to protect or someone whose intelligence is not high enough to know what people think."

John resigned himself to the answer he knew he had to give.

"Okay. I'm just repeating what I heard. People label you a sociopath. They say you are responsible for more death than a war."

"All unproven," Ben interrupted.

"I believe you are one of the most feared men on the planet. Some say you are the closest on this earth one can come to meeting the actual devil."

Ben smiled, this time pleased. "I congratulate you on having taken the first step toward building trust between us."

"Since you seem to want us to be open can I ask you something?" John inquired.

"Don't ask if you can ask. Just ask."

"I don't want to insult you. Believe me: that is the last thing I want to do. I just want to know if it's true. Or at least do you consider it true, that you are evil?"

"That question tells me you haven't yet shaken off the naivety of your youth. If it weren't so dangerous to have idealism at your age it would be cute. Do you know what the antidote for idealism is? I'll tell you. It's reality.

"Everything in your world has a simple definition and a simple answer to complex situations. Black or white, good or evil, is so much easier to determine than the gray that reality presents. Those who use their misinformed understanding of the world are the ones who label me evil. Then one day some event forces them to accept a new reality, change their perception of the world they only thought they understood, and judge me differently."

"There's something else I have been told," John continued, "that you despise Ted Carrington."

"I have heard that as well."

"I know the two of you battle it out all the time. He's stolen deals right out from under you."

"And I him," Ben interrupted again.

"They say he has crossed you many times. Given your reputation, people wonder how it is he still walks this earth."

"The absence of information can lead one to such conclusions. Now, John, it's my turn to be honest. I'm not interviewing you because of your skills or intelligence. It's apparent you possess neither. No, the reason you are here is because you work for my friend, Mr. Carrington. You indicated you have information that could destroy him."

"You have been correctly informed," John said, pulling a small flash drive from his jacket pocket.

Ben's entire face lit up. "Okay, you have my attention."

"Ted may think he is smart, but he has really terrible security with his computers."

Ben took a deep slow breath, like that of a child hardly able to wait with patience for some glorious treat.

"How good is what is on that drive?"

"Unbelievable. It takes some analysis, but when you connect the dots, there is enough to do away with him forever. Ten times over actually."

"Who knows about this?"

"Just us for now."

"Good. Keep it that way. I don't want to be in a bidding war, and I'm serious about that. If you share this with anyone, I will take you down so fast you won't even know it's happening.

"Well, I'm sure we can come to an amount, and a job too. I'll be needing one. I want something that will advance my career."

"The money part and the job, that's easy. But aren't you forgetting the most important thing?"

"What would that be?"

"Protection. Protection from Ted Carrington when he finds out."

"He doesn't concern me. Did you know he's mentally defective?"

"You need to be more careful of how you assess people. Yes, he is on the spectrum. But his being different has caused him to struggle and compensate his whole life. That daily fight leaves him more formidable than the two of us combined, although you don't add much to the equation. Believe what you want, but I'll tell you this. Coming to understand the reality of the world turned me into a snake. But Ted, Ted Carrington, he was born that way."

That was the only warning John was to receive. Thereafter, Ben's tone mellowed dramatically. One would think he and John were old friends, even sharing a glass of his special occasion private reserve scotch.

They agreed there would be a payment. The amount yet to be determined. As far as the job is concerned, what Ben offered him was quite strange, unless one were to consider the truth lies behind the pieces that are out of place. Without any background, training, or even a word of the native language, Ben offered John a job to be his international liaison to Indonesia.

Avalanche

Winter 1978

Friendship with Itch declared dead, Ted was a despondent twelve-year-old reaching out to replace his best friend. There wasn't a line of people wanting to hang with him, so options were limited. Rip would have been a natural choice, but he didn't want to get roped into working out with him three days a week. The prime candidate was a short Italian classmate named Geovanni whom everyone called Geo. Oversized hooked nose and large ears jutting from his short, straight, greasy black hair, he resembled a gremlin.

The first day following winter break was cold, with snow still on the ground from a recent storm. They agreed to hang out after school, Geo suggesting they peruse a nearby record store so he could find out if the latest Kiss album was available.

Geo seemed a nice change from Itch, at least initially, as they joked along the way. Far less abrasive, no constant "good-natured" insults. When they arrived, Geo went to the counter to check on the album while Ted moved to the country music section and picked up the latest release from John Denver.

Two minutes after, the door opened, ushering in a blast of cold air, and in walked three girls from their class, Lisa, Christine, and Ashley. While they had gone to school together since first grade, these girls were far too popular to want anything to do with the two of them.

Lisa and Christine were among the prettiest in the class, but Ashley was a vision of heaven. Tall with long, flowing, golden-blond hair, striking blue eyes, and a muscular body shaped by constant exercise and seasons on the soccer field. Ted envisioned a halo floating just above her head. Upon sight of the boys, Lisa rolled her eyes, Christine let out a muffled groan, and Ashley took a step back as a suggestion the three of them leave.

Before they could do anything, Geo was upon them, going all-out to trap them into some small talk. Ted threw down the John Denver record, not wanting to be caught dead showing an interest in country music, and made sure his shirt was neatly tucked and his tie perfectly straight. Moving next to Geo, they chatted, but Ted was too distracted to say much.

Jackets open, revealing their tight white shirts and burgundy plaid skirts, hiked up to show off sheer leggings, he found it impossible to keep his eyes from rolling over them like a paint brush. After a few minutes of pointless conversation with Geo and uncomfortable ogling by Ted, the girls made an excuse to leave and walked out, only to find themselves followed.

Once outside, Geo yelled, "Snowball fight!" and threw a fist of loosely packed snow in their direction. Not to be outdone, and figuring numbers were on their side, all three girls grabbed handfuls of snow and returned with a couple. The boys dodged, then returned with more of their own.

With Ted the only one wearing gloves, all other hands soon froze, and the little melee, in theory, ended.

The girls naively thought all they had to do was walk away. It might have worked with Geo, but Ted wasn't going to let go of their attention that easily. At first, they laughed, albeit nervously, as they tried to outpace their two admirers while Ted hurled snowballs toward them at every opportunity. When they ran faster than Ted could keep pace, he switched to crude catcalls as the distance became farther than he could throw. The girls headed for a park, hoping a walk through a few inches of snow would thwart the boys' persistence. They scaled a small chain-link fence, but skirts made the maneuver tricky, which gave Ted the time needed to catch up.

From opposite sides of the fence, the girls demanded he stop. Ignoring their pleas, Ted grabbed at the links and started to climb. The three tried to run but paused when they found themselves in front of a snow drift. That was all Ted needed. Scaling the fence, he put together a snowball and hurled it at Ashley. The snowballs up to that point had missed, but this one found its mark, hitting her just under the back of her knee. She turned and wiped off the bit of snow still clinging to her leg while Ted readied another.

"Knock! It! Off!" she shouted, anger spiraling in its tone, making it clear enough to sink into the thick layers of Ted's skull they were done. This left him with a decision, he had one last snowball in his hand. It was a beauty—large, perfectly round—and he hated to waste it. What to do? Throwing it high into the air in their general direction, he turned to leave, but just inside his peripheral vision watched the snowball come down to land like a mortar shell onto the back of Ashley's neck. Most of it disappeared down her shirt, the sight leaving his mouth open. He was unable to utter a word even if he had a clue what it should be.

Fists and teeth clenched, Ashley spun with a fire in her eyes like a bull seeing red. She was on him so fast he had no time to react other than to raise his hands, more pleading than in self-defense. Overcome with fury, wanting to beat him all over, she raged, contemplating where to begin her attack. It was decided when she jammed her palm up into his chin, slamming his mouth shut. That was followed by a hard slap of her hand against the side of his face. She then grabbed a large clump of his hair, violently tearing, attempting to rip it out. As this pulled his head forward and down, she planted a kick into his thigh.

"Ashley, no!" Lisa yelled, realizing ahead of Ted what was about to happen.

Her next strike landed with full fury exactly where a boy never wants to be kicked. He could feel the entire contents of his stomach rise into his throat. A shock went through him accompanied by pain like he'd never experienced, a feeling as though every organ in his lower body was being twisted inside out. Collapsing instantly, he caught Ashley's leg on the way down. Causing her to lose her balance, she nearly fell on top of him.

No sooner had she risen to her feet than she was shoved from the side by Lisa.

"You never do that to boys! What is *wrong* with you!" Lisa screamed with extreme emphasis on the word *wrong*.

While Lisa scolded her friend, Ted lay on the ground, thrashing desperately before letting out an inhuman groan and rolling into a fetal position. There he remained unable to do anything but rock in the snow, moan, and fight an intense urge to vomit.

Geo was gone. It was only Ted laying in the snow with three freaked-out girls standing over him not knowing what to do. After waiting a bit and seeing no improvement, Christine knelt to inspect him closer.

"Ash, I think he's hurt for real," she concluded after shaking his shoulder.

Ashley, now concerned, shook her head hoping to deny her friend's conclusion. "I've done it to my brother lots of times, and he's always been okay."

"We need to get help!" Christine insisted.

Hearing the panicked chatter reverberating between the girls, Ted's concern now was to avoid the extreme embarrassment of anyone else getting involved. Drawing from everything within, he forced himself to lean upright on one elbow. That was as far as he could get.

The rise of Ted's "corpse" ended their debate, but they realized he wasn't getting up when he began to shiver as snow melted under him. Huddling together, they decided on a plan, came back, surrounded him, put their arms under his shoulders, and helped him up.

Continuing to provide support, they guided him to a nearby bench where he was able to sit. They had never before witnessed anyone's complexion that shade of green. The streak from a single tear that had squeezed from one eye remained on his face, the droplet still hanging off his chin.

Ashley, anger having been eclipsed by concern, said words that were as foreign as unexpected to Ted.

"I'm sorry. I honestly didn't mean to hurt you like that. It's just you got me so mad. But that wasn't right. I shouldn't have done that."

Ted apologized too, but as he did and stared at her face, all he could think of was how much he wanted to strangle her. He pictured it clearly, his hands wrapped tightly around her neck as she slowly fell into the snow and died. As much as he wanted to do it, he barely had the strength to remain upright.

They exchanged several more mutual apologies, but for the last, Ashley made it a point to crouch down, bring her face within inches of his, and look him straight in the eye.

"I'm glad you're okay, and again I'm really sorry," she said softly, clutching his shoulder as she spoke to him.

Lisa then came up with the suggestion that she could get her mom to drive him home.

"No, no, no, no, no!" was Ted's emphatic response. That would add another whole level of humiliation to the entire thing. Mustering all his strength and with knees shaking, he struggled to rise.

"I'm fine now," he declared, straining as he said it.

He deliberately took time to tuck the tails of his disheveled shirt neatly back into his pants and pulled his tie nice and straight, attempting to retrieve the smallest amount of the dignity he just lost. Forcing a smile onto his face, he aimed it at the girls and, with robotic motions, started to limp forward, causing them to erupt into an irrepressible giggle. They asked again if he was okay and offered to walk him home, but he assured them all was fine.

A walk that should have been ten minutes took over a half hour. He snuck into the kitchen, put a few ice cubes in a towel, and slinked to his room to apply the cold pack. A long evening of avoiding his parents was followed by a good night's sleep. By the next morning, while still sore, he was well enough to focus his attention on a topic of supreme importance, the demise of Ashley. He believed the worst of it for him was over. Now it was her turn to suffer. He would be greatly mistaken.

Reliance

All the way to school Ted plotted the murder of his new nemesis. He devised a plan to cut the brakes on her bicycle, causing her to roll into traffic and get killed. Details—if she owned a bike, where it might be kept, how he would get to it, why she wouldn't notice there were no brakes—could be worked out later. His mind was too pleasurably filled imagining her final scream as the tire of a bus rolled over her head.

His pleasant musing was suddenly interrupted. He knew there was a problem when he heard as he approached the schoolyard. "There he is!"

Rob was first and set the tone.

"Hey, Teddy, how are your goodie bags?"

There was no chance to respond as others immediately followed.

"How come Ashley gets to beat you up? When do I get my turn?"

"Be careful, Ted. I hear the first graders can be pretty tough."

"Aren't you in the wrong uniform? Where's your skirt?"

While Itch never would have done it, Geo told anyone who would listen about the fight, even embellishing details to make it sound worse.

"She wailed on him like a kicking machine. He cried like a baby," Geo insisted.

It did not take long for Ted to discover there was no faster way for a boy to fall to the lowest rung of the lowest social ladder than to get beaten up by a girl. During every break, in every class, in the halls, schoolyard and even as they assembled for mass, he was verbally pounded to a pulp.

"Hey, Teddy, are your balls still round, or do they have dents in them?" Ciro called from the other side of the cafeteria to the amusement of all around. Ted, with his only remaining friend, Rip, by his side, was frustrated.

"Why don't you do something? You let them talk to me like that?"

Rip was confused, if not a little in shock. "Why am I supposed to do something?"

"Everyone's afraid of you. You're supposed to be my friend."

"Me! Me? You have got to be kidding me! It's my fault you never learned to defend yourself. No, it's always been a big joke to you, never doing a thing *for yourself*. No, you want everyone else to do everything for you. I'll stand up for you the day I see you lift a finger, just one finger, to help yourself."

Ted eyed him angrily, then backed it up with words. "Tom was right about what he called you. I can see now why no one wants to be friends with a —" The racial epithet he ended it with was not to be tolerated.

The response was surprisingly fast. Rip grabbed him by the throat and cocked his arm back. For a tense moment, neither of them knew what the outcome was to be before Rip relented and released his neck. A habit he'd always had was to speak in Spanish when he was furious.

"Eres no vale la pena" (You're not worth it), he declared as he rose from his seat, carrying his lunch with him. "Don't ever speak to me again."

Ted was already profoundly regretting this terrible mistake against his last friend.

"I'm sorry. We can still be friends, right?"

"Stay the hell away from me."

As if the day could not get any worse, he knew it was going to.

Compassion

Despite having no one to talk to and people making fun on all sides, something was bothering him more than anything. It was his last class, a gauntlet he would have to pass, the single class he shared with Ashley, and he considered what he was facing. She was going to administer a final coup de gras, a deathblow. It was left to his imagination as to how.

Close to retching, he entered the class and took his seat as though it were an electric chair. The teacher talked to another outside, allowing a group of boys behind him to humiliate him further. Ashley was not there yet, and he could only pray that perhaps she had gone home sick.

The wisecracks continued to sting at him like a swarm of five thousand angry hornets.

Unable to cope, he dropped his head to the desk and covered it with his arms, trying to at least partly muffle the cackles that were all about. Counting the seconds, which seemed like minutes, he knew class was to start shortly. Then Ashley entered the room.

"Hey, Ashley's here, Ted. Don't worry. I'll protect you," one of the boys chided from behind.

Even though she sat on the opposite side, he knew she was hearing it all. What fun she must be having with the thoroughness of his destruction. All he could do was await her anticipated deathblow.

It was true. Ashley was listening to the banter bouncing off the walls, and she looked at Ted whose arms were over his head trying to cover his ears. She slammed her open palm against her desk to generate a loud bang.

"Hey!" she yelled at the boys laughing behind him. "Why don't all of you shut the hell up?"

A loud "Oooooh!" went through the air before the room went silent.

"You think you're tough? Any of you want to come over here and see if you do any better? The reason he lost"—she paused to think something up—"the reason"—she paused again—"the only reason he lost is because he refused to hit me back. He won't hit a girl. He's a gentleman. That's more than I can say for any of you! Does anyone else have something they want to say about what happened?"

She waited long enough to confirm a response wasn't coming.

"I didn't think so!" she screamed across the room, accompanied by a pound of her fist before slamming herself back into her seat.

It's a rare occasion that you can hear yourself think in a room of unattended sixth graders, but the class remained quiet as a graveyard until the teacher began the lesson. Ted raised his head as it started. Had he been permitted to speak, there would have been nothing.

Confused, *No deathblow? Why did she do that?* he wondered.

This had been the second time in as many days she had picked him off the ground. The deep hatred he held melded into indescribable gratitude, and he wanted to thank her before she could regret it. Throughout class, he looked over in her direction trying to get her attention, but she was focused on the lesson.

Finally, their eyes met. Knowing his expression could not convey the depth of his feelings, he mouthed a silent thank-you. She looked confused, so he repeated it, carefully exaggerating both syllables. This time she understood but shook her head no. With her eyes looking as though they would burst into tears, she placed her open hand on her chest and mouthed back the words, *I'm so sorry*.

His mind started to spin. He became so dizzy that, had he been standing, he would have fallen. His head, too heavy for his shoulders, dropped to the desk in disbelief. He had seen magic, a miracle, something he didn't believe could be real. Compassion. She had defended him in an act of compassion.

Ashamed, recalling what he wanted to do to her that morning, he was unable to hold his head upright. A wave of understanding washed over him. Like a fog dissipating, leaving visible the pure truth, he realized she had in fact struck that much feared deathblow. Done in such an effective and thorough manner, it was far beyond anything he could have predicted.

It never bothered him when someone was better at something, which was pretty much all the time. But the one thing he believed he held over her, and everyone, was that he was a better person. In this way, he knew she had undeniably proven she was better than him in every conceivable way. He closed his eyes to absorb the level of perfection to which she had scored on him her deathblow.

Coming in the door from school, he told his mother the biggest lie of his life when she asked how his day went and he replied, "Fine." He laid face down on the floor of his room and focused sight on the tiny fibers of fabric in the carpet wishing he could become so small he'd be able to hide within them. He imagined having a secret power that would allow him to stop breathing. Five minutes and it would all be gone. What an extraordinary ability that would be.

Refusing to give up on life that easily he sighed, sat up, and then took a much deeper breath than the one his body was forcing him to take. His world was collapsing, him with it. Worse was coming.

Exile

The focus of kids' attention moves on quickly. By the next day, Ted was old news.

And that was the problem: no one paid him any attention at all. He was alone in the schoolyard. No one talking with him in class, sitting by himself in the cafeteria; by lunch, it was driving him crazy.

Acceptance. For millennia, the survival of an individual depended on it. For centuries, banishment was equated to the death penalty. Get thrown from your tribe and you were most likely to die. Locked deep within our bones is a need as significant as food and water, to be accepted, loved, even popular. The desire for this essential element of our well-being holds great influence over our behavior.

Across the lunchroom, one row over sat Ani-mul, by herself, empty chairs on both sides. It was apparent to Ted that she had become a grandmaster at being an unwanted nobody. Somehow, every day, she endured a routine of being shunned. He reasoned there must be some secret she kept that allowed her to keep coming back for more.

The second half of his day continued just like the first. Even on the trip home from school the kids he usually walked with deliberately outpaced him.

Sitting silent in his room, it struck him he hadn't spoken a single word to anyone his own age all day. That night, laying despondent in this bed, he decided it was time to seek help from the class pariah.

Vesuvius

At lunch the next day, as usual, Anna was sitting alone at the foot of one of the cafeteria tables. Same as every day, two empty chairs remained on each side with her jotting in her notebook. Ted approached to a suspicious look from a pair of staring eyes as she snapped her book shut. Selecting an empty seat two away, he asked if she minded if he sat.

They had never before exchanged a word. She preferred to be alone, and Ted was one of the last people she desired to change that. Her first impulse was to tell him off, but she could never turn her back on someone with an expression like the one on Ted's face. Ted, for his part, assumed she would be thrilled to have anyone bless her with conversation.

"It's a free country," she replied. "But not that seat," is what she tried to say as Ted sat, unwittingly squashing her imaginary friend Penelope.

"I'm working on a sort of project, and believe it or not I think you can help me."

"A school project?"

"No, it has to do with how you deal with being such a reject around here." He mistook her frown as acceptance and added, "You don't have to worry. It won't interfere with you choking down your food."

She squinted. "And what do I get if I help you?"

"Isn't it enough that I'm talking to you?"

When she didn't answer, he thought for a second, then came up with his version of a generous offer.

"I know. If you help me, I'll agree to stop calling you Ani-mul for one month."

Her mouth dropped, and her face carried the stunned expression worthy of the years of insults he had inflicted upon her. Dormant, quiet, unassuming Mount Annabelle, with Ted perched on the summit, would at this moment violently erupt.

"Y-you...you stupid stinking jerk! You lousy snake!" she stammered before focusing on what she couldn't gather fast enough to say. "Don't treat me like a piece of garbage! All the things you say about me! Well, *you* are the piece of garbage! The nerve of you wanting my help! How come you didn't greet me like you usually do by screaming, 'Elephant loose in the school'? Last week you said they could press my face in dough and sell monster cookies. You said if they gave out gold medals for being fat, ugly, and stupid, I could go to the Olympics and come back a millionaire. I can't even remember all the dumb, heartless things that have fallen out of your mouth!"

Ted shook his head, eyes fixed on her, panicked and in shock she wasn't grateful he was talking to her.

"I never said any of those things to you."

"No, you never talk to me at all. A whole year and not one word! It's all behind my back because you, you miserable coward, you don't have the guts to say it to my face!"

Now rising from her seat, face red with anger, she paused to catch her breath. Ted had seen the type of rage filling her eyes in the eyes of another girl quite recently and decided it would be a good idea to stand and take a few steps back, thinking, and not trying to be funny, that if she got her hands on him, she could crush him like a rampaging elephant.

"You're a rotten, terrible, horrible, miserable person! Why don't you do the world a favor and die!"

A lunch aide came over demanding, "What happened? What did you say to her?"

A girl further down the table who was watching chimed in. "He didn't do anything to her, Mrs. H. She's just weird. She'll be fine once they get her back to the zoo."

Anna had been entirely focused on Ted but awoke with the comment, looked around, and froze. All the attention in the now silent cafeteria was aimed at her. Eyes filled with terror, like that of a mouse surrounded by cats, she started to scream.

"What are you looking at? Stop looking at me! Stop it! Stop it! Stop it! I just want to be left alone!" She seemed to run out of energy, hovered as if about to lose her balance and collapsed onto her chair.

"I can't do this anymore. God, please, I don't want to live anymore!"

Covering her head with her arms, she cried with a high pitch, the sound resembling that of a distressed infant.

"Pleeeease let me go home! Please God put an end to this! I want my nana! I wanna go home! Pleeeeeeeeeeease!" she screamed. She continued to cry out, but everything after became unintelligible.

As the lunch aide moved to comfort Anna, Ted took several steps backward. He wanted to deny this was happening but found himself unable to take his eyes off the tragic sight. To his knowledge, no one had ever witnessed Anna show any emotion, and he considered the kind of monster he was, that it took to break her.

Nothing in what had already been the worst week of his life had come close to this. He backed away, aghast by the results of his stumbling stupidity. There was a sensation his hands were dripping blood; her screams were those of a person dying. Murder. He had just committed murder.

He could take no more, turned, and tucked himself in at a table of fifth graders, unnoticed by the monitors, who were busy comforting Anna. Caught in the truth, it stood a most devastating realization, he was nothing like the person he believed he was or wanted to be. He had experienced the stuff of nightmares. Something most people never get to see. Anna's eyes had become mirrors, and he, for the first time and in horror, saw an unfiltered, unbiased reflection of himself.

A tornado of emotions—guilt, shame, sadness, and self-loathing—enveloped him and battled for the lead role in his torture. Anna was escorted from the room, supported by lunch aids as she cried and screamed curses at everyone that no one else would have been allowed to get away with. Everyone looked on dumbfounded, the single exception being Ted. He sat with his head down on the table, hands covering his ears, attempting to bypass having to process the sounds. Their eventual disappearance down the hall did not bring any of the relief he'd hoped. It wasn't until the cafeteria had returned to relative normalcy that he raised his eyes and fixed them to the crucifix that hung on the wall. He had a most troubling question. How could it be that he'd attended this Catholic school for six years and learned nothing?

Anna could be right in what she said. Maybe, he considered, he should do the world a favor and die.

Nightmares

Ted staggered home, suffocated by self-hatred of an intensity that removed his ability to say even a single word to his mom without giving away his disposition. He sat in his room with his face in his hands, not a thought given to anything but what happened in the cafeteria. A feeling as though the knife he had plunged into her heart was also in his.

He found it hard to sit upright for dinner and picked at the food just enough to keep his mother off his back. It surprised him anything stayed down. The sound of Anna's mournful screams, like that of a tortured baby, removed all desire to breathe, let alone eat. After dinner, guilt enveloped him as though a giant version of the snakes he kept.

"I made her not want to live anymore." Ted shakenly remembered as he lay in bed, a sleepless night already a foregone conclusion. Laying spread-eagle, straining to stretch out his arms and legs as far as they would go; it was to him the best position to express surrender. He closed his eyes, imagining, hoping a small meteor would crash through the ceiling and cut him in half.

Focusing on his breathing, he tried with increasing desperation to somehow stop it. Each time he held his breath, his chest ultimately rose to suck in air, filling him with renewed frustration.

Early in the morning hours, demoralized, unable to rest, he searched for permanent sleep. Then a wonderful warm feeling washed from head to toe as he realized the answer—his father's gun, kept on top of the breakfront. All he would have to do is creep into the living room, get on a chair, and the resolution would be in his grasp.

The sigh of relief was audible as he turned onto his side, only then realizing just how uncomfortable he had been. Before he could execute his plan, his eyes closed, just for a moment he told himself. Instead, he fell asleep. His final thoughts were of the movie *It's a Wonderful Life* and how great it would be to have never been born.

But it wasn't a wonderful life. His eyes cracked open shortly after six to the sound of his alarm. He touched his temples with his fingertips on each side, checking for a bullet hole. "I can't even get that done," he lamented with eyes partly closed to shield them from the assault of the garish morning light forcing its way through the window.

He reached over to end the racket of the alarm and dragged himself from bed, knowing he had a 7:00 a.m. mass that he didn't the night before expect to serve. His mom was occupied preparing breakfast, allowing him to slip past as soon as he was dressed, only calling to her as he shut the front door to head for the church. Throwing one foot in front of the other, more stumbling than walking, he didn't care to zipper his coat against the eighteen-degree morning air.

Arriving impractically early, being the only person in the cavernous church, he walked up to the altar and fell to his knees. There he did something he had never done before, he prayed. There had been countless times he had mouthed rote words and memorized orations of praise but had never captured the true meaning of prayer like the ones offered that morning. Sincere and pleading, he begged God for a single gift. A chance to set things right.

Preparing for the mass and the time it took to collect himself left only three minutes before its start. Since communion could only be received by a sinless soul, it was not uncommon for altar boys to request confession before mass. The priest, visiting from another parish and not one Ted had worked with before, was suffering from a slipped vertebra and fighting an incredible amount of pain. Ted interpreted his expression as an indication he did not wish to be disturbed by whatever trivial matters plagued his soul. Desperate, though, putting aside reservations, he approached anyway.

"Mass is about to start. You got one minute," the elderly priest snapped, conflicting with Ted's image of how a holy man should respond.

"Father, bless me for I have sinned," Ted opened with the exact words always recited to begin confession.

"Okay, what do you want to confess?" the priest asked, looking at his watch, breaking standard protocol, trying to rush the process so as to be able to start on time.

"I've committed a mortal sin. I'm guilty of murder."

"You are saying someone is dead because of you?" the priest replied. If the voice were not condescending enough, the eyes would have been.

"Well, not exactly. But I treated someone so badly I think it's the same thing."

"Anything else?"

"No."

"Okay, for your penance say an Our Father and a Hail Mary. I absolve you of your sins in the name of the Father, Son, and Holy Ghost."

"That can't be it, not for what I did."

"I understand what you did. It's 7:00 a.m., son. Start the mass."

"This is a mortal sin. I just want to make sure you know that."

"It's not a mortal sin. Start the mass."

"No, it is. I'm not forgiven yet. You don't understand."

"All right, say the prayers then go to this person, apologize, and ask them for forgiveness. Now begin mass. I'm not telling you again."

"And what if she doesn't forgive me. Is there still a mortal sin on my soul?"

"Start the mass. This is ridiculous. Do I have to report you to Father Tom?"

"No, Father."

Ted turned and faced down the long aisle, looking toward the altar, his afterlife now having been placed in Anna's hands.

Reconciliation

The classes he attended that morning were nothing more than noise, a background against preparation for his upcoming request. Wanting to get it over and afraid he'd chicken out if he put it off, he decided the cafeteria would be the best place.

He entered at lunchtime and saw Anna at the far end of the room, sitting alone and scratching into her notebook. His throat seemed dry as a desert as he took a deep breath and wondered if he would be able to do this without collapsing. The few sentences he had put together were already fuzzy in his mind.

"What?" she barked as he approached, snapping her notebook shut just as she had done the previous day.

Stopping short, too far to lean against the chairs or hide behind anything, he stood in the open, keenly aware of his vulnerability. His frayed nerves caused him to need to catch his breath. Anna looked at him with daggers and while most of her focus was consumed by hate a small part couldn't help but wonder why he was trembling. With a swallow and at a level not much above a whisper, "Anna, Annabelle," he began before blanking on everything he had planned to say.

Desperate to begin but having nothing to start with, the words that followed were from his soul.

"I haven't stopped thinking about what you said. Everything you said that I said is true. I've also said many things you don't even know about that are worse. You see, I was just trying to get a laugh. I never meant any of it."

"Do you know how much you hurt me when you did that?" Anna asked, surprising him she would speak to him at all.

"I do."

"You do? You mean you knew, and you did it anyway! How sick are you?"

"No, no. I didn't before, but I do now. I didn't think about what all of that was doing to you."

As the sentence rolled off his tongue, it struck like lightning why what he had done was so wrong. Just like himself, she was a human being with feelings and emotions. But the cold truth was that she had suffered through bad days of a magnitude he had only just now and ever so briefly tasted. How she kept her sanity while being forced to drink from such a chalice every day made him shudder. Physical size having nothing to do with anything, he suddenly felt so small standing before her.

If the effect you have on others is all that matters, he reasoned in disgust, then what have I done?

He stopped to absorb it all and held on his face a look of horrid amazement that even made Anna wonder what had just happened. Struck by his revelation, he forced himself to look straight at her.

"Anna," he stated her name as if trying to get used to it, "I didn't think of you as a person. I never considered it. The things I did and said, the way I made you feel, there's no excuse. You called me a terrible, horrible person. I don't want to be that anymore. I need to change."

He paused, knowing there were no words to heal what he had done.

"I don't think it's possible for you to understand how sorry I am, and I don't deserve for you to even listen to me, but I swear to you, and I swear to God, I'll never treat you like that again."

Too ashamed to continue looking into her eyes, he gazed to the side, bringing into view several girls who were seated nearby pointing at him, poking fun, making the next part all the more difficult.

"And I wanted to ask."

He stopped, unsure where to look other than the floor.

"If you would forgive me."

That was met by a burst of laughter from the nearby girls while Anna was indignant.

"No," she responded, then repeated it twice more to be sure he understood.

"I don't forgive you one bit. Now go back to those idiot friends of yours and leave me alone."

He wanted nothing more than to be able to, but those "idiot friends" weren't speaking to him. It didn't matter anyway. He needed to sit undisturbed until there was relief from the dizziness that filled his head.

He let out a moan amid the witch's brew of emotion bubbling inside, and worried. There was a mortal sin on his soul that would be there until Anna forgave him. Not bad enough that he had messed up this life, but now eternity as well.

Sunrise

Fear, embarrassment, remorse, desperation, isolation, misery—all are excellent motives for change, but king is fear of death. That was the one that took over as he lay in bed that night, demoralized and depressed. He believed his only options were to change his life or die.

His sleep, as had been all week, was fitful and restless. His mind perpetuated in cold isolation, a deliberate banishment from emotions set to attack the moment there was recognition of their existence. The only warmth he drew upon was the apology he had made to Anna and the logic that if what he had done to her bothered him so much, somewhere inside his conscience must still be alive.

The day following was Saturday and light snow had fallen. Waking up at 7:00 a.m., unable to return to sleep, he rose, dressed, and went outside to clean the stairs and sidewalk. Next, he was off to the great hall of answers, the library. His mission was to find some way to fix himself.

Having struck out in the self-improvement section days before, he explored meditation. Itch had told him a friend told another friend, that he was told by his father that thirty minutes of meditation eliminated the need for sleep. Ted wasn't sure if he was joking but thought he'd check it out anyway.

Plucking a book on meditation, he read with fascination. There was nothing about a magical replacement of sleep, but it did seem to offer tranquility. To a boy who hadn't had restful sleep in days, it seemed like a ticket to heaven.

All attempts at the technique failed miserably from the interruptions of his mother's near-constant yapping to his own innate inability to remain focused.

The miracle happened that Monday after he served a 7:00 a.m. mass. Attendance at weekday service this early was always sparse, and the church emptied entirely after. There was a brief span of solitude until the 8:00 a.m. mass. Lying in the first pew, he closed his eyes and began the breathing exercise he had read about.

There was something mystical about the church's vast emptiness, with its silence only broken by seemingly distant echoes. It was like the time on the lake with Billy, the nothingness enveloped him and carried his mind to a place as peaceful as it was beautiful. There were moments he was sure he was in the presence of Almighty God.

Serenity was broken by the creak of the great door in the back and the sound of shuffling feet from an elderly lady who came each day to attend the 8:00 a.m. mass.

Ted rose from the pew, smiled at her, then left through the side door.

That span of meditation provided wondrous relief, if only brief, from his overwhelming anxiety. Like the best amusement ride he'd ever been on, he wanted to do it again. With a plan, Ted went to see Father Tom.

"I'll take all the weekday 7:00 a.m. masses," he offered. "Just don't schedule anyone else with me. I like doing them alone." Altar boys were always assigned in pairs. The only reason Ted was alone that morning was because the other kid blew it off.

Father Tom looked around and over his shoulder toward the closet expecting someone to jump out and let him in on the joke. In twelve years of running the program, he could not remember even a lone request for the 7:00 a.m. mass and tried to make sense of it.

"Does your father drop you off on his way to work or something?"

"No."

"Having problems at home?"

"No."

"You sure?"

"Yeah, definitely."

"Okay I'll assign them to you, but it doesn't seem fair."

"The other kids won't mind. You should hear them complain when they have to get up that early."

"No, I mean not fair to you."

"Oh no, I want them. Please, I really do."

"Monday through Friday, you'll do all of them, and you'll tell me if you want to stop?"

"Yes, Father."

"Just help me figure out why you want to do this."

"I suppose I had an epany."

"Epany?"

"Yeah, you know, when you suddenly realize you're meant to do something, a lightbulb goes on and you just realize it out of nowhere."

"Do you mean an epiphany?"

"Yeah, that's it. I had an epiphany."

Father Tom suppressed a laugh and readily granted his request.

Ted's new daily routine was to serve mass, then after, lie unseen in one of the front pews and meditate until he heard the old lady come in. She came in like clockwork, seven fifty every morning.

For a few weeks, he laid low. Kids still chided him about what had happened with Ashley and having absolutely no one to talk with was depressing, but just focusing on the moment and dealing with everything as it came began to bring an extraordinary serenity.

For those glorious weeks, his dreams stretched no further than one day forward. He stopped buying the *Journal* and put aside thoughts of becoming pope. The only person he needed to impress was himself. Never believing it possible, he learned a lesson few ever do, that the most incredible peace is hidden within everyday routine. It was fortunate he picked up this nugget of wisdom quickly because one thing that never changes is that everything does.

Happiness

Weeks of uneventful routine.

Change

Three Weeks Prior To His Fateful Decision

Someone dropped an orange in the cafeteria, and as it rolled across the floor, Ted's foot found it. It burst open and slid as he stepped, stretching out his leg, causing him to do a split as he fell to the floor. His rigid body was not agreeable to splits. Muscles pulled he didn't know he had; his shriek was met with laughter from every direction. A dark-skinned hand to help him up appeared in front of his face. This was an opportunity Ted was not about to squander, as Rip helped him up.

"Rip, I'm sorry, you know, for that thing that happened and everything I did and that horrible word I called you. Who cares if you grew up in a bad neighborhood? I didn't mean anything by it."

"I thought about it. The truth is, you were my first friend here. I don't think I would know how to fix a tie if it weren't for you. We can get past this. What do you mean about my neighborhood?"

"I won't repeat it. That word I called you because you are poor."

"You mean the word you used that ticked me off? Do you even know what it means?"

"Yeah, of course, and it doesn't matter you came from the ghetto."

"Ghetto? What you called me is a bad word to call someone who is Hispanic."

"Hispanic?" he questioned, confused. "What does that have to do with anything?"

"You're too dumb to stay mad at. Come on, give me a hug," he chided, exaggeratedly throwing his arms open wide before putting Ted in a headlock and roughly scraping his knuckles across his scalp.

Like food to a starving man, delight ran through Ted when Rip suggested he sit with the group for lunch.

"Hey, guys," Ted said cautiously as he sat next to Rip and across from Itch and Upchuck.

Itch pounced. "What's that dirtbag doing here?"

"I invited him," Rip responded.

Itch grabbed his lunch tray and stood, with Chuck following.

"If that's the kind of company you keep, I've lost a whole level of respect for you."

"I guess they aren't ready," Rip noted as he picked up his lunch tray and left with them, leaving Ted, once again, by himself.

That afternoon, he stopped in at the library hoping to find more answers. There sitting on the table was a *Wall Street Journal*, just teasing him to open it. He hadn't checked his stock in weeks.

He thought it an incredible coincidence or more likely an act of God when the stock he had recommended to Walter was featured in an article on page two. The application for their revolutionary drug had been refiled with the FDA. Last time he looked, the price had been $2.75, and now, it closed at $8 5/8. While experiencing both elation and concern, he was glad to see it soar but wondered if Walter Burke remembered any of their conversation.

Forgiveness

Checking the altar boy schedule posted by the principal's office door to confirm his schedule, he found something unexpected. The next day he was scheduled not just for the 7:00 a.m., but also the 8:00 a.m. mass with Itch. Father Tom figured, if he was there for the earlier one, it only made sense to put him on the next with his best friend.

"I'm not serving with that jerk. I won't do it," Itch complained to Father Tom when he happened upon him in the hall.

It caught him off guard. Father Tom knew they argued like an old married couple, but in truth there were no two kids tighter than them, or at least, he thought.

"May I ask why? I thought you were good friends?"

"Not anymore. Ted's a"—Itch was about to curse but changed it to—"turncoat."

"You guys have a falling out?"

"You learn things about people. You think they are one way and then find out they are another and I'm not serving with him. Never again. Not together."

"That's not a very Christian way to serve the Lord. I'll change this one mass, but when you serve God, you have to do things for the Lord and not yourself."

The vehemence of Itch's conviction concerned him enough to pull Ted out of class and ask about it.

"What happened between you two?" Father Tom inquired. Disappointment carried in his voice.

Ted offered few details, but stressed it was his fault.

"I don't know what to do with myself. I wouldn't want to be my friend either.

The worst part, the thing that bothers me most is he called me a snake."

"Anyone can call you a name it doesn't mean..."

"Father, the problem is he's right. I am a snake; it describes me perfectly. God made me a snake. What am I supposed to do about that?"

Father Tom could see the boy standing in front of him was reaching a significant and upsetting milestone on his journey toward maturity. The realization that what is told to children the world over that they can be and achieve anything was a lie. There were options open to some that others will never have; limitations that dictate what could and could not be done. None of it was fair, but our brains instinctively demand that we attempt to shun this truth. Ultimately, the only unalienable right afforded to all was the ability to decide what to do with the options available.

Father Tom disagreed wholeheartedly with Ted's self-assessment but knew arguing against perception was futile.

"Why is that so bad? Snakes kill rats and keep birds from destroying crops. It's what you do with who you are that matters. I don't know what God made you, Ted, but if it is a snake, then take the characteristics that come with it, use it for good, and be the best one you possibly can."

"Now what about your friend?"

Ted stood silent for a while as he thought before speaking. This meant so much to him he wanted to be sure he didn't screw it up.

"Father, he was my best friend and deserved so much more from me. I was such a jerk. I know now what I am, but I am doing everything I can to change it. I'm different now, really, and I wish he could somehow know that. If he forgave me, I'd be the best friend he ever had."

"Well, Ted, I'll say a prayer that you get a chance to show him."

Preaching

Father Tom knew prayer without action is meaningless. The next morning, he took the place of the scheduled priest and a few minutes to talk with Itch. He reminded Itch of the good times he and Ted shared.

Itch stood the whole time with his arms crossed staring at the floor, but as the conversation continued his defiance drained like a deflating tire.

Father Tom changed the Gospel to a reading from the book of Matthew. Part of it stated: "For if you forgive other people when they sin against you, your heavenly Father will also forgive you. But if you do not forgive others their sins, your Father will not forgive your sins."

His homily, uncharacteristically long, especially for a weekday mass, focused on the same subject.

"Let me get right to the point of what this Gospel means in your life. I'll begin with a quote for you to think about. The first to apologize is the bravest, the first to forgive is the strongest, and the first to forget is the happiest.

"Every significant relationship you have, whether it be to a spouse, family, or even your best friend, somewhere, forgiveness will eventually come into play. People don't live up to our expectations, they will disappoint us. Think of all the times they may have helped you and the many qualities they have. Ask yourself, should I throw it all away?"

Itch wasn't stupid. He knew this homily was directed towards him. And as rough as he could be he also wasn't heartless and began feeling deep remorse. Despite what Ted did, he had turned his back on one of the few kids willing to put up with him.

"Forgive and forget. The words give and get are contained in them. What is it that you are giving when you forgive? You are cleansing the soul of another human being. What power. What incredible power God has given us to be able to do that. You can buy a present, spend a lot of money, add a touching card, but anyone who sincerely wants to be forgiven will tell you that gift is appreciated more than anything money can buy."

"I said you get too. What is it that you get? Well, when you cleanse their soul, you will find you have cleansed your own as well. It shows God and all those around you the goodness inside yourself. But there is something even better, miraculous. Someone truly repentant has changed. Imagine after you have given the gift of forgiveness what kind of a best friend they will be to you from that day forward."

Finished, turning around to glance where the altar boys sat, he caught Itch looking down at the floor, fingers wiping his eyes.

The next part of his plan was to provide a temptation he knew neither could resist.

Sacred

Ted was assigned a 9:00 a.m. mass! Allowing him to skip first class, it was never assigned to new altar boys. It would be the first given to any of their group.

For a moment, he was excited, giddy, in fact, when checking the week's roster just after lunch to see this prestigious honor. It all crashed when he looked to find Itch's name next to his.

"Figures," he mumbled, planning to give it away. Before he did, though, he decided to make sure Itch hadn't had some unexpected change of heart.

Just before dismissal, he approached him sitting at his desk. Staring straight ahead, focusing on the blackboard, he didn't move, even as Ted stood next to him and started speaking.

"Itch, I got the 9:00 a.m. mass tomorrow with you." He paused and lamented the sacrifice he was about to make. "I can flip it with someone if you want."

Itch remained focused on the board, ignoring Ted as he had done for the past two months, before taking a deep breath, which only added to the moment's drama and replied with unexpected softness.

"I'll see you tomorrow at nine."

Just hearing Itch acknowledge him made his heart pound. After school, he ran most of the way home.

"You're awful hungry," his mother said as he shoveled in dinner that night, not able to tell her the real reason for his suddenly found appetite. He told her the good news about his 9:00 a.m. mass instead. She interrupted to tell her story of what happened at the butcher that day and how she wound up buying lamb instead of pork. No matter, he listened to her uneventful drawn-out story and put aside his own. Nothing could dampen his excitement for the next morning.

Nervous, he showed up ten minutes earlier than necessary and found Itch already prepping in the sacristy. Upon sight, Itch flatly gave instructions.

"Don't say a word. When mass is over, do all the cleanup and then meet me back here."

The twenty-minute mass seemed hours long as the two sat silently side by side. When it was over, Itch disappeared into the sacristy and closed the door while Ted put everything neatly in place, more carefully than usual, taking time, hoping to calm his nerves. Finishing, Ted saw it was the moment of truth. With a deep breath, he grabbed the knob of the sacristy door and swung it open.

Inside, Itch was standing next to a small table on the far side of the room where he had set up two large gold chalices and placed an unopened bottle of altar wine between them.

"I owe you an apology," Itch began as Ted entered.

"What?" Ted replied, now worried Itch was being sarcastic.

"No, I do. You've had some rough times, and I knew you needed my help, but all I did was act like a stuck-up jackass. Listen, what you did sucked, but I should have been the better man. This school is full of jerks, but you aren't one of them. I want us to be friends again." He put out his hand as he said it.

"Itch, I was a total dirtbag, but please know I would never do anything like that again," he said as he walked across the room, grasped his hand, and shook it long enough for Itch to ask if he could have it back.

"Talk is cheap, but I suppose we'll see. A little surprise," he said as he picked up the altar wine and twisted open the screw top. "Let's have a toast to our friendship."

Ted's eyes bulged as Itch emptied half the bottle into each chalice. *A bit much*, he thought, but voiced nothing.

Itch handed him one and took the other. Holding his up, then clicking it against Ted's, Itch proclaimed, "To friendship."

"Wait," Ted said before it had touched either of their lips. "I want to tell you something. Itch, if you ever need my help, I swear on this holy blood of Christ, I will defend you even at the cost of my own life."

Itch could feel the sincerity of his words. "And, Ted, I swear on the blood of Christ I'd do the same for you."

They then raised the chalices for a toast that had transformed from a mischievous celebration to a most sacred vow. Crossing their arms around each other, they locked at the elbow and began to drink. Ted took a sip of the sickly sweet wine and wondered how he'd possibly down it, but despite almost retching in the process, he finished it to the last drop.

"Hold out your hand," Itch told Ted as he cracked open a pack of mint Tic-Tacs. Pouring half onto Ted's palm, then the rest into his own, he plowed them into his mouth. "Chew them good and let's go. We don't have much time before the wine kicks in."

The two made it to class shortly before their ability to walk straight would have been gone. Ted was clueless how close the vow he had just made would come to costing his life. He sat at his desk, thoroughly enjoying the buzz but finding it incomparable to the joy of having his friend back.

He looked forward to the cafeteria that day, finally getting to sit again with the group. He might have been less enthusiastic had he realized he was about to face a test of a different type than those he routinely failed in school. This test, he absolutely had to pass. His entire future was to be determined by it. Stacked up against everything that happens in life, the event that followed was quickly forgotten, yet it signified a turn to a path that altered his life. Decision day and hour was upon him.

Decision

Decision Day

They sat in the cafeteria, the group of four back together with jovial chatter filling a space where recently there had been none. As Anna walked by on her way to her place of exile, Itch took the stage.

"Boom, boom, boom," he uttered, insinuating an elephant was walking by.

It was the moment Ted had feared. A fork in the road. Insignificant decisions can have such cascading effects. It was at this moment he set a domino in motion that would have life altering implications.

We remember the big events in our lives, but truthfully, our path is determined by everyday small decisions. A golfer knows a 2-inch putt counts the same as a 200-yard drive. Life is very similar, except there are innumerably more 2-inch putts than 200-yard drives. For Ted, making a vow, swearing to God, deciding to change, even involving things seemingly insignificant, held meaning. The difference, as his life unfolded, had he decided to relapse into his regular routine and join in with his newly reconciled friends and make fun of Anna, would have been enormous. A new path was set following what had been a long buildup to what any but of the keenest of observers might otherwise view as an anticlimactic moment.

"Guys, do you think we could stop doing that?"

"Doing what? Ani-mul?" Itch questioned.

"That's another thing. Could we stop calling her names? Call her Anna from now on?"

"Why?"

"Because that's her name. We should start using it."

"What's it to you?"

Upchuck saw an opening he'd been waiting on for years.

"Hey, guys, I know you think it's funny and all, but since we're talking about nicknames, do you think you could stop calling me Upchuck?"

"See, everyone hates their nickname," Ted chimed in.

"I like mine," Itch said.

"If you want to lose a finger, call me Ricky," Rip added.

Upchuck continued, "Newsflash to you, guys, the joke was over a long time ago. Could you guys stop?"

"What the heck are we supposed to call you?" Itch responded.

"How about just Chuck?"

Ted jumped on it. "Guys, allow me to introduce our new friend, Chuck. We can only hope he's an improvement over the old one."

Itch, disliking anytime Ted moved on something faster than he did, ended his resistance. "If it bothered you so much, you should have said something. I hereby baptize you Chuck in the name of the Father, Son, and Holy Spirit." He put his thumb on Chuck's forehead and signed a cross.

"How about you Ted?" one of them asked. "Anything you don't like to be called?"

"Never call me Teddy. I detest Teddy, and not Theodore, and if you ever call me Teddy Bear—"

"How about Theodora?" Itch interrupted.

The look on Ted's face negated the need to reply. He returned to his original topic.

"So, it's Anna from now on, right?"

When they just stared, he persisted.

"Come on. Just agree. Don't make me bust your heads."

Rip had trouble keeping a straight face. "If I wanted to, I could tear your arm off and beat you to death with it, but yeah, whatever."

He had never stood against peer pressure or anyone in that way before. Nerves shot, he felt like he had just fought a lion. He focused his attention elsewhere and stumbled upon a favorite eavesdrop.

"Hold up, guys. I want to hear this," Ted said, raising his hand to silence the others. They complied, but never understood his fascination with a game the girls would sometimes play, which he would try to overhear whenever encountered.

Usually played by three, they would pick someone famous, and each would have to come up with one word that offered the best description of their character. After each gave a suggestion, a vote was taken on the best description.

Harrison Ford was their selection, and they came up with fearless, courageous, and bold. Courageous won.

The next name was Anna, but it was regarding an actress he had never heard of, but it made him wonder. If he had one word to describe the Anna he knew, what would it be? He had no idea why but the word he kept returning to was *amazing*.

Incense

It is easy to be fooled. Despite appearances of holiness, altar boys are, underneath it all, adolescent monsters. If the choice were to get a laugh from their friends with the consequence being eternal damnation from an unseen yet all-powerful deity, the decision is obvious. Things like sneaking a few sips of altar wine or wetting the wicks of ceremonial candles to make them impossible to light during mass celebrations were common. What happened in the church in April 1978 was over the top even for the worst of them.

Someone had lifted the cover of the radiator in the sacristy and urinated on the boiling-hot steam coil. The result was a thermonuclear mushroom cloud of stench. The beautiful church, with its marble floors, ornate chandeliers, intricate stained glass windows, and life-sized statues of saints was reduced to the environment of an ill kept men's room. Multiple incense burners had been lit to counteract the effect, but it only bonded with the odor to produce a perfume from hell.

The altar boys, every last one, were assembled in the church among nuns who paced the floor like bees from a kicked over hive. Each boy would be interrogated individually, but Father Tom wanted to address them first as a group. Although he didn't know positively, he assumed the culprit was among them.

"One here among you does not appreciate that this is God's house. I don't think I really need to tell you what happened here this morning. You can smell it for yourselves."

There were giggles from the crowd.

"None of this is funny. What you are smelling is sin, raw, pure, disgusting sin."

The giggles became cackles, and from much greater numbers.

Realizing the need for a different tack, he reached into his wallet, pulled a twenty, and held it high over his head. That got their attention much faster than the possibility of damnation.

"See this twenty? It goes to the person who reveals the culprit. Let me assure you we will find the guilty party, and when we do, they will have a new understanding of God's wrath. Am I clear?"

The response was a universal, "Yes, Father."

Days of questioning followed. No threat or reward uncovered the guilty party.

That person, alone in the knowledge of what he had done, rather than remorse, reveled in the thrill of having singlehandedly, no pun intended, pissed off every priest, nun, and teacher in the entire school. He would strike again, but with the radiators being shut off for summer, patience would be required.

Indifference

The best days of our lives and, happily, the most numerous, consist of dull routine. Sorely underappreciated, they provide necessary pauses between spurts of growth. Ted would have been perfectly happy to continue his routine unbroken, but as always, events, usually beyond our control, dictate otherwise.

Interruption came during a walk home from school as he stopped to chat with a couple of classmates. He leaned against a six-foot-high chain-link fence that surrounded the parking lot of a supermarket beside them.

This day in May was gorgeous, and they lamented that most of it had been wasted in school. A moment later, the calm of what should have been a lazy afternoon was shattered by the screams of a child. A girl, no more than five, was being pulled to a car by a large muscular man.

"Holy cow!" one of them yelled at the sight of the man, who scooped up the struggling girl screaming for her mother.

Of the three standing there, the last anyone would expect to burst to action would be Ted. Compelled by an almost supernatural force, he tore at the fence's links, scaling it at a speed that would have impressed a drill sergeant. As he landed on the other side, he believed his two companions were just a step behind. Hyper focused, his world now consisted of only three simple variables, the girl, the man, and his need to break her free.

His eyes fixed on the thrashing of her arms; her screams only propelled him forward with more power. As the distance between them closed his mind recorded the details of the monster he was to attack. A large man, gray muscle shirt, head shaven, thirties maybe, tattoos on both arms.

As Ted rapidly approached from behind, the man put the girl down to get his keys but retained hold of her arm. Ted was now the only thing preventing her fate. Using inertia and total surprise, he slammed into the man, taking advantage of his awkward position and causing him to fall forward to the ground. The grip on the girl was broken, and she fled through the parking lot back toward the store.

Ted's attempts after that to subdue this bear verged on comical. Finding himself lying on top of the man's back, Ted tried to get his arm around the man's neck, which was covered in tattoos of flames. One would never guess he was trying to get him in a chokehold. A fast, upward elbow into Ted's ribs ended the melee. The wind knocked out of him, he rolled to the ground face up with no fight left.

The man rolled too, instinctively, on top of him with his arm coiled far back and fist tight, ready to slam down into his unknown attacker's face.

"Please don't kill me!" Ted strained to say, in pain and under the pressing weight of the man. Catching sight of the fist hovering in a strike position, he mentally prepared to see stars and figured after that everything would fade to black.

The man, met by the sight of this ridiculously young schoolboy, cursed then jumped up to run after the girl.

"Sophie, Sophie stop!"

"He knew her name?" Ted reckoned for a moment, afraid to process any further the implications of such a fact. Joining the pain in his ribs was a column of bile from his suddenly nauseous stomach that made it halfway up his throat. He cautiously struggled to his feet. The girl ran straight into the arms of her mother, who had abandoned her cart full of groceries. Carrying the girl, she walked forward to meet the man with whom Ted had just had the altercation.

"David," she yelled, "what the hell happened?"

"That kid," he said, pointing at Ted. "You know how she gets. He must have thought I was trying to kidnap her."

The woman strained her eyes to get a better look at him through her glasses while Ted closed his. Embarrassment is a terrible feeling, and Ted was doing laps in an Olympic-size pool of it. He visualized a sign over his head, the size of a city block, with the word *moron* written on it and an arrow pointing at him. He'd just made a laughingstock of himself and everyone who for years claimed him a genius.

The opening of his eyes confirmed his worst fear; this was real. As soon as the woman holding her daughter was in earshot, he began a running monologue of apologizing and explaining what he thought had been happening. She abruptly cut him off.

"Kid, are you alright?"

She meant physically, but Ted was convinced she was referring to his mental state.

"I'm fine!" he snapped, even though he was beginning to think maybe he did have mental problems.

"No, it looks like you might be hurt."

He did his best to spiral anger in his tone. "Yes, I'm fine. Can I just go?"

"What you tried to do was incredibly heroic. What's your name?"

Ted shook his head.

"Heroic? Is that what you just called him? He's a f—ing idiot!" David yelled.

The woman looked at Ted, eyes apologetic, then noticed David's nose.

"You're bleeding!" she exclaimed in surprise.

By this time, David had the groceries in the car and seemed as eager to leave as Ted.

"It's just allergies," he snapped back. "Get in the damn car!"

Ted pulled a handkerchief from his pocket, one made of cloth, the kind any professional nerd would carry. Holding it out toward David, he was ignored.

The woman went to hand Sophie to him so she could look for a tissue in her purse. Again, she began to scream, an alarming, instinctively primordial scream that, unless heard, cannot be justifiably described. A stark look of terror filled her innocent young face. Her mother ended the search and instead buckled her into her car seat. Ted peeked in, silent, observing the lost, helpless look on the girl's tear-stained face.

They got in the car, David's bloody nose unattended, and, with a slight spin of the tires, pulled away. To Ted, who hoped David would acknowledge his apology, the rush to leave seemed odd, but he was otherwise relieved it was over.

Now alone, he wished that by some miracle a hole would open in the ground and swallow him. His sense of stupidity increased with each step on the return to his friends, who had not moved an inch from where they had been standing.

One of them yelled as Ted approached, “Did you see that?” As if he had not been part of it. “Oh my God, that was freaking awesome!”

He and the other kid began retelling the story with Ted’s performance becoming more exaggerated with each repetition. He hated to interrupt their telling of his heroics, but his ribs were bothering him something awful. He wanted to be rid of these two so he could let down his veneer of bravery. He did his best to pretend he was unaffected, only telling them he was due home and walked off, ignoring their questions about why he was dragging his schoolbag.

Something that had been missing right to that moment suddenly presented itself. It was fear, and as if triggered by a push button, it shot throughout his body from seemingly nowhere. Irrational thoughts assaulted his psyche. Maybe this guy would be looking for him. Perhaps he was in his car circling around like a shark so he could run him over. Pain shot from his ribs as he dragged his schoolbag, but he plodded forward, focusing on the safety only home can offer. It felt to him like he was leaving a war zone as he passed through the front door.

His mom was downstairs doing laundry, allowing him to sneak in, go straight to the bathroom, and lift his shirt to look at his ribs. To the right side of his chest, about four ribs from the bottom, a large black-and-blue mark was already well formed. Aside from a few scrapes on his shoulder, everything else appeared okay.

He went to the kitchen to get ice, but the trays were empty. There was a bag of frozen peas that might do nicely. Breaking them apart against the refrigerator door, he pressed them to his ribs, a perfect fit!

Feeling as though his joints might shake apart, rather than homework, he turned on the TV, settled deep into one of the armchairs in the living room, and held the cold peas to his chest. The makeshift ice pack was just starting to provide some relief from the wincing pain experienced with each inhale when his mother came up from doing laundry. Tossing the peas to the floor, he straightened, trying his best to give the impression everything was normal.

"What is that?" she asked, pointing to the bag.

"Frozen peas," he said, as if giving a matter-of-fact answer might stop the questioning.

"Why do you have those?"

"I'm playing with them," he replied, unable to contain a sarcastic tone.

"Do you want peas for dinner?" she asked.

"No, absolutely not."

"I'll make peas with dinner," she replied, trotting off to the freezer to look for another bag.

"I thought I had more," Ted heard her say to herself. Coming back into the room, she spoke again. "I need those peas."

"Can I have them for a while?" Ted asked, hoping his annoyance was clear enough to dissuade her.

"I don't have another bag, and I want to make them for dinner. Besides, why are you playing with peas anyway?"

She didn't wait for an answer before returning to the kitchen. Ted's eyes rolled to the ceiling and stayed there. That woman had the God-given talent for doing the exact thing nobody wanted. He reached down, grabbed them, and stood up, but a bit too fast, causing a lightning hot shock of pain to race across his chest and take his breath away. He was quick enough to get his hand to his mouth to muffle the squeak that had spontaneously erupted, then moved more cautiously.

Thankfully, in the kitchen, facing the sink, her back was to the door, allowing him to quietly place them on the kitchen table before slinking to the shelter of his room. There he faced a no-win decision. Standing upright hurt, sitting hurt, laying down hurt, moving hurt. Choosing an evil, he picked the chair at his desk and sat. Emotionally exhausted, feeling his eyes getting watery, he pushed back, wanting to be a man and deny the release. Unable to steady his mind or his hands enough for homework, he sat stoically, head down on his desk, and waited a torturously long time for the call to dinner.

Emerging into the kitchen, it took his father, now home from work, one look to realize something was horribly wrong.

"Call an ambulance!" his mother screamed when Ted lifted his shirt.

"Don't panic, Ann. Let me have a look." Yeah, this was a trip to the hospital, but not in an ambulance. His dad grabbed the car keys and did what Ted thought was the ultimate favor in convincing his mother to wait back at home.

Like the detective he was, he peppered Ted with questions on the drive over, beginning with, "So, why don't you tell me your version of what happened?"

At first, Ted tried to pass it off by saying he was horsing around and fell against a mailbox, but his father blew holes in that story, already assuming he had been in a fight.

"Was it Tom? Did Tom do this? Be honest. There's something wrong with that kid, and he could really hurt you."

In the waiting room of the ER, Ted gave a full account and concluded with sheepish regret. "This is all so embarrassing."

Following an evaluation, X-rays, and a long wait, it was confirmed that Ted had a hairline fracture. The only treatment was ice packs, Tylenol, and according to the doctor, "He should not play sports for six weeks."

"Ow, ow, ah, only six weeks! Don't make me laugh. It hurts too much," Ted pleaded.

Arriving home after ten, his father confirmed he'd be out of school the next day and they'd see about Monday.

With help from his father, he settled into bed and reviewed the entire incident in his head. He reasoned this as more evidence in an ever-growing pile that he was an imbecile. The emotion filled cloud of confusion settled down to be replaced by an all-consuming sensation of helplessness.

"What's wrong with me?" he asked when his father came in to check on him. "Why was it me who reacted that way? There had to be a dozen people in that parking lot, my friends too. I was the only one that stupid."

His father went to sit on the bed but stopped, realizing that might upset Ted's carefully managed position. He knew the answer quite well; he saw it every day in his job.

"Ted, let me ask you something. When you were on the ground and you thought the man was going to punch you, did anyone try to stop him?"

"There wasn't enough time."

"Okay. But after, did people come running over to help you?"

"No, but I didn't want them to. I just wanted it all to go away."

"What did your friends do?"

"They were just watching."

"Do you know what that is Ted? Something you will see a lot in your life. It's called indifference. It's people not wanting to get involved. If you want your life to really matter, Ted, don't let yourself become indifferent."

"I'm going to let you in on a secret. I'm going to tell you the secret to being an adult."

Ted loved keys to life and listened with extra attentiveness.

"Can you guess what makes you an adult?"

"Your age?"

"Technically, yes, but no. Growing up, being an adult, is all about taking responsibility. Whether it's fair or not, whether at fault or not, an adult takes responsibility. There is no should or shouldn't. It's about standing up every time and doing what you know in your heart is right. Ted, when you grow up it is going to amaze you how many people never do that. A person can be any age, but that doesn't mean they ever grew up.

"And I'm proud of you. You might think what you did was stupid, but we all make mistakes. All I can see from what you told me is that you are becoming an adult."

He sealed it with a kiss to his forehead and headed for the door, his words having gone much further than the Tylenol in easing his son's pain.

"If you need anything during the night, don't get up. Call for me."

"It really isn't that bad, and wait, Dad. You want to know the truth? The day you adopted me was the luckiest day of my life."

"Mine too," his dad replied as he exited the room.

Still haunted by those horrid screams, the look of terror on the little girl's face, sleep abandoned him. He lay on his back doing his best to remain still, fingers gently stroking the sore spot on his ribs. His mind filled with thoughts of Sophie that made him question everything about his judgment. In the end, he decided there was only one thing he could do.

* * *

"I prayed for her, then I prayed even more for myself," Ted reflected to those in the office, now decades past the incident. "Sometimes you do what you can and sometimes there is nothing you can do. But within that incident, it was the first time, and it deeply disturbed me, I truly understood, that I was different and there was something wrong with me."

"That woman was right. You are a hero," Sister Margaret interrupted.

"Oh, I did not feel that way at all. I still cringe whenever I think about it. Everyone does stupid things when they are young that, as an adult, they try not to replicate. My ribs had long healed before I was sleeping soundly again. Such was the anxiety generated by the belief that I was not like other people. I suppose the only good thing to come of it was how it helped my reputation at school."

Ted was the main topic of the scuttlebutt that passed around in a schoolyard the next day. So opposite his image, no one would have believed one iota of the story had there not been two witnesses. Several versions of his performance circulated with the only commonality being the claim that he broke the guy's nose.

He had been lucky that day. David, a violent cold-blooded felon who'd served time in maximum security for manslaughter, was not one to hesitate striking back, even against a child, and could have killed him with one punch.

It was Ted's autistic tendencies that caused him to interpret the world in a way most people would not. Clearly, he had been wrong about the kidnapping, but he was never able to shake the feeling Sophie was in mortal danger. Judging Ted's actions as heroic or idiotic depended upon the information presented and the interpretation.

At school, his two friends made it sound like it had been a fifteen-round prize fight.

Ted believed they battled at least thirty seconds; other witnesses would have reported half that. With exact facts on any event impossible to ascertain, everything in this world, great and trivial, is incomplete, misreported, and misinterpreted. Skewed by our perception, fundamental biases and inexact facts, distortions occur even when directly experienced, much more so when not, and filter through a lens that never allows us to see what is exactly right.

For the record, it was not allergies, but years of heavy cocaine use that was responsible for David's nosebleed. The fight, which was made to sound like a world-class heavyweight boxing match, lasted, start to finish, all of 3.8 seconds.

Little Sophie's fate was unchanged that day despite Ted's truly heroic actions. Irrespective of whether it had been deliberate or unintentional, due to the indifference exhibited by everyone else present, Sophie, most unfortunately, did not live to see her next birthday.

Acquiescence

Off school on Friday, Itch called over the weekend to inform Ted that he was all the buzz. Putting aside a little pain in his chest, Ted returned Monday to bask in it, but that wasn't to happen. Kids move off topic faster than lightning. By the time he returned, his story was relegated somewhere behind the weekend's TV shows and the latest baseball scores.

Regardless, the incident left him shaken into realizing he needed to be able to defend himself. Pride swallowing would be required if he were to ask the one person he knew could help. Rip had stopped extending invitations ever since their altercation, so collecting his nerve, he brought up the topic as they lined up to head for the cafeteria for lunch.

"Rip, I don't know how to ask, but remember how I used to make jokes when you would ask if I wanted to work out and learn to fight? I decided I'm done being a jerk and thought maybe you might still want to teach me."

Rip's eyes lit up; his words jumbled in the excitement.

"Really! After school today! Just got two new twenty-five pounders I'll show you. The sparring gear might be a bit big, but we'll put some padding underneath. We'll do warm-ups first, but you have to be serious. If you're not going to be serious don't bother. Three days a week, Tuesday, Thursday, and we'll do Saturday mornings. Sunday can be a makeup day if we miss one. So, what time?"

"Hold off a sec. I want to do it, I swear. I promise I'll do the whole schedule, but I don't think I can today. My chest is killing me because of last week."

"Yeah?"

"Well, you know how I beat the guy up pretty bad, but you said it yourself—they can always get a lucky shot. He got my ribs."

"Show me," Rip said, pulling Ted's arm as the other students began following the teacher out of the room.

"You coming?" Mrs. Butterman called from the front of the line.

"Ted and I want to study during lunch, so we need to get a book."

That should have been a tip off of the lie, but she ignored it.

"Hurry up," she called back as she broke off to head toward the teacher's lounge, leaving the line of students to guide themselves to the cafeteria.

The two boys went to the back of the room where Ted undid his shirt's buttons and raised his undershirt.

"Holy crap! What did your folks say?"

"My dad took me to the hospital, but they said it just has to heal on its own. Maybe six weeks. Looks worse than it is. If I don't move the wrong way, it doesn't really hurt. My mom gave me Tylenol this morning."

"Well, you can't work out until it heals, but after that..."

"I know. I will. I promise I'm serious about it. Three days a week, no exceptions, no excuses."

"I'm holding you to it."

Just then Steve, having returned for something, caught Ted in the peculiar situation. Red faced, Ted yanked down his shirt and fumbled to get some of his buttons closed.

Steve shared his thought. "Ted, do you ever get tired of being a faggot?"

The echo of his words still hung in the air when Rip grabbed him by the throat and thrust him solidly against the back wall.

"¿Cómo llamaste a mi amigo? ¡ no le vuelvas a decir eso! ¡Entiendes! ¿Quién te crees que eres un maldito vago apestoso? ¡ debería romperte la cara aquí mismo! ¡ Si no te disculpas con Ted este maldito instante te voy a quitar la cabeza!"

Few things are more terrifying than having your life threatened in a language you don't understand. Steve didn't have to know Spanish to almost lose control of his bodily functions. The deployment of Spanish curse words became so liberal, Ted, who only knew those, was almost able to follow along.

Finally, Ted interrupted, "English, Rip. Speak English."

Rip loosened his grip on Steve enough to let him breathe again.

"I wasn't talking to you!" Steve pleaded following a violent cough.

"You talk to him, you're talking to me. Lift your shirt, Ted," Rip ordered.

Complying, Ted once again exposed the bruise.

"Look at that," Rip demanded, taking Steve's chin in his hand, and forcing him to look. "Look at it good. That's what your face is going to look like if you ever talk to him like that again. Now get out of here before I kick your ass."

Steve, no longer caring to retrieve whatever he had come for, ran from the room empty-handed.

"I learned that in my neighborhood. Remember it."

"What's that?"

"When people don't want to give you respect, fear changes their mind pretty quickly."

Ted liked the sound of that, a lesson he would liberally apply later in life.

Reprieve

It was three weeks before Ted called to resume his 7:00 a.m. mass schedule. He felt he had let Father Tom down. Father Tom was glad to see him back but had already filled the roster for the next month.

Instead, he had something special. Unheard of for a first-year altar boy, with the likelihood of a tip, he was given the most coveted assignment of all—a wedding mass, and not just any.

Along with three of the finest and most senior altar boys from the eighth grade, similar to a royal wedding of old, the marriage was between two powerful mafia families. Resembling a scene from *The Godfather*, a church too large to be filled on Easter Sunday had standing room only, filled with floral arrangements lining the side aisles, front to back.

On a Saturday in late June, it took place on what would be one of the hottest days of the year. The mass itself ran two hours, then two more for photos. The boys were nearly passed out, panting and sweaty by the time it ended.

Disappearing into the small room just off the entrance, they were grateful to finally peel off the stifling layers of their religious garb. This was followed by a knock on the door from one of the ushers. It was the moment they all had been waiting for.

"Wonderful job, boys. The bride and groom wish to show you their appreciation," he said as he handed each an envelope.

Containing themselves, they acted like it was no big deal until he left and the door closed, then tore them open like gifts on Christmas morning.

"A hundred dollars!" one of them yelled, holding up a crisp bill in his hand.

"I would have smiled a lot more in those pictures if I knew this was coming," Ted commented, holding another in his hand.

"Definitely," another agreed before asking Ted something they were all wondering. "You're in sixth, right?"

"Going into seventh."

"This was the mass of the year. How did you get assigned to it?"

Ted gave a response that made them all laugh, borrowing from the style they'd been subjected to all morning, even imitating hand gestures.

"Ayyyy…., I got connections!"

CHOICES

Eighteen Years Prior to Present Day

Indifference within himself is not something Ted could tolerate. Karen had been working for Ted just a few years when she saw how this dictated his thoughts and actions.

It was related to a subpoena she had once received from the State Department regarding her knowledge of what Ted had labeled "Operation Purify." This resulted from a chance encounter he had while visiting a small island off the coast of South America to close a potentially lucrative business deal. He was to provide full financing to a struggling oil exploration company. Had the deal closed, he would have made tens of millions, but fate moved in a different direction.

The rain from the morning had turned a sunny day into a tropical steam bath. It was the kind of day people begin sweating from just looking out the window. His two bodyguards advised him to be inconspicuous. They were beside themselves when he insisted on being the only human on the island to dress in a dark business suit on a sweltering 104-degree day. He stuck out among the hundreds of tourists walking the streets like a giant American thumb.

Henry, the bodyguard who was always by his side when he traveled abroad, felt he needed to try to match but had not packed for it. The closest he had was a suit from a trip to Bermuda the week before, including the famous shorts. He barely pulled it off in Hamilton with his hairy legs, but here he looked ridiculous. Not half as much as Ted, though, who had added blindman-type black glasses and a baseball cap to his already ludicrous, out-of-place appearance. Ted hadn't previously met his second bodyguard but the man, Paulo, was a trusted local with an excellent reputation. He fit in perfectly with the natives and trailed the pair some twenty paces behind.

This destination was selected for the meeting due to its seclusion. It turned out to be a wrong choice as Ted was never going to make the meeting.

There was time to kill before the signing. Ted decided to window shop along the main streets, allowing himself to be accosted by store owners promising bargains and cold air in their shops. Most of the jewelry stores were traps, ripping off American tourists unable to convert the price of an ounce of silver into grams, so he didn't bother going in.

After being stared at like a freak by most shop owners, he assumed it was because of Henry and asked him to drop back so he could walk alone. Paulo still followed inconspicuously. Walking just a couple of blocks off the main street all the tourists disappeared. The shops became notably run down and the streets occupied by only locals. This was the part of a country he liked to immerse himself in and explore. A man in a doorway stepped in front of his path and asked in the locals' accent, holding his thumb and index finger up to his lips, "Signor, you want to smoke?"

Having lived his entire life in New York, it was second nature to just walk past and ignore someone like this.

"Hey," the man said, tapping him on the arm as he tried to bypass him. "Do you want to buy some smokes?" He repeated the gesture with his fingers.

"I don't smoke," Ted replied, making the mistake of acknowledging him. He was short, nicely dressed, looking gentlemanly in an expensive Stetson cowboy hat. A gleam in his eye instinctively indicated to Ted he was not to be fooled with.

"How about something young and sweet? Huh? You like girls?"

Not sure if he was offering what seemed to be implied, Ted tested. "Now there's something I like. What were you thinking?" Both their faces brightened.

"I'll get one for you. Whatever you want. So, what do you like? Pretty? Young?"

"How about pretty young?" Ted said, his face becoming serious, causing the man to smile ear to ear, exposing three gold teeth.

"Costs, but if you want, I have it."

"How much?"

It would have been fifty dollars, but he said, "Two hundred," on account of his mark's well-to-do appearance.

"And that gets me?"

"Anything, everything. Let me see the money, and I'll take you."

Ted plucked the top two bills of a roll in his pocket, both hundreds, and showed the man. That got another smile and a motion for him to follow to a destination just a block away, a dingy white two-story stucco building, cracks running all along the facade. From the number of windows, Ted estimated ten rooms.

"You pay me now and then go in. They'll take care of you," the man said.

Ted smiled, genuinely enjoying the kindred spirit of a man who apparently also liked to play on words.

Smart enough to remain outside, he pushed back. "I'm not giving you $200 until I see what I'm getting. I want young. Real young. Show me."

"Come in, I'll show you."

"No, I'll wait here. Bring her out," Ted insisted as a standoff developed.

"I'll be back," the man said after looking over his mark head to toe and realizing this wasn't negotiable. Left alone, Ted waited outside, observing the beehive-like activity of the men coming in and out the door before the man returned and pointed to a window on the ground floor. A girl appeared with someone behind her apparently holding her in place by the shoulders.

Ted knew such places existed, but they were always somewhere else. Now, being at one, a place where this was really happening, he felt lightheaded with an uncomfortable twinge passing through his center. The girl could barely have been thirteen.

He gave a wave, but she remained motionless, stoic, with eyes under her straight brown hair fixed as if staring across a field rather than the street. She seemed like a shell-shocked soldier who had been through too many battles.

"No deal. I want really young," Ted said.

The man responded by gripping his arm firmly, prompting Paulo to appear from the shadows.

"Espere que no hoya ningana' problemas." *I hope there are no problems,* he stated while momentarily, as if it were unintended, exposing the gun he was wearing to the man holding Ted's arm.

They traded grips as the man let go of Ted's left arm while Paulo grabbed his right and tugged, extricating him from the situation.

"You want her? One fifty!" the man shouted, not comprehending the transaction was over. "No good? I got younger." He called at the pair before slapping his hand against his leg in frustration.

"That was stupid!" Paulo chastised in his thick Spanish accent as they hurried away. "The locals use that place. It's not for you. They would have killed you in there."

"I wasn't going in," Ted assured.

"It's a bad place. Bad people. I'll get you a woman if you want. Stay away from little girls," Paulo lectured.

"It was just reconnaissance. I have a daughter who is eleven!" Ted shouted. "Why don't the police do something about that place?"

Sad as the situation was, Paulo had to cover his mouth to hide a chuckle over the naivety of this otherwise intelligent man.

"That guy you were speaking to, his brother is the chief of police."

Ted stopped to absorb the information, frustrated at how stupid Paulo just proved him to be. Glancing at his watch, about to be late, he instead turned for his hotel, giving no consideration to the meeting or Henry whom he left stranded. His feet pounded the pavement in such a way everyone in his path could tell failure to move might put their very life in danger. Paulo had never seen such a look on anyone. *There is no taming insanity*, he thought but tried anyway.

"This isn't a crusade you can win," Paulo reasoned. "These kinds of things are all over the place."

"I'm not taking up a crusade," Ted replied, "but now that I have seen it with my own eyes, I know it exists and where it is, and critically, there is something I can do about it. It now becomes my responsibility. I cannot ever allow myself to become indifferent."

Into the elevator at his hotel, he pounded the button to his floor nonstop like a jackhammer. Getting to his room, he slammed the door in Paulo's face, locked himself in, and tore toward a solution.

By the time he was done two days later, the deal was in tatters. Ben Arlington had swept in and stolen it out from under him. Panicked by his no-show, the company executives had allowed Ben to negotiate the deal of a lifetime.

There was nothing for Ted to do but FedEx to Ben an envelope containing a piece of paper with just two words. Without knowing all the information, and skewed by preconceived understandings, the message would seem strange. Written by Ted's own hand, it read, "I win." Ben would never allow such an affront to go unanswered.

SALVATION

On the morning of the raid, the fourteen girls were more confused than frightened, as it all happened too fast to comprehend. They walked past their captors, who were laid face down with their hands in twist ties behind their backs. All this under the eyes of men with the largest machine guns they had ever seen. They were led out of the building into sunlight so blinding they had to tightly close their eyes. Quickly, they were hustled onto a waiting luxury bus, one usually used to shuttle tourists.

Under military escort, they moved at high speed to the airport, which was close enough to almost be seen from their location. They had, for as long as they had been at the house, heard the roar of jet engines overhead and sent countless prayers that, one day, one of those birds would carry them away. Today, that bird awaited, awake and at full power at the end of a nearby runway.

Control of situations in a foreign land can be quickly lost, so the jet was prepared for a fast takeoff. The roar of its engines became earsplitting as their bus approached directly on the tarmac. The side emblazoned with a large sunflower, the door open, its stairs hanging down as if fingers were carrying them to freedom. They barely had time to climb aboard and buckle before the jet was rolling down the runway, then airborne. Its destination was a rehabilitation facility in Texas where staff awaited their arrival.

Following a long day of processing and orientation, the girls remained unconvinced salvation had arrived. They wondered how it was possible to be in a place as beautiful as they were without having to die to get there. The girl Ted had seen in the window, Mariella, who at fifteen was a bit older than he had guessed, awoke the next day after having slept fourteen hours in the plushest bed she had ever experienced.

That morning, she enjoyed a pleasure so simple that most would never give it a second thought. The marble tile and granite countertops in the bathroom were meaningless. She ignored the enriching smell of the lilac soap in her hand and the mint essence added to the shampoo. She never would have believed the faucets were plated in real gold. For her, the greatest pleasure of that morning was having privacy.

"Ohhhhhhh." She cooed when she stepped from the shower and put her arms through the sleeves of a brown cashmere robe that had been provided. Noting it was time for a special welcome breakfast and liking the robe so much, she kept it on when joining the other girls, veterans of the same war, in the dining hall. The selection and amount of food was more than she thought anyone with reason would allow to exist in one room.

After filling a plate with delicacies, she was guided to a round table sized to accommodate everyone from their group. An uncomfortable silence hung in the air. Although some occasionally communicated through eye contact and facial expressions, each girl seemed captured within her own thoughts. All were under the watchful observation of several counselors who would begin the process of putting them back together later that day. Finally, one of the older girls asked what everyone else was thinking. All were afraid the question might break the magic spell that apparently had been cast.

"Por quayé algin hacek este para nosotros?" (Why would anyone do this for us?)

The lead psychologist could have provided some incomprehensible answer but instead considered how Ted, who had founded and operated the facility, might respond. She pulled open the curtain covering the windows that overlooked a large field of sunflowers, then stated in their native tongue, "Those sunflowers, that is why you are here."

Karen's only part was compiling information on a number of individuals and continuing follow-up on their impending trials. Knowing her boss's pastimes and the fact that in his mind he'd blame them for the busted business deal. She could assume he was going out of his way to make their lives as miserable as possible as they languished behind bars.

Karen knew, in executing this operation, Ted had violated numerous US and international laws. Deeply shaken by the subpoena, she asked what she should do.

"Nothing. Ignore it," he replied without looking at her or putting down his paper in a manner so casual one would think he was answering the question, regular or decaf? "I'll make a few calls. You won't hear of this again."

With karma hard at work, for those who believe in such things, the missed meeting and broken business deal had a golden lining. Another even more lucrative opportunity presented, and Ben Arlington, tied down financially, lost it to Ted.

Later that day, a FedEx arrived from Ben Arlington. Ted giggled like a schoolboy when opening it to find two words. "I win." Taking the envelope down to his library, he placed it alongside a half dozen others containing the exact same message.

"No way is he going to get away with this," Ted muttered to himself.

Control

Fall 1978

Summer passed in the blink of an eye. His promise to Rip to work out was unfulfilled. He did make use of the time serving masses, reading at the library, and tracking his fictitious multi-million-dollar stock portfolio. It was performing exceptionally well because of the stock he'd recommended to Walter Burke, which soared from its two-dollar start to nineteen dollars.

Other things weren't as promising. This school year was the last opportunity to boost grades, ace entrance exams, and get into the high school of choice. For years, Ted was in denial. Now it was a growing quandary. That weekend, they had just taken the COOPs—the Catholic High School entrance exams. Itch and Chuck aced it while Ted put on a brave face and pretended the same.

Ted always assumed he'd go to school with his friends. It just felt like the natural order, but Itch and Chuck were set on applying to one of the more prestigious Catholic academies. There was no way such a school would ever accept someone like him. Even lesser private schools, ones where Rip was applying, seemed out of the question. The catch-all was public school and the abyss of kids whom he didn't know. And once they got to know him, the odds were it would be downhill after that. He tried to focus on something else.

He imagined himself a fellow millionaire sitting with Mr. Burke over coffee or fine tea, neither of which appealed to him, at a fancy breakfast talking business on what was his last Sunday morning before the beginning of the school year. The fantasy was rudely interrupted when he opened the newspaper to find an advertisement with two pictures of Ashley modeling clothes. There she was, the girl who beat him senseless on her way to becoming a super model, and worse, she looked damn good! In one photo, she was wearing snug jeans and a frilly pink shirt, in the other a one-piece swimsuit. He'd turn the page, then turn it back, hating himself for the inability to stop looking.

Just fantastic, he thought. *Now she's going to be all the talk, as if people didn't make a big enough deal over her already.*

Ted had a knack for being right whenever it regarded his humiliation and needed to go no further than his first five minutes that morning back for confirmation.

"You guys see Ashley in the paper?" Ciro asked the group of four, Ted, Rip, Chuck, and Itch, making sure all were together to maximize the impact of his upcoming insult. "So, Ted, you can be honest with me. You have to be hoping she beats you up again."

Ted huffed but dared not offer a comeback, afraid of Ciro's potential response.

A rumor was spreading that Ciro got in a fight with some kid over the summer and beat him up so badly he was in the hospital for days. Unlike most of the false gossip that circulates in a schoolyard, this happened to be true.

Interesting them all, but nothing said at first, the girls somehow seemed different. Ted noticed most, with his head swiveling each time one past, but it was Itch who broke the ice.

"Hey, guys, have you noticed something different about the girls?"

"What do you mean?" Ted said, trying to play it cool.

"Their shirts. They were like flat bags of popcorn last year. Now, pop, pop!"

Ted murmured back. "You think so? Really?"

"Come on, you're turning your head so much it's going to spin off."

"I'm just excited to see everyone."

"I bet. Speaking of Ashley," Itch said enthusiastically, "did you get a load of her? *Kaboom!*" he shouted, holding his hands in front of his chest. A nun walking by stopped and eyed him.

"Yep, that's right, Fourth of July was great, big explosions like that," he continued, quickly covering.

They only laughed after she cleared.

Ted looked across the schoolyard for her but instead caught sight of one person none of them wanted to see. All sensed it simultaneously, a dark presence entering their atmosphere. It was Tom and in disbelief, mouths agape, they all had thoughts.

"I think he went through puberty twice over the summer," Chuck observed.

"What are they feeding him?" Itch responded.

Rip, as horrified as the others, contributed. "He mutated! That Neanderthal's got to be six feet!"

Chuck continued. "He isn't right in the head. What do you think the odds are he kills someone this year?"

Itch had more. "And all that muscle controlled by a brain the size of a walnut. Every day last year, he bullied me into letting him copy my homework."

Ted had his own complaint. "Last year he took my lunch money. Some days I couldn't even buy the *Wall Street Journal*."

Itch and Chuck stared at each other racing for the first comment. Itch won.

"You know, Ted, if he kills someone this year, I really hope it's you."

The morning bell rang as Ted fished for a response and all rushed to assemble.

Minutes later they sat in an overheated classroom meeting their homeroom teacher. Theirs was a short, morbidly obese woman with black hair named Rita Butterman. They referred to her as Butterball, but never to her face.

Following a brief orientation, the teachers settled them down to prepare for what seemed only to them the most glorious event of the day, the celebration of mass!! Just hearing the term *religious ceremony* was enough to make most kids' eyes roll.

The church was hot, the students restless, and none of them wanted to be there. Soon, row after row of the pews were filled with grades one through eight to await the start. Keeping the kids silent, as they were supposed to be, proved impossible. Chatter emanated from everywhere with the teachers making their best attempts to keep it under control.

Ted and Itch, sitting next to each other, were no exception, and in fact were already riled up having spent the previous ten minutes arguing, without resolution, about the maximum potential sharpness of a pencil point.

Itch was in a mood to drive Ted crazy, all pent up and waiting for the fun of bragging to him about summer camp. He decided a little early antagonism would provide a warm-up. Knowing he couldn't resist a philosophical question he asked, "Do you think God is a man or a woman?"

Ted of course took and swallowed the bait, and after thinking a moment posited an answer.

"I think He's a woman. That's because women are the ones who bring life into this world, and God created life. Makes sense, right?"

"If you believe that, then why did you just call God a He?"

"It's a figure of speech. He's all powerful. He can be both."

"Wait, wait, wait, you have me confused. Let's say God had to go to the bathroom, which one would He go into, the men's or women's?"

"Itch, you are a certified moron."

"Shhhhhh!" they heard from the end of the aisle; a finger shaken at them by "Butterball."

Both quieted, but only while she lingered.

"You just got me in trouble Itch, first day!"

"Well, if you could answer a simple question like I asked I wouldn't be correcting you."

"You didn't correct me, maybe if you knew anything about anything, you wouldn't be asking such dumb questions."

"And you say that after I won the pencil argument."

"Oh, that is such bull. You lost, and you know it, graphite..."

"Hey!" their teacher grumbled, this time turning every head in the pew. "I'm not telling the two of you again, sit still and be quiet!"

They settled but only because mass was starting. Kneeling, standing, sitting, going through the motions, all present listened to two readings from the good book, then the Gospel. It was followed by a homily of a length that just invited the kids to misbehave. Alongside a line of girls sitting in the pew directly in front of Ted was Ciro and his favorite partner in crime, Steve. Like everyone, they too had matured over the summer, but in their case not really in a way anyone would have wanted.

To alleviate their boredom, they decided to play an incredibly obnoxious game called a 'pup tent contest.' Played by slipping a hand into their pockets. they would arouse themselves until a 'tent' appeared. The winner was the one able to create the largest bulge, and they would always try to get some hapless girl to serve as judge.

It didn't matter that prayers were resonating off the walls, Jesus was front and center depicted suffering on a crucifix, and the priest's homily focused on self-control. These two contestants discreetly readied themselves.

The largest bulge came from Ted's eyes as he peered over the pew noticing what they were doing before elbowing Itch and tilting his head forward. Itch did a double take, his mouth dropping before he threw one hand up to his forehead just as Ciro tapped the girl next to him. It was Audrey, one of many girls he'd been crudely flirting with the year before. Steve leaned forward to give her an ear-to-ear grin, prompting Ciro to ask, "Who's got the biggest?"

"You're disgusting," she replied after glancing down then looking away.

Ciro, never giving up that easily, especially with a girl he's attracted to, for some reason the world will never explain, felt this was the right moment to ask her out in a way only he could deliver so crudely.

"How about we meet up after school? We could check out the mall or cut through the crap and just make out," he whispered.

Itch could no longer hold back and poked his head between the two. "Pardon me for overhearing, but as a member of the male persuasion, I feel it my obligation to advise you that this one here is defective."

"Shut up, dickhead!" Ciro snapped.

Ted leaned forward. "Hey, don't you dare call my friend a dickhead. He's an asshole!"

"Got that right," Itch proclaimed in agreement.

"Hey! The three of you, get over here!" There it was again, this time with a demand to get up, somehow squeeze past the others in the tightly packed pew and get to the aisle. Ted and Itch complied but Ciro didn't move.

"Now!" Butterball insisted, aiming her finger at Ciro.

"Can you give me a minute?" he asked.

Itch almost fell into the lap of one of the kids as he desperately tried to stop laughing and remain upright. Ted, confused and clueless, pushed at him to keep moving.

"Stand up!" she insisted again. Ciro closed his eyes and stood up, praying that the situation might somehow resolve itself. No such luck, quite the opposite.

"Sit down! Sit down!" she called in a panic while waving her hands furiously for him to sit.

Ted, now catching on, joined Itch in laughing so hard tears were beginning to fall from their eyes. Leaving Ciro behind, the cackling two were hauled outside by a teacher now free to yell without restraint, which she did abundantly. They finally got hold of themselves and following a lengthy tirade and a string of dire warnings, were led back into the church.

Things would have gone better if it weren't for a few of the kids in the row spreading out to take advantage of the extra room, leaving only enough space for one to sit comfortably. Itch plopped down taking most of it, laughing at Ted as he stood with no place to sit. Ted flashed him the finger before dropping hard into the little gap that remained. Itch pushed at him, Ted pushed back and next thing they knew both were outside again with a half-crazed teacher ready to strangle them both.

Jealousy

"How is that fair, tell me how that's fair? I get five detentions and you get one, when you did most of it," Ted complained to Itch at lunchtime.

"Well, Ted, I'm a straight A student, and you are...well, you know, you...if it makes you feel any better, Ciro got three and they didn't even know what he was doing. Plus why were you giggling the whole time in the office?"

"You know I have that nervous laughter. I can't control it. Ciro knows it too and he was making faces behind Sister Bethany."

It wasn't so much the detentions; his real concern was "Butterball." Not only homeroom, but she also taught social studies and had a well-established reputation for sending kids to summer school. San Quentin, Alcatraz, Leavenworth, summer school; it was all the same. By the skin of his teeth, he'd always manage to avoid it, usually coming up with a last-minute miracle on his finals.

This year that wouldn't work, in fact in the first class she laid down simple rules: study hard, pay attention and most important, hand in all assignments on time or get zero. Ted was likely to strikeout on all three. Worse, the projects, counting 50 percent of the grade, were said to be arduous while Ted's SOP was to procrastinate. A zero on one assignment and he'd be toast.

Expecting her class to be the worst, it was soon topped by others as homework quickly piled up. First day, no mercy. It took him an hour to do it that night but should have taken three had he done it right. The English assignment, which he had two days to complete had him baffled.

"Who the heck am I supposed to write about?" Ted quipped to Chuck at lunch the next day, referring to the essay they had to write about someone they admired, relatives excluded.

"That's easy," Chuck suggested. "Pick someone you think is a buffoon, then be sarcastic. Just don't be obvious."

The next day Ted proudly handed in "Jimmy Carter: The First President to Know More about Peanuts Than Politics."

Ted bragged of his cleverness to his friends, but the boasting was short lived. Itch always had to outdo him and had all the ammo he needed with his tales of summer camp. This year had something new, *girls!*

He and some of his buddies contacted a Girl Scout camp on the other side of the lake. Late at night in the darkness after lights out they would sneak down to the shore, launch a rowboat and meet with a pack of Scouts on the other side. Ted's mind filled with the possibilities and along with the others, begged for details. Itch brushed them off, proclaiming a scout never kisses and tells.

The result was just what Itch craved; loathing jealousy painted across Ted's face.

Ted, looking to change the subject, turned to Rip.

"What did you do over the summer?"

"Not much, didn't go anywhere, worked out a lot. By the way Ted, that reminds me, you were supposed to call me; we were going to work out."

"Uh, people to do, things to see, presidential meetings, travel, you know."

"You mean you're full of it, you had promised."

"Yeah, I remember, all right, when do you want to start?"

"How about after school today?"

Ted was afraid he'd say that, and the long pause stated as much. "Yeah, okay," he relented wondering what in the world he'd just committed to.

If there were an opposite home to Walter Burke's mansion, it was that of the Ramirez family. A single fourteen-inch black-and-white TV, ceiling fans instead of air conditioning, dinner table surrounded by cheap plastic chairs, and the couch looked like it had been plucked from someone's trash. Unknown to Ted that happened to be the case. The floors were unfinished and begged for carpeting. It was, however, impeccably tidy and clean.

Ted was warmly greeted by Rip's mother. They'd met a few times at school functions, but she seemed especially pleased to see him today. Embarrassed by his living conditions, Ted was the first friend Rick had ever brought home from school.

"Can I get you anything?" she asked sweetly as he stood in the living room.

"A glass of wine would be nice," Ted delivered as a reply with such an emotionless expression she could not be sure if he was joking.

Peeking out from behind the door that led to the kitchen was Rip's sister Isabel. Ted knew her already from the many times she'd unsuccessfully tried to tag along with her brother in whatever Rip was doing. Impatiently, Rip cut short any conversation and led Ted to the basement. The portion of it not taken up by the hot water heater and furnace was devoted to his workout equipment. Shocked by the equipment's sophistication, he wondered if the stairs had led to someone else's basement.

In front of him was a room full of professional grade benches, barbells and a punching bag hanging from a ceiling beam. Lining the walls were posters of Chuck Norris and Bruce Lee.

"How did you manage this?" Ted asked, thinking of the contrast from the furniture upstairs.

"I got an inheritance," he replied, sounding as though he'd been left millions.

"My Uncle Bert left me $400 and my Papi said I could get this with it, as long as I use it."

"Now here are the rules. Most important, you never touch anything without someone else here. Also, you got to do what I tell you. We work out three days a week. We do warm-ups, then lifting, then sparring. After that we run three miles and finish with some cool down exercises. Any questions?"

"No, sounds great," Ted replied. Rip made it sound easy breezy.

Just then Isabel came down with a pitcher of ice water with fresh lemon slices floating in it and two glasses. No sooner had she placed it, she darted upstairs.

"What's that all about?" Ted questioned.

"She's just glad you're here, I'm not allowed to work out alone, so my mom makes her stay when I'm down here. With you here she doesn't have to do it anymore."

"First Ted, I need to teach you the most important lesson."

With that, holding back just a little from full strength, which would have put Ted on the floor, Rip punched him in the shoulder.

"What do you do?" Rip asked amidst Ted's surprise, confusion, and fear.

Ted was baffled. "Duck?"

Rip repeated it again, and a third time.

"What is the correct response?"

"Stop doing that, it really hurts."

"Wrong!" He shouted and did it again. "There is only one correct response. When you take a hit Ted, in anything, fighting, life, whatever it is, there is only one correct response. You hit back! You get up, pull you ass together, and hit back! Apply that to everything in life."

Intro over, warm-ups began. The initial stretching wasn't hard, but it was followed by sit-ups and push-ups. Rip knocked off fifty of each before Ted finished ten of either.

"Can that be it?" he asked breathlessly, face down on the floor.

"Get up, we haven't started," Rip laughed, really believing Ted was joking.

More stretches, chin ups, hitting the bag, Ted was already in pain before weightlifting began. Rip, not wanting to show off, set his bench press for 160 pounds. Ted could not budge the forty-five-pound bar.

"Oh God! Oh God! Oh God," he repeated through each set of the hour and a half session.

"Let's go for the run," Rip stated when they finally finished boxing, with Ted serving as a padded punching bag.

"I don't have the energy to get up the stairs," he complained as he looked up from the bottom when it was over. "I'm done. I'm so done. Let me go now, and I promise I'll come back on Saturday."

Disappointed, Rip called it a day.

"How did it go?" Mrs. Ramirez asked as Ted emerged, literally crawling up the last two stairs, poking his head out and laying on the floor for dramatic effect.

"Mrs. Ramirez, your son is trying to kill me."

"He did great," Rip exclaimed, stepping over him and into the kitchen.

"Do the stretches I showed you tomorrow, and you'll be ready for Saturday," he instructed.

What force of hell ever made me promise this? Ted thought as he dragged himself home, already feeling the onset of soreness that would last for days.

Misstatement

Ted's muscles' soreness the next day was all but forgotten when his English essay was returned with an unexpected A. He beamed over his cleverness, running into the cafeteria to rub it into Itch's face, but stopped short to keep from plowing into Anna as their paths crossed.

He was taken aback by her sad expression as she stared toward her seat of banishment. Observing the courage it took for her to keep going filled him with regret. Who did he admire? It should have been about her! The opportunity the essay had afforded him was now lost. Enthusiasm fading like the dreams she used to have, Ted tore the pages to pieces and threw them in the trash.

Over the summer he happened upon a poem in a book at the library that caused him to think of Anna. He'd photocopied it, toying with the idea of giving it to her and reached a decision. Retrieved that night from a desk drawer, he carefully checked to be sure nothing might give him away as the sender.

When the kids changed for the last class, he casually walked past her momentarily empty seat, knelt as if pretending to tie his shoe, and quickly threw the paper into the cubbyhole under the chair. As he rose, he came face to face with a girl named June. Her reputation was sweet and friendly, but she had no affection for Ted.

Back in the lower grades he had tortured her over her severe overbite, referring to her as "Mr. Ed the Talking Horse," and sometimes neighing when she walked in the room. The braces which she still wore, had mostly corrected the problem, and they hadn't crossed paths in years.

"What are you up to?" she snapped, knowing how cruel he could be, her ever-present smile becoming a cold glare. If looks could kill Ted would have been six feet under.

Leaving her question unanswered he raised his finger to his lips hoping she would keep quiet before darting off.

Anna returned noticing the folded paper but not the eye Ted was keeping on her. Her lips moved as she read the words, passing over them twice before crumpling it into a ball and shooting it toward the garbage. Missing, June, curious to see what that demonic miscreant had done, jumped to retrieve it. Anna saw it but didn't care.

Once class started, when no one appeared to be looking, she took out the page and read. When finished, her eyes moved to Anna, then to Ted. The message in the poem to Anna was clear but she was most surprised by what it implied of the messenger.

To Anna:

Don't Quit!

When things go wrong, as they sometimes will,
When the road you're trudging seems all up hill,
When the funds are low and the debts are high,
And you want to smile, but you have to sigh,
When care is pressing you down a bit,
Rest, if you must – but don't you quit.
Life is queer with its twists and turns,
As every one of us sometimes learns,
And many a failure turns about,
When he might have won had he stuck it out;
Don't give up, though the pace seems slow,
You might succeed with another blow.
Often the goal is nearer than
It seems to a faint and faltering man,
Often the struggler has given up,
When he might have captured the victor's cup.
And he learned too late, when the night slipped down,
How close he was to the golden crown.
Success is failure turned inside out—
The silver tint of the clouds of doubt—
And you never can tell how close you are,
It may be near when it seems so far;
So stick to the fight when you're hardest hit—
It's when things seem worst that you mustn't quit.

—Anonymous

Grace

This year, for Ted's science class there was a request for an exotic pet. Ted argued his corn snakes were perfect and his teacher agreed. He loved showing them off, and was especially excited to demonstrate their feeding, hoping the class might find it repulsive.

It was three weeks before all was ready, and Ted kept them unfed so they'd eat when the time came. Standing before the class he rattled off facts and took questions then proceeded with the main event. Explaining how they would be strangled then engulfed by them, he opened a box and held up a small white mouse in each hand.

"Awww, you can't do that!" one girl called out.

"God makes the rules, not me," he shot back, amused by her concern.

"Do the mice have names?" another girl asked.

He had names for none of the mice but considered it for a moment.

"Ciro and Steve."

"Which one is which?"

"Ciro is the fat one," he answered as he dropped both into the tank.

Some looked in fascination, others away as the snakes went to work.

Ciro sat, unamused and imagining what he might do to fix this outrageous affront. Ted should have been a bit smarter. Ciro sat behind him in that class, one row over, putting him in perfect position to hurl a whole variety of objects at him when the teacher wasn't looking. He'd done it the prior year, betting with Steve what things he could get to stick in his hair. Typically, it was gum or small wads of tape. His high score had been with strips of paper coated with chocolate pudding.

Ted lost his smile as he returned to his seat and noticed Ciro rhythmically pounding his fist into his palm. Paranoid, he turned repeatedly through class to see what he might be doing. On one of his swivels something unexpected caught his focus. Further back, in the last seat, diagonally past Ciro, sat Anna. Her head was positioned straight down at the desk, hair forming a curtain around her face. It looked as though she was studying but Ted's angle provided a different perspective. In her palm was a balled-up tissue that she repeatedly raised to her eyes. There were tear drops on the desk.

His blood went cold. The mighty SS *Annabelle*, powering through the worst of storms appeared to be falling apart. It was like witnessing the sinking of the *Titanic* and he could imagine what those in the lifeboats must have felt as the great ship disappeared beneath the surface. The sight of her slightly quivering body and the imagined sound of sobs haunted him the rest of the day.

At home that night he tried in vain to work on an important social studies assignment due in two days. In front of him were two world maps, one from 1900 and the other

1970. The project was to identify as many countries that had changed borders in the intervening years and state the cause. His plan was to take his usual lazy shortcut and answer that WWII was responsible for everything. Procrastinating once again, he decided to go to bed and work on it the next day.

He hoped sleep would bring him peace and began to dream as he drifted off. He found himself sitting at a kitchen table in a house he did not recognize. Across sat Anna with tear streaks running down her face, yet unlike he had ever seen, she was smiling. She said to him softly, "I did this for you," then stretched out her arms, which had been cut with razors and were profusely bleeding.

Eyes snapping open, wide awake, Ted lay shaking like a rattling engine. This was a message from God. Anna was dead and remaining unforgiven, he was eternally damned. He jumped out of bed to his dresser, pulled the rosary he was given for his communion, knelt and began to pray.

"Please God, I don't want all the stupid things I've asked for over the years. Let Anna be alive, watch over her tonight, be generous with your mercy. Almighty God if you must take a life tonight let it be mine and not hers."

He then began the long series of prayers that made up the rosary, completing it more than once before finally taking another try at sleep. Heart pounding like a drum, lungs huffing and panting, eyes refusing to stay closed, sweat accumulating across his chest, it was useless. He needed to know she was okay and hoped dawn would bring the answer. His eyes frustratingly poked the dark sky from his bedroom window, searching for any hint of the morning light.

Anxiety tore at any sense of peace. In his chest, there was a pounding, a sensation as though he were riding atop a lightning-fast steed, and yet, swift as it traveled, he would never reach his destination in time.

Frustrating hours passed before the first hints of light began to chase away the darkness. Light, redemption, he had never been so happy to see a sunrise or have a 7:00 a.m. mass and hurried to the church. Arriving early and alone, he repeatedly walked its circumference, praying as he passed the stations of the cross which depicted the suffering of Jesus during the crucifixion.

He felt better, almost silly about the thoughts that had robbed him of sleep. Still, he fretted what to do before deciding to talk to the priest. The one serving this mass, the most experienced in the parish, a man in his seventies, he felt fortunate to have his perceived wisdom at hand.

At mass's end, he approached, but as soon as the priest heard it involved a student, he cut him off and recommended he see Mr. Maze, the school's guidance counselor. Ted had been hoping for a better response but considered it.

"Mr. Maze, huh? That guy."

At the beginning of each school year, Mr. Maze, a short, balding man with thick black glasses, sporting an oversized mustache above a warm smile, would give a speech telling the students that he was their friend, and they could come to him with anything. The younger kids ignored him while the older ones snickered through his presentation.

The man had a psychology practice in the evenings, but his true love was working with children. It was a rare treat that any of them would reach out, and he couldn't help but feel excited when he found Ted waiting by his locked office door that morning.

"What time are you supposed to be in?" Ted asked, bypassing a more traditional greeting.

"Eight a.m.," he replied.

"That says five after. I thought maybe the clocks in the school were off."

Mr. Maze was a bit taken aback by his snarky comment, not understanding that Ted was serious, really thinking he might need to tell the school their clocks were off.

"I'm late, very sorry about that."

"Ted," he said, holding out his hand, "I'm Ted."

"I know who you are. I know the name of every student in this school. It is so nice to see you this morning at my office," Mr. Maze said while reaching out to shake his hand. "Please come on in and sit down, and call me Matt."

"Okay, Mr. Maze," Ted confirmed. He never would call him by his first name.

Ted took one of the two chairs placed in front of the desk. Mr. Maze threw his coat onto his chair behind the desk and took the seat next to Ted.

The look of apprehension on Ted's face communicated he didn't appreciate Mr. Maze's attempt to be friendly. He reached out and snatched a business card from a holder on his desk and viewed it suspiciously, then darted his eyes over the degrees on the wall.

"Addiction counseling, that's my specialty, I have a private practice off hours," he explained. "Would you like some jellybeans?" he said, pulling a glass dish on his desk filled with them closer to Ted.

Ted thought, *He must think we are all idiots, putting a bribe of candy out so we come in here like flies.*

"This isn't about me. I don't need any mental help from you," Ted clarified.

"Just because you came to see me doesn't mean that, it doesn't at all, tell me what you want to talk about."

"It's about Anna."

Mr. Maze maintained an expressionless face, but his heart skipped a beat. He counseled her three times a week and was already deeply concerned.

"Do you know if she's here today? Please tell me first that she's okay."

"You seem concerned, don't worry, they'll take attendance."

"No, I need to know *now*. Is she here? Did she come to school today?"

"Would you like me to look and see if she's in the schoolyard, she usually gets here early?"

"Please, would you? I didn't see her before."

As he opened his door Sister Howard was hobbling on by. She'd just come from the schoolyard. Yes, she had seen her, Anna was there.

Ted overheard and took as deep a breath as he could force into his lungs, held it, then let it out. Returning, Mr. Maze couldn't help but notice how his demeanor had so radically changed, looking both relieved and exhausted as he now slouched in the chair, arms hanging over the sides. He reached out and plucked a couple of jellybeans from the candy dish.

"Ted, do you have a favorite thing, something you like more than anything else?" he asked as he closed his door.

"Don't think I do," he replied, too quickly to have given it any real consideration.

"Would it be all right if I shared with you mine?"

"Sure."

Sensing Ted's apprehension this time he sat in the chair behind his desk. Ted smiled slightly, seeming to relax.

"I love it when someone comes to me and tells me everything that is on their mind, openly and freely. To think of me as a friend and someone who's whole purpose in life is to help as best I can. So, I'm going to start by sharing something with you. It really brightened my day when I saw you outside my office this morning because that's what I thought you might do."

"Have some more," he added, pushing the candy dish a bit closer to him.

"These are really good," Ted admitted, reveling in a treat he knew under any other circumstance would be forbidden this early in the morning, and took a generous handful, "Okay, here's the deal on Anna."

Mr. Maze's pen blazed, sheet after sheet filled with notes as they conversed for more than an hour. He kept the tone light and friendly but inside was horrified. In session, Anna told him of parties she attended, friendly banter she had with girls in her class and even her occasional unreturned flirtations with Ashton. According to what he heard from Ted, all of it was pure fantasy.

"I understand Debbie has a big birthday party Saturday. I thought all the girls were invited, you don't think she will be there?" he tested, having been told by Anna all the previous week how excited she was to be going.

"It's more likely I'll finish the year with straight As than Anna gets invited to any party so no, not a chance. Just sitting next to her lowers you three pegs on the popularity scale. That's why all the chairs around her at lunch are empty."

It took effort for Mr. Maze to keep from dropping his head into his hands as his concern became panic. He had been pitching the school to put her into an intensive two-week socialization program, primarily meant for moderately autistic children. It was expensive and the school was very hesitant to allocate precious charitable funds toward it, but he was fighting hard for her. Ted had now handed him everything he needed.

Concluding the conversation and putting his notepad down, Mr. Maze thanked Ted and gave him a permission slip allowing him to be late for first period.

"One more thing, Ted," Mr. Maze added as Ted went to leave, "if you ever need someone to talk to, I'm always here."

"I don't need to talk to anyone, there's nothing wrong with me. Why, do you think there is?"

"I'm just saying it's very unusual for someone to come and see me to talk about someone else."

Ted didn't like the sound of that. "He thinks I'm nuts," Ted told himself as he entered his class, relieved again to see Anna present in the back. Math, science, English, all he could think about was why Mr. Maze wanted to speak with him, until the need to make up for his previous sleepless night began wearing down his ability to continue.

"Ted! Ted! Ted! Theodore! Theodore Carrington!" His teacher didn't have to go that far. She had him at the much hated "Theodore."

"What?"

"I asked you a question."

"Could you repeat the question?"

"New question, why weren't you paying attention? Pay attention Ted."

He did, for the next thirty seconds, then it was back to trying to solve the Mr. Maze puzzle and fight to remain awake. It took all day, but he was convinced he finally had it.

"I'm not like Anna," Ted blurted, unannounced, standing in the doorway of Mr. Maze's office after dismissal.

Completely confused, Mr. Maze let Ted speak.

"It all comes down to how we see other people. You think people care more about people they think they are like. When we don't care about someone, we justify it by seeing them as different from us. We find an excuse. So that means I care about Anna because I see myself as like her, but you are wrong."

He straightened to stand a bit prouder, "I got it right, didn't I?"

Mr. Maze heard for years Ted was different but experiencing him first-hand was more interesting than anything that could be captured on paper.

"Ted, all I meant is that you are an extraordinarily caring person."

Zero

Lack of sleep was catching up and the last thing he felt like doing after school was working out with Rip, but it was Thursday, and a promise was a promise. Sit ups, push-ups, weights then sparring. All Ted wanted to do was lay on the floor and sleep, but Rip pushed, and he pressed on. Dragging himself up the stairs, Rip's mom was concerned enough to insist on driving him home. Once there, he called Father Tom to cancel his 7:00 a.m. the next morning.

Ted's mother's remedy for anything was a good meal. Ted hoped it would give him enough energy to get his critical social studies assignment done.

Finished with dinner he retreated to his room and put the maps on his desk. Feeling his head fall forward, he set his alarm for 6:00 a.m. in case he fell asleep, then sat back at his desk and hovered over it.

Next thing his eyes cracked open to a bright room. He was lying in bed where he had been placed by his mom after she came in to check on him, still dressed in his school uniform, collar unbuttoned, minus the tie, which he would never have so much as loosened with his uniform shirt still on. Waking in school clothes was odd, but he felt good, well rested, and slowly turned to look at his clock to see how much more time he might have.

The clock read eight thirty-nine. *Oh,* he thought for a moment before it hit him like a truck. Blasting out of bed, "Oh my God, it's eight thirty-nine!" he shouted to his mother, scrambling to grab clothes before realizing that he could wear the wrinkled clothes he already had on.

Grabbing a new tie he threw his books and the blank page where the assignment should have been into his school bag and raced for the door.

"My alarm didn't go off!" he yelled to his mom, brushing past her in a panic.

"You looked so tired last night I shut it off. I wanted you to sleep late, you don't have to go in on time."

"I have something due first class!"

"Oh, then you better hurry, you're going to be late."

"I know that!" he screamed full force, waving his arms in frustration.

Thanks to the regular workouts he was doing, even with the extra weight of books he was able to run the entire way and catch his class line just as it was entering the building. Swishing his fingers through his hair as a makeshift comb, the hope was his teacher might forget to collect the assignment. That was dashed moments into class when she went around the room. Ted had nothing, not even a page with his name on it.

"I forgot it at home," Ted offered as she passed his desk.

"Want to call home from the office and have your mother bring it in?"

"No," Ted relented as he hung his head, "I didn't do it."

Her response was blunt. "Nothing could have been more important than your assignment, zero, Ted."

"This weekend, I'll spend all weekend doing it."

"I think you should, these assignments are for your own benefit, but you still get the zero."

Maybe if I do a great job, he thought, hoping to save himself. He fretted through the next class and was still perseverating when he caught sight of Ciro in one of his pathetic attempts to flirt. Once again it was an attempt to gain the affection of Audre. Why, Ted would never know, but she laughed with exaggeration as Ciro joked with her, thoroughly enjoying the attention, and wanting him to know it.

"I'm going to the mall on Saturday, if you're nice to me I might let you tag along," Ciro said.

"I'm busy Saturday, grandparent's house, otherwise I'd go."

"I guess I'm just going to have to ask someone else," he replied, sticking his nose in the air to ensure she knew he was teasing.

"Hey, why don't you ask out Ani-mul? I'm sure she's not doing anything," Audre chided.

"Nah. She's uglier than a warthog and I only date my own species," Ciro shot back with a laugh.

Anna reacted the same as always, flashing her eyes away, looking into the distance, detaching. They closed tight as Ciro's next words bit into her.

"Besides, I don't have enough money to buy all the food she'll need."

Seeing pain written across her face, Ted boiled.

"Look at the pot calling the kettle black," he mumbled, wanting it to count for something, but hoping too low for Ciro to discern.

"Did you hear him?" Audre said to Ciro.

"Did you say something to me? You got something you want to say to me, Teddy, Teddy Bear?" Ciro barked.

Ted wanted to say no and strained to push it out, but his throat refused the command. Furious, unfiltered words began spewing from his mouth.

"Obviously, Ciro, there are no mirrors in your house, or you would realize I just insulted you. But that just tells me you're stupid too, so let me make it clear for you. I just called you fat and stupid. It went from my mouth to your ears. Ciro, you are fat, and you are stupid. Can I help you with anything else?"

Ciro sat motionless, not able to comprehend the words that had passed his ears. No one ever dared speak to him that way.

"You going to let this loser talk to you like that?" Audre said, pointing at Ted laughing.

"You are dead. Do you want me to explain how that works to you? Schoolyard, today, 3:00 p.m."

"No, I'm not doing it, not fighting."

"'Cause your chicken shit."

"No, I'm not getting suspended. That's the reason."

Eyes to Audre, Ciro concluded, "Believe me: when I'm done, he will regret this."

Settlement

Most of Ted's weekend was spent at the library, pulling together the social studies project. What he put together would have garnered an A had he handed it in on time.

Monday morning, he decided to call in a little divine intervention as he knelt to pray before the 7:00 a.m. mass. Thoughts of the assignment filled his mind as he opened the door to the sacristy and hit the light switch.

For a split second, he thought someone had moved one of the saint statues into the room. This was no saint. An instant later, he was on the receiving end of a punch to the center of his gut. Groaning loudly, he fell to his knees then put his hands out to keep from falling flat.

"If you said to my father what you said to me, there'd be a bullet in your head." Ciro shot the words into Ted's ear before exiting the room.

Ted could hear the clanking echo of his footsteps slowly fade before disappearing as Ciro strode down the long aisle and out the door. Ted breathed in and out a few times deeply to work through the pain, then grabbed at the doorframe and pulled himself up while keeping one hand over his stomach.

The worship of God did nothing to calm his nerves as he wondered if Ciro was waiting outside to pulverize him. When the mass was over, dread followed. Ducking through the door and down to the schoolyard, he thought he had made it unscathed.

One of the nuns waved for him to come into the office before the morning bell. His science teacher gave him the news sympathetically, but in a quick shot to spare drama, that his snakes were dead. The only reaction from Ted was the loss of the fake smile he always wore. They assured him they would find the cause, but he already knew.

Ciro's first reaction to anything was violence, but his preferred method was humiliation. More of an art, his goal was to make a person want to kill themselves. Ted calculated this was next and reasoned the only possible out was to apologize. He did it immediately in the schoolyard, sincerely and at length, with no mention of the assault that morning or the snakes.

"You know what my father says?" Ciro offered once Ted had finished. "People only apologize when they are weak. Only cowards do it. I would have had more respect for you if you had come out here and tried to deck me."

"Come on, Ciro, kick his ass," Steve goaded.

"No, I am going to plan out his destruction, make this bastard suffer. You know something, Steve. He actually is a bastard. He's adopted. No parents, real ones, that is. Even as a baby, his own mother couldn't stand him. Imagine that," he concluded as he moved his face close to Ted's, eyes locking.

"So, you going to let me talk to you like that, Teddy Bear? Come on, tough guy, set me straight. See, Steve? A coward."

Ted swallowed hard knowing pleading would only make it worse. It had been a disastrous morning, and he all but gave up hope Mrs. Butterman would accept his assignment.

"I heard about your pets. I'm sorry. Are you okay? If you need any quiet time in the nurse's office at any point today, please let me know." Her tone was unexpectedly warm and surprisingly human.

"I'm fine, I was hoping you would accept my assignment, I know you never— "

She snatched the papers from his hand and began flipping through.

"This is something you have never handed in before. It's the work you are capable of." She tapped her finger against the pages. "This one time, I'll accept it."

He knew it was probably because of the snakes, but he'd take it. As the way everything works in life, one anxiety is traded for another.

Lucky

At lunch he sat with his face in his hands staring through fingers at a sandwich that would never be eaten. His thoughts were of the one feeder mouse still sitting in a cage at home; he had never named it, but it was his favorite. It had a small brown patch above one eye and he always passed over it at feeding time. It had always been extraordinarily affectionate, licking his hand whenever close enough and nuzzling every time the opportunity presented.

He prepped the pitch to his mom as he walked home from school. He'd begin by telling her about the snakes, gain sympathy, then hit her up about keeping it.

None of it worked. The school had called to tell her what happened, and she was ready, secretly thrilled the snakes would never be seen again. After feigning sympathy, she shut him down in the middle of his plea.

"Let it go in the yard. I don't want it in the house tonight. The sooner you get rid of it, the easier it's going to be."

She wanted it gone before his father came home to intervene.

Pleading for his mom to give him just seconds to sort something out, through eyes so watery he could hardly make out the numbers, he dialed Itch. His sister loved animals and had a collection of them including guinea pigs and rabbits.

Excitedly jumping up and down on the other end of the line, she agreed to give it a good home. Reluctantly, kissing it once on the head, Ted placed it in a shoebox with some torn newspaper and walked over to Itch's house.

"He's a great mouse," he said when handing it to her.

"He's wonderful!" she acknowledged. "He's licking my hand. What's his name?"

It dawned on him the mouse had no name. There was a measure of comfort that his final act would be to give him one.

"Call him Lucky," he said before asking to hold him one last time and then having to quickly return him. With a girl present along with his best friend, there was too much risk of the disgrace of showing emotion.

Inaction

"That stock I keep telling you about, the weights, sparring, I'm probably developing some fatal condition I don't know about because things never go this well for me," Ted explained to Itch.

"I can explain it, you are full of crap. There is no way you bench pressed fifty pounds once, let alone ten times. Sparring, your stock, it's all made up."

"No seriously, I did. I knocked Rip down for the first time ever boxing. He was so excited he had his mom invite me for dinner and insisted she use the good dishes. And here, look at the stock yourself, loser."

Ted shoved a *Wall Street Journal* before his eyes, pointing at the price of the stock he had recommended to Walter Burke and mentioned to Itch a hundred times since. He was happy enough when it had risen to twenty-eight dollars the month before. Now it had just been announced the company was being bought out by another at forty-one dollars!

"Wait, wasn't that two dollars?" He remembered Ted showing him a long time before. "It's forty-one dollars. Are you sure that's the same one?"

"I told Ashton's dad about it at that price."

"Yeah, so what?"

"So what? I hope he remembers."

"And then what?"

Ted thought for a minute. What would he do?

"Well, I'll need to meet him again," he began as the lead into his contrived plan.

"And how is that going to happen?"

"I have a plan."

Itch rolled his eyes. "Oh God, here it comes."

"Fine I'll keep it to myself, but if you must know..."

"I don't want to know."

"What I'm going to do is wait until I see him at a school function. Okay, then."

"And when is that going to happen? Even Ashton told me he never sees his dad. That man is not going to waste his time coming to some dumb school function."

"You didn't even hear my plan."

"I don't have to. Why don't you pick up the phone and call him? You always make everything so complicated."

"There's a problem with that. You see I kind of well, let's just say I sort of lied to him and said I was a millionaire."

For several minutes Itch had an uncontrollable laughing fit. He'd stop, take one look at Ted, and start all over again.

"Oh, I have to stop, my sides are hurting. Why would you say that?"

"I just did. Okay. So now what am I supposed to say to him? Hi, you probably remember me as the jerk who made an idiot of himself at Ashton's birthday party a couple of years ago."

"At least it's accurate."

Ted hung his head in frustration. Itch readily jumped at any chance to kick him, but he'd always make it up with some advice that would earn his keep.

"Ted, one bit of action is worth more than all the thought in the world. You know what your real problem is? You are afraid of what might happen, but is that better than nothing happening at all?"

Vanished

Fall had just begun. It was that time of year temperatures were cooling but remained pleasant and the leaves on the trees took on a golden hue. Holiday celebrations were getting almost close enough to begin planning. The heating system in the church had just been turned on and, finally, the mad pisser had struck again.

This time it was Sunday. and the parishioners coming for the 10:00 a.m. mass was greeted by the devil's perfume. Inquisitions, offers of rewards, more threats of expulsion, nothing exposed the culprit. Had he shared his deed with anyone, he likely would have been found out, but he had kept it to himself, loving all the commotion and the insanity it caused.

As a countermeasure, a security lock was installed on the sacristy door. In theory only the priests and Sexton had the key, but a copy was hidden in the church where it was thought no one would look, on a small nail hammered into the wall behind the crucifix hanging over the altar. It took a longer time for Jesus to resurrect from the dead than it did for every altar boy to know where that key was hidden. Insulted by the simplicity of the effort put in to thwart this mastermind, the mad pisser was already planning his next airstrike.

Everyone was so occupied with talk of the church incident that no one seemed to notice Anna was missing! She was not to be found in the schoolyard, in class, anywhere. The girl who never missed a day had disappeared as if plucked by a UFO. Her books remained untouched in her desk; a sweater she had brought stood hanging in her locker unmoved. Even the teacher didn't bother to call her name at attendance.

Exchanges

"Hey, Ted, hold up," Ashton called from behind as he exited the school at dismissal.

"Yeah, what's up?"

Ashton was a little breathless as he caught up. "Kept forgetting to ask you something all day. My dad wanted to know who your favorite sports team is."

"Your dad! What about your dad? Your dad said my name?"

"Yeah, well…"

"He meant me, right? Did he say just Ted or Ted Carrington?"

"Ted, he meant you. What is your favorite sports team?"

"I don't have a favorite team. Now tell me what your dad said."

"I told him that, but he wanted me to ask you anyway."

He got into Ashton's face. "You got to tell me why he said my name."

"He said a long time ago the two of you talked about a stock in some company."

Ted knew he was acting like a crazed six-year-old and tried to cool it by switching to fix his tie. "He remembered it? Did he tell you the name? Did he get it right?"

"He bought some and said it did really good and wanted to give you tickets to a game as a way of saying thanks. You can go to anything you want. We have season tickets to the Knicks, first row if you'd be into that. Sometimes you get to be seen on TV."

"Your dad will take us?" he asked, the excitement unhidden.

"Probably not, Vince always takes us."

All Ted could think about was spending several hours with their driver/chaperone pretending to be interested in some game. "I don't know about Knicks tickets. I've never been into hockey."

That comment was enough to convince Ashton that sports wasn't going to work.

"How about a Broadway show?" His father hadn't suggested it, but Ashton knew it would be okay. "We go all the time. I'm sure he'd give your whole family tickets."

"Uh, maybe. I heard some plays have nudity. Do you think we could see something like that? Female nudity, of course."

"My dad is not going to give your family tickets to a play with nudity."

"Oh," Ted replied, losing interest as it dawned on him all the embarrassing ways his mom might behave at such an event anyway. "Hey! Your father works on the stock exchange. Do you think maybe he could get me a tour? You know, on the floor?"

"Well, my dad doesn't work on the actual exchange, but he knows a lot of people. I could ask him."

"Would you? That would be awesome. And, Ashton, just curious, how much of that stock did he buy? A hundred shares?" He guessed, hoping Ashton would blurt the actual number.

"Wasn't it like two dollars?"

"Yeah."

"My father would never do anything that small."

"Come on, Ashton, do you know how much he bought?"

"Yeah, but I'm not allowed to talk about it."

"Pleeeeeease! I swear I'll never tell another living soul. Come on, I'm the one who told him about it."

"I guess you did. All right, secret, though. He said he bought fifty thousand shares."

There was a long twenty seconds before Ted blinked again. He wasn't even sure how he got home. The next thing his mind registered was sitting at dinner listening to his mom drone on about her day. She hadn't picked up on his comment that his day had been "pretty darn good" rather than his usual "fine."

Contact

The earth turned, the sun rose and set, and homework was assigned. Time passed without Anna, and no one paid any attention. Gone, all but forgotten. Even the chatter didn't pause in the classroom just before Friday dismissal when the teacher mentioned she would be back.

"Class, Anna will be back on Monday. I would like everyone to be especially nice to her."

Ted didn't give it much thought over the weekend and, having forgotten, was surprised to see her sitting at her desk Monday morning. She was oddly different.

Sitting upright, her hair, which had always been a jumbled mess, was clean, combed back, and tied into a ponytail. Her nails were done in a light-pink polish, and her face held a hint of makeup. The threadbare secondhand uniform that had been her identity was replaced by one neatly pressed and brand new. Initially, she looked around with an expression of excitement as though it were her first day.

Ted recalled, when Ashley was out a week after breaking her ankle, they all but threw a ticker tape parade upon her return. With Anna, silence. The hopeful expression that had been in her eyes faded as the morning wore on. She refused the humiliation of sitting alone in the cafeteria and instead chose to eat her lunch with Mr. Maze in his office.

By the time she joined her class in the schoolyard, she was broken, sitting on the short wall with a despondent expression painted on her face. Her head was balanced on her knees, arms grasping her legs, not even the notebook with her. The only thing that moved were her eyes when Ted approached, which turned to small slits.

"I like what you did with your hair," he said. Her lack of response made him feel compelled to add to it. "Pulling it back, it lets everyone see your pretty face."

"Thanks," she grumbled angrily, body poised to lunge if he dared finish it with the insult she expected. She assumed he had forgotten the punchline when he departed without delivering it.

By the end of the day, her head was face down on her desk. Whatever she had hoped would happen, clearly had not. Yet the sun each day rises and brings with it new hope to people like Anna who, despite all adversity, never stop reaching for it.

If there is a world record for the most amount of time attending a school and not making a single friend, it is likely held by Anna. Her streak was broken that afternoon after two years, two months, and four days. It happened just minutes before dismissal.

Two girls in the row next to her were talking. Dorothy, a devout loner, was tall, thin, with long red hair and a pale complexion. The only person she truly liked in the school was June. June was the girl with the ever-present effervescent smile who caught Ted delivering the poem to Anna earlier in the year. Short, dirty-blond hair, and brown eyes, average weight, they were members in the school's high academic achievers' club.

June's start as an ugly duckling was changing to that of a swan with each passing year, and more recently, each passing day. Her personality, quick wit, and beaming smile made her a candidate for the popular crowd, but she was ridiculously selective. Like June, Dorothy was genuine, fiercely loyal, and never had a bad thing to say about anyone. To date she had been the only one meeting June's high standards.

Among other things, the program Mr. Maze had sent Anna had encouraged her to be more outgoing, and the conversation she overheard offered the chance.

"Not regular braids, I want French braids," Dorothy said to June.

"I don't know how. A regular braid will be fine," June responded.

Everyone has something that terrifies them. For some its heights, or death, or public speaking. For Anna, it was anything that attracted attention to herself. Such a small act, so trivial to practically anyone, the fear she felt speaking her next words was nearly enough to make her pass out.

"I think French braids would look better. I can do French braids," she breathed, barely able to keep her voice steady.

June and Dorothy looked at each other thinking the same thing: *She can speak. She can actually speak.*

"Serious, where did you learn that?" Dorothy asked.

"One of my foster moms, she was a beautician, she taught me."

"Well, okay. We're going over to my house after school, you want to come?"

Anna thought she must have misheard. "You want me in your house? After school?"

"Yeah, I live close. A few blocks. How long do you think the braids will take?" Dorothy asked.

"Not long. You'll like them, I promise," she answered, her tone notably perked.

Anna always looked forward to dismissal. Today the anticipation was the same, but the reason very different. Believing neither of them wanted to be seen with her she trailed ten feet as school let out.

"What are you doing back there?" June turned and asked. "Let's get going."

"I thought I dropped something, but I didn't," Anna said, surprised they would allow themselves to be seen walking with her.

Braids, hair style ideas, tips, and techniques, Anna had an impressive array of skills when it came to beauty. The irony was not lost on June or Dorothy that before that day she had never applied those skills to herself.

The wishes of children range from the insignificant to the impossible. Dorothy's desire was simple, and she came in with it the next day, beautiful French braids. At least to her, Anna's wish seemed to verge on the impossible, but she walked in with it the next day too.

Passed over so many times by the wand of her fairy godmother, this day it appeared she was on the receiving end. We can seldom claim to have been given our heart's most profound desire, the one wish that is included in all our prayers. There it was in her possession twice over, two friends. The wait was long but had been worth it. Given the loyalty of those two girls, she had hit the jackpot.

News of her palling around with June spread across the class like fire. Although June was mostly rainbows and sunshine, the intervention of God might be the only thing to save anyone she heard disparage one of her friends, as evidenced the next day in the cafeteria.

Always sitting alone, on this day Anna's two new friends insisted she sit with them.

"I didn't know these chairs could support elephants," a girl across from the trio quipped.

"I can leave," Anna whispered to the pair.

"No, stay where you are, this will only take a minute," June replied as she turned and then pounded her hand repeatedly onto the girl's tuna salad sandwich until it was flat as a pancake.

"You have any more stupid things you want to say?" She retorted with her nearly always present smile gone from her face.

The girl quickly gathered her things and moved away.

For years Dorothy and June had been fixtures in the schoolyard, joined at the hip. In short order it became the three that were inseparable.

"Nana, I'm going to a friend's house after school, so I'll be home late today," she called as she walked out the door the following week, hardly believing the words she was saying.

It seemed so foreign, fantastic yet impossible. Trotting down the stairs of her house and continuing with a bounce in her step she headed for school, not consciously registering, this was the first time she had been looking forward to being there.

Pissed

It was another in the marathon of his 7:00 a.m. masses, and Ted was up to the part he most looked forward to, laying in one of the pews meditating. Sometimes, as was the case on this day, he would lightly doze. It was the reason he didn't hear someone enter from the outside through the side door of the room next to the altar. A slight echo reverberated across the expanse of the church raising Ted from his nap. A gut feeling told him something was off; it was too early for the old lady. Then he heard it again, sounds, as if from a scurrying mouse, coming from the sacristy.

He figured it was Father Tom or another priest, but oddly the door was closed with the light on. Still not suspecting what he'd find when he opened it, a friendly "Hey" hung on his lips to greet whomever it was. Stopped in his tracks, breath frozen, it was David standing on a chair urinating on the radiator; his signature mushroom cloud of stench already filling the room.

David, the king of confectionary delights, premium pastries, luscious Linzer tarts, creamy cheesecake, and so many other treats. Anyone but him. Why couldn't it have been Geo? Ted wished he were anywhere in the world other than where his feet were planted.

"What the hell, David!" he shouted.

The shock of seeing Ted standing there made him jump, causing the stream focused on the radiator to hit the back wall.

"My God, where did you come from?" he shrieked, before zipping up and jumping from the chair.

His choice was to beg, or threaten and he chose liberal use of the latter.

"If you tell anyone, Ted, you'll be the one hanging from that cross out there. You hear me? I'll get every damn kid in this school to beat the crap out of you."

"I won't tell anyone, I swear."

"I want you to swear on your mother's life you won't tell anyone."

"Yes."

"Say it. Swear on your mother's life."

It may have just been words, but at that age no one would utter them casually.

"I swear on my mother's life I won't tell anyone."

Needing some alone time, with a motion of his hand he instructed Ted to get out. Ted stepped back and pulled the door shut as he left. David braced himself against the wall. He decided, despite the stink bomb of evidence circulating around him, to wait just a minute to catch his breath and for his heart to go from his throat back into his chest.

Just then he heard the unmistakable sound of the door being locked.

"Oh no, oh no, no, no," he said to himself in a panic then ran to twist the knob. It was useless. "Funny, Ted, let me out, come on Ted. I was joking about beating you up. I got your point! Ted! Come on Ted! Theodore, so help me when I get my hands on you!"

David's pleas may have been heard by God, but no one else. Ted had already rushed out of the church. In the schoolyard he moved to the furthest corner so he could contemplate alone the potential consequences of what he'd just done.

The wait wasn't long.

Prayers

"Sister Howard wants to see you," one of his classmates called out as he ran up to him pointing at the main entrance of the school where she was standing.

"She seems really mad."

"Oh crap," Ted declared.

"What's going on?"

"Everything is fine," Ted replied, suddenly wishing he'd stopped at the bathroom on his way to the schoolyard knowing this was not going to be pleasant.

Sister Howard didn't move as he approached, just stood there doing that shaking thing elderly people do when they stand still for too long.

"Yes, Sister Howard?" Ted asked as if oblivious.

Not a word, she just took hold of his earlobe and pulled.

"Owww!" Ted cried, not in pain as much in surprise that this frail old lady had this kind of strength.

Ear firmly in her grasp she pulled him along to the school's office where David was already seated in one of the two chairs directly in front of the principal. Ted occupied the other without having to be asked.

Sister Bethany faced both from behind her desk. She had this habit when she was bubbling with anger. She'd hang her mouth open and push her tongue against her lower front teeth. It concerned them she was doing it now.

"So, Ted, what happened?"

"What do you mean?" Ted asked.

She pounded the top of her desk with her open hand. "What in the name of heaven would ever possess you to go to the bathroom in the radiator?"

"I don't know what you're talking about."

"David said he saw you do it and when he tried to stop you, you locked him in there."

"What are you going to do to him?" David asked, moving from a slouch to sit forward.

The look she gave him negated further questioning.

"I didn't do anything," Ted pleaded, shaking his head. "You have to believe me."

"I don't have to believe anything. Were you in the church this morning?"

"Yes Sister. I served the 7:00 a.m. today. I do that every day, almost every day. I left right after mass was over. You know, after I put everything away. I don't know what David's talking about."

"That explains why Ted was in the church. How about you David?"

"I just went in to pray," he responded.

"Who wants to go first?" The question came from Father Tom and preceded his entrance.

Both boys eyed Father Tom. David put his hand up, almost enthusiastically. “I’ll tell you everything.”

“Okay, I’m listening,” he said, leaning against the desk with his arms folded.

“I was in the church this morning praying and I heard something going on in the sacristy, so I went to investigate and there was Ted, doing it, right before my eyes. I told him to stop, and he just came up to me and pushed me out of his way and ran out the door. So, I figured I’d at least try to get some of it cleaned up before I reported him and then he locks me in there! He was laughing, thinking this whole thing was funny.”

Ted sat in disbelief, leaning forward and slowly shaking his head throughout David’s rendition.

“Your version, Ted?” Father Tom inquired.

“I don’t know what he’s talking about. You put me on the 7:00 a.m. as usual. Why would I do that after my own mass? I put everything away and left, that’s all I know.”

“So how do you think David got locked in?”

“Maybe it was the work of God.”

“I see. By the way Ted, I couldn’t find it, where did you leave the key to the sacristy?”

“I put it on the center of the alt—” Ted froze, realizing too late the trap he just fell into. David smiled.

“Okay, I locked him in but I swear to God I didn’t do the other part,” Ted pleaded, his head collapsing into his hands.

“We do not swear!” Sister Bethany corrected.

“Sorry, sister.”

Ted looked at the floor and said nothing, then looked up at David.

"Can I ask a question?" Not waiting for a response, he asked anyway.

"David, what were you praying for?"

"What do you mean?"

"You said you came to church to pray. What was it you were praying for?"

"I wasn't praying for anything."

"That is something that is out of place. Nobody comes in early just to pray without asking for something. Like for example, sometimes I pray that the truth will come out. I pray that it might be understood there is a reason I could not tell anyone what happened. I pray that the people in this room who know me will have faith in me. That's what I'm praying for right now."

"So, what do you think Tom?" Sister Bethany asked.

"Ted had nothing to do with this, other than locking David in of course."

"You don't think there's any chance they were both involved?"

"If Ted did this then I have lost all faith in humanity."

She thought for a moment.

"Get to class," Sister Bethany barked at Ted.

"Yes, Sister," he replied and left, David now wearing an expression that alternated between shock and panic.

Not long after, Father Tom was at the door of Ted's class to pull him out to talk in the hallway.

"Ted, you know you can always come to me."

"Sorry about that. I'm just glad I was able to convince you I didn't do it."

"You didn't convince me of anything, give me a little credit. I asked you about the key to see if you were involved, but I knew that it wasn't you before I came down. It doesn't matter, David confessed to everything right after you left. Now I'm not just asking you but telling you not to tell anyone else about this."

"Sure, no problem."

"I'm serious Ted, I don't want anyone to know it was you who caught David, and no one will as long as you keep quiet."

"I promise, so what is going to happen to David? He's not going to be expelled, right? Please, I don't want that."

"That hasn't been decided. I can tell you he's being defrocked as an altar boy."

"So, I guess he won't be one of the servers at my funeral. You should probably reserve time for it in the church now. The other kids are going to kill me."

"As long as you don't say anything, no one is going to find out."

There was a fact not shared with Ted. When David's father came to the school to retrieve him, they were advised expulsion would be automatic if any of this came back at Ted.

"Father, am I in trouble?" Ted asked.

"Why would you be in trouble?"

"I didn't tell the truth. But you see I couldn't. David made me swear on my mother I wouldn't tell anyone. Locking the door was the only thing I could think to do."

"That wasn't your only option."

"What else could I have done?"

"Think Ted, there was something else."

Ted stood with a baffled look on his face contemplating.

"I have no idea what it could be."

"You could have done nothing, you could have walked away and done nothing."

"How could I do that?"

"See Ted, you didn't even think of it as a possibility. That is what you are made of and that is why I knew it wasn't you. And here's the twenty dollars I owe you."

"What? For getting David caught? No, I don't want it. Not this way. Put it in the poor box."

"If you want it in the poor box do it yourself," he said, shoving it into Ted's shirt pocket before sending him back to class.

He reluctantly accepted it but might have done so more readily had he known it would become instrumental in the next phase of his life.

Gifts

Talk of the "church incident" was soon pushed aside by the Christmas season with all its festivities. A favorite was secret Santa, where each student would pick a name from a bowl, get them a gift, and give it to them on the last day before vacation break.

Boys and girls segregated, the fishbowl of anticipation was passed, and each drew a name. In theory, a person was stuck with whomever selected, but kids would sometimes swap.

Moving down the aisle, Itch drew Steve. Ted was next.

"Geo! Damn it! I don't want that gremlin. I can't stand him. I'll trade you."

"Nah, Steve's easy. I know what to get him already."

"Come on, Itch. I hate that kid."

"Nope. Maybe someone else will trade."

"Hey, I got Geo. Geo the gremlin, anyone want to trade?" Ted whispered at a level allowing those nearest to him to hear.

A girl toward the back thought Geo was cute and long had a crush on him. She figured the teacher would never catch this violation of the coed restriction and jumped at the opportunity.

"We have a bingo!" Ted exclaimed as she agreed to take him. "Who do I get?"

"Fatso Anna, and if you're looking for suggestions, I'd go with a bag of peanuts."

Ted took the slip of paper but not the suggestion. *What to get her?* he asked himself. He had never purchased a gift for a girl.

Then he looked over and saw her chatting with Dorothy and June and decided his next move. Anna had extra help the following morning. This provided the perfect opportunity to ask them.

"Oooohh!" They sounded off when he disclosed why he needed to speak with them.

"Step into my office," June joked.

"How in the world did you get Anna?" she questioned.

"I traded her for Geo. I hate that kid."

"What's wrong with Geo?"

"Tell me one thing that's right about him."

"I suppose I see your point. Anyway, what did you come up with so far?"

"Well, the spending limit is five dollars, so I was thinking maybe a box of chocolate."

"Bad idea," Dorothy interrupted, "that's going to send the wrong message."

"Well, do you know what she likes? What do you suggest?"

The two girls briefly debated before coming up with an idea.

"Maybe posts," June summarized, pulling at one ear.

"What are they, like earrings?"

"Sort of. She was talking about wanting to get her ears pierced. These keep them open. She'd need them."

"Look for them in costume jewelry. You can get them for five bucks," Dorothy added.

Jewelry, of course! Girls love jewelry. There was a jewelry store along the way home he could stop in.

"So, is that a good gift? I kind of want this to be special. You know, send the right message as you said."

"And what's so special about this message?" Dorothy asked, curiously.

Ted realized he'd accidentally stepped into an area he'd prefer left untouched.

Deflecting it, or trying to, what he stated next only brought him further into the pit.

"We had a fight a long time ago and I wanted her to forgive me, but I'd like to get her something nice and I don't want her to think it's because of that."

"Then what's the reason?" Dorothy asked again, now even more curious.

Backed into a corner, he carefully worded his answer, which ultimately became more of a confession.

"Anna is different. She's not like anyone here. She's so much greater. Everyone beats on her. I don't know how she takes it. I never thought anyone could be that strong." The two girls stood in unexpected amazement as he spilled his deepest feelings. The diatribe of admiration that followed lasted several full minutes, finally at the end, "I think I can sum it up this way..."

Both girls looked on, waiting with intense anticipation for the punchline.

"Do you remember a while ago we had that assignment where we had to write about someone we look up to? Someone who is a hero to us?" He paused a final time before letting go. "Anna is mine. That's the message I want this gift to give."

The two girls looked at each other. "Oh Teddy," Dorothy snapped.

"Teddy Bear," June followed.

Ted straightened. "I came to you for help, and what do you do? Make fun of me."

Disengaging, the conversation finished, he rushed off, leaving the two bewildered.

Planting

Later that day, following yet another detention, he milled about a local jewelry store. He found posts for eight dollars, but they seemed so ordinary. *What kind of special message is that?* he thought. Instead, he began to peruse the showcase, looking across sparkling rows of diamond rings, earrings, and other baubles. His eyes stopped at a stunning diamond and emerald wrist band.

"How much is that?" he asked the saleslady, a woman in her early twenties who was busy talking with another customer.

"Eight hundred dollars," she replied without looking at either him or the case, guessing the wrong price but knowing he wasn't going to buy it anyway.

Then he spotted a gold chain accompanied by rose pendant with a small diamond chip in the center of the flower. A rose! It was her favorite flower. This was meant to be.

"How about that gold chain next to it? The one with the rose?"

"Let's see. It's $149 plus tax."

"Can I see it?"

"Sure," she said, "it's beautiful, isn't it? Is it for someone special?"

Ted stood staring at the chain as tension oscillated head to toe. The exact moment he made the decision was not determinable but after a pause he responded.

"Yes, someone very special. Could you put it aside for me? I have to get more money, but I definitely want to buy it."

"Of course, we are open until nine tonight for the holidays." Then unable to suppress the salesperson in her, she confirmed in a whisper, as if telling him a secret, "She's going to love it."

At home, Ted gathered his money. Untouched was the crisp hundred-dollar bill from the wedding mass tip and the twenty-dollars reward money Father Tom had given him. He had dreamed of buying his first stock with that, but this felt so much more important.

After the two large bills and a couple of singles it degraded into piles of change.

He gathered it all, every penny he had on earth and ran to the store without counting it, not wanting to know if it wasn't enough.

"So, you want it?" The woman confirmed. "That will be $161.65," she said, then held back rolling her eyes as he stacked his limited bills before emptying a giant bag full of coins onto the counter.

Following two lengthy counts Ted confirmed he was ten cents short.

"Do you think you could loan me the ten cents?"

A man in line behind him tossed a dime onto the counter.

"I hope she's worth it," he said with a smile.

Thanking him, his life savings along with the dream of buying his first stock was swept away into the register.

"Not that box," he said as he saw her snap it into one that was long and rectangular. "Put it in a square box."

He didn't want to give any hint as to what it could be before she opened it. He then asked if she could gift wrap it.

"It's two dollars. I'd do it for you, but they count the number of sheets. If you want, I can wrap it with a nice bow."

She opened a cabinet containing different color ribbons on spools.

"What color?"

"White," Ted responded as if it had picked itself.

"I think red would look nicer."

"White is honesty. It's pure. It's all the colors coming together, can I have white?"

"You seem sure. White it is. She's a lucky girl."

"I don't think people would call her lucky. I just want to see her smile for once," Ted responded.

"Well, then this should do it."

Transaction complete he ran home, each step increasing his excitement. Lying in bed he went over a dozen different ways he might present it to her, deciding to break the anonymity of secret Santa. He imagined the beautiful scene that would unfold. Rays of sunlight would gleam over her shoulders accompanied by a stunning smile.

Things would turn out differently.

Finest

Ted wasn't the only one who traded their secret Santa pick. Ciro, through detective work and a few threats of violence, managed to procure Ted. He wanted to create an extra special experience for Ted and was more than willing to put in the necessary effort.

His sister had a pet canary. It didn't matter that she loved it. It smelled and made a ton of noise and Ciro hated it.

First thing, the morning of the exchange Ted opened his locker to find a small beautifully wrapped box. He moved close to his locker to avoid other curious eyes and carefully peeled away the wrapping to open the top.

"Yikes!" he gasped, almost throwing it back into the locker while, behind him, Steve gave Ciro a high five. Shock passed but with his heart still racing he peered again into the box, which he now realized was decorated to look like the inside of a coffin. Next to the dead bird was a note, "To remind you of your grandfather."

Ted knew it was Ciro, or one of his goons, but realized tattling to anyone would make it worse. He collected himself, put the lid back on the box along with the usual fake smile on his face and, doing his best to go unnoticed, placed it in the garbage.

It took practically all day for Ted to draw his courage, which left Anna one of the last to receive her gift. She seemed unphased and sat chatting with Dorothy and June.

A final intake of oxygen, he braced, then approached. Anna gave her usual suspicious look.

"Hey, Anna, I'm your secret Santa," he began, propping up and down on his toes in excitement with the gift held behind his back.

"How the heck did I wind up with you?" she asked, her disappointment unhidden.

"Someone else had you but I traded them."

"What rotten luck."

"No, I got you a really great gift," Ted countered.

"The greatest gift you could give anyone would be to drop dead," she replied, delivered with a tone as serious as it was sincere.

"Anna stop! You're being rude," June scolded in a whisper.

"He probably put a lot of thought into it," Dorothy added into her other ear.

"No, he didn't, he's a jerk," she replied, confirmation of her opinion contained in her voice.

While Anna ignored him, her companions watched the blood leave Ted's face. A wave of shock reverberated through his body. He looked down to see if the javelin he felt piercing his heart, driven by the words from a girl he honestly admired, was real or imagined. He moved his hand from behind his back and gently placed the box on her desk. Putting on a brave face, the last thing he wanted to do was show any indication of how much that hurt.

"Merry Christmas," he whispered, despite it all, still trying to be sincere and saying nothing more for fear he might break.

The two girls hunted desperately for words they never found. "Wait," was all Dorothy managed to say before Ted retreated to the cover of his desk and struggled to get through the next twenty minutes until dismissal. Like a gunfighter in some late-night movie, the wound he had received was much more severe than he was willing to recognize.

His last check confirmed the gift was still sitting where he left it, unopened. Despondent, he managed to avoid human contact when school let out and dallied so he wouldn't have to walk home with anyone.

Arriving at one of the busier intersections he noticed a bus coming down the road. He momentarily considered jumping in front of it before turning in the opposite direction, returning to school.

Breakdown

Reentering the building, the festive Christmas decorations adorning the halls were in such sharp contrast to the sensation inside his chest. As much as he hoped Mr. Maze was in his office, he also wished he wasn't. When he arrived the door was open, the light on and there he sat.

"Mr. Maze?" he questioned, then halted to improve his demeanor.

"Hey, Ted, come on in. To what do I owe the pleasure?"

"Oh, I just came by to wish you merry Christmas."

"Well, merry Christmas, Ted."

"And do you remember when you said if I ever needed to talk?" he asked with a voice that raised two octaves on the last word. His eyes betrayed the wall of emotion behind them.

"Sure Ted, sit down, I'll shut the door."

Ted looked with relief as he sat back behind his desk and not next to him like he had the first time they met.

"You look troubled."

"I don't really know where to begin," he started, a depressive sadness built within his posture and tone.

Much as he wanted to forget what had happened, there was solace in sharing the details. He went on to explain everything. How he had treated Anna in the past, the eternal damnation he believed he was condemned to suffer due to her unwillingness to forgive him and finally, what happened with the gift.

"This must have been very upsetting," Mr. Maze began.

"It didn't upset me, nothing does. I'm very strong."

"I see. Well, tell me this then. When Anna said those things, how did it make you feel?"

Ted's eyes betrayed panic. He didn't want his streak of avoiding his emotions to end in this office.

"I felt nothing, I swear. You see, things don't really bother me. I didn't even cry when my grandfather died. I wanted to so badly, but I didn't," he said, straightening up to look stronger.

"I'm sorry about your grandfather, were you close to him?"

"Yeah, he was great. Such a kind man, generous too. He might have been the one who paid my tuition a few years ago. I wouldn't be here if it hadn't happened. But I think it was my mom, my birthmother, you see, I was adopted, but she has never come forward, so I don't know for sure. My parents think it was him, it doesn't matter though, I miss him so much."

"Sounds like it. So why were you afraid to show how much he meant to you when he died?"

"I wasn't afraid, men aren't supposed to."

"Who says that?"

"That's just fact. Everyone knows it."

"Showing your feelings doesn't make you any less a man."

"It doesn't make you more of one either."

"Ted, I can't impress upon you enough how important it is for you to experience your feelings."

"Even the bad ones?"

"Especially the bad ones. Ted, pushing away your feelings is a terrible thing to do. It's how addictions get started. It spirals into suicide. Being in touch with them is part of being human. I've got news for you, you're human. What you did for Anna today, what a beautiful thing. You put your entire being into it, and then for her to react that way, it's okay for you to feel hurt. When you block all these emotions bad things happen."

"What kind of bad things?"

"Denying them allows us to do things we might never do otherwise. You've studied about the holocaust, right?"

"Yeah, last year in social studies."

"I'll tell you something they might not have taught you. There were doctors, medical doctors who worked in the concentration camps, sworn to help humanity, but they didn't help anyone. Instead, they would select people to die. They would make the decision. They sentenced thousands upon thousands of people to death. How do you think they did it? They put aside their feelings. I'm sure they didn't cry about it, but that didn't make them men, it made them animals. Don't ever be afraid to feel what is inside you, take pride in being able to do so."

Eyes focused on the floor, Ted recalled something and began to talk softly.

"One time when I was very young, I found a book with horrible pictures about the holocaust. There was this one with a man hanging on a fence, all by himself, dead. He was so alone. He seemed so cold. No one cared, it was terrible."

"It sounds terrible, but you said something, you said no one cared. Ted, you saw his suffering in that photo and you cared. Even though that poor man will never know about how you felt for him, it still has meaning. Anna may also not know how much you care but try to understand it doesn't make your caring about her any less important."

Ted hung his head and thought but didn't answer.

"Tell me, what are you feeling?" Mr. Maze asked in an especially calm voice.

Ted remained silent, hoping the question would fade away, unanswered.

"How are you feeling right now?"

A reddened strained look filled his face. "I'm fine," he whispered.

"I don't know about that. I think you are holding back, and I think you need to reach inside and recognize that."

"I'm fine," he stated again, only this time with a higher pitched quivering voice as he dropped his head into his hands. "I am not fine, I've never been so far away from fine," he admitted before throwing his hands down onto his legs, his face showing the stress of pain. "Coming here was a mistake, I'm going to go."

"Before you do, tell me what you are thinking about right now."

He hesitated at first but then answered, "She is the most pure and honest person I know, and she hates me. That hate is as sincere and genuine as it comes, and I hate myself for making her hate me. And I can't fix it."

At this point his eyes held too much water to see clearly, yet not a single tear rolled over his face.

"She just didn't understand. Please Ted, tell me how that's making you feel."

"Who cares how I feel!?! Why should I answer such a stupid question?" he shouted.

"Ted, it's an important question. You gave Anna that beautiful gift. You reached out to her with the very best of intentions and she responded as she did. Admit at least to yourself how hurt it has made you feel."

"Damn you!" he squeaked, tears now falling from his eyes.

Hovering for just a moment, he made one last futile attempt to push it away before collapsing forward face down onto the desk, overcome with emotion.

"I'm sorry," he whispered breathlessly as he began to sob hysterically.

Mr. Maze quickly moved to the same side as Ted to sit in the chair next to him. He pulled a box of tissues close and began gently rubbing his shoulder.

"Ted, you don't need to be sorry, I'm the one who is sorry. I'm so sorry about your grandfather, I'm sorry for your loss. I'm sorry about what happened today with Anna."

Watching Ted wail uncontrollably, he found himself unable to shake the feeling that he'd just committed some form of child abuse. He knew it needed to be done but nothing in his education or training suggested he force it in such a way. This can sometimes be the chasm between what we are taught and what we do when the fear of being wrong is overcome by our intuition and the will to do what is right and necessary.

After a few minutes, Ted turned toward him, providing the opportunity and apparent invitation to be hugged. Mr. Maze didn't hesitate and pulled him in close enough to allow his tears to land on his shoulder. Ted surprised himself by how much the warmth of the embrace comforted him.

At least a third of the tissues in the box were gone before he collected himself. Now it was clear to him why he had given Anna the chain.

"I wanted her to have that chain to make her happy," he began softly as the intense release of emotion finally subsided. "Just once I wanted to see her smile. Mr. Maze, she never smiles. No one has ever seen it. She goes through her day, and she is so strong, so incredibly strong, no matter what is thrown at her, but in her eyes, there is so much pain.

"But it's more than just that," he continued, his voice cracking as fresh tears refilled the streaks that were already across his face. "When I was buying that chain, there was a man in line behind me who said, 'I hope she's worth it.' The reason I bought it is because I was trying to find a way to show her that she is."

Now it was Mr. Maze who was starting to get choked up. He marveled at how such as act of love had the potential to do more to help Anna than years of therapy.

Ted lowered his head into his hands in defeat. "I've messed everything up. I'm just no good."

"No, no, no. I'll permit almost anything to be said in this office Ted but not that. You don't do what you did today and put yourself down. I won't stand for it. You've done more for her than you will ever know. It's just that you don't see everything the way it is. I am sure that gold chain will come to mean the world to her once she figures it all out."

"She might have thrown it out for all I know."

"I'm sure she didn't. She'll open it and one day recognize it as the most meaningful gift she's ever received."

Panic suddenly filled his eyes, thinking somehow, she'd find out about all of this.

"Don't tell anyone what I said," he pleaded. "And please, please don't tell anyone about this part." He held up the wad of tissues in his hand.

"Ted, this is just like a confessional. Everything we talk about here is completely private. You know how a priest can be excommunicated if he ever tells anyone what's said in confession? Well, I would lose my license if I did that. You are safe here to tell me anything." He reflected for a moment. "Your parents must be so proud of you."

"Yeah, well, that's a discussion for a day that isn't going as lousy as this one. My mom is going to freak. I wasn't thinking when I did this. She knew I had money, and now I can't buy gifts for anyone. She's going to want to know what happened to it."

"She's not going to freak. Tell her the truth. What you did is a beautiful thing."

Ted shook his head and sighed. "I think it's time for me to get going."

"Before you do, is it okay to ask? How are you feeling?"

Ted dabbed his eyes. "You know, I feel much better." He paused to consider it further. "I really do," he repeated, surprised by his own words.

"You sure?"

"Yeah, Scouts' honor," he said, holding up two fingers, apart.

"Oh, you're in the Boy Scouts?"

"No, but my best friend is in the Scouts. I could never measure up to those kids. Well, thanks for everything," he said, reaching out to shake his hand as Mr. Maze stood. "Have a merry Christmas."

"You have one too, Ted. Would you like a fist full of candy for the trip home?" he asked, moving the candy dish to the edge of his desk.

"No thanks, that's okay, I'm good," he said as he left, shutting the door behind him.

Plucking a candy from the dish, Mr. Maze looked at the door and stated to the empty room, picking on those last words. "How on earth is it you don't see that about yourself? We are going to have to work on that."

Bonding

Ted went home and, wanting to get it done, broke the news by saying to his mom that he'd lost his Christmas money. Following a tyrannical inquisition, his mom concluded he must have bought drugs with it and spent hours tearing apart his room. Finding nothing, she threatened to ground him for the entire vacation.

Salvation came when his father arrived home from work. Speaking with him one-on-one in his room, his father got him to circle around the issue.

"Dad, I blew it all on a girl."

His father smiled. "Who is she?"

"I don't want to talk about it. Please don't make me talk about it. It was a disaster."

"I don't think there is a guy out there who hasn't made that mistake. Here," his father concluded, handing him two twenties, "buy some presents. This is between us. Tell your mom later you found the money you lost. It will get her off both our backs."

Without thinking, he moved to give his father a hug, and found it returned unhesitatingly. The words *thank you* became unnecessary.

"Dad, just curious about something. Mom wouldn't listen, and I gave you no proof at all. Why did you believe me?"

"Because you have never given me a reason not to."

Giving

The top gift under the tree for Ted was a beautiful ten-speed bicycle, but the thing he cherished most came two days after, when he learned a tour of the New York Stock Exchange had been arranged! His mother received a call from Walter Burke, or more accurately, a secretary from his office. The trip was set for the last week of February, just after his birthday, on a half day when parent teacher conferences were scheduled. Ashton would accompany him.

Anna didn't get anything fancy like a bike for Christmas. She was happy to receive a couple of secondhand school uniforms. She sat at the breakfast table alone four days after Christmas, only remembering the unopened gift from Ted when she noticed the box with the white satin ribbon in her book bag on the floor.

She traded the spoon she was holding for the package. With one hand, she shook it by her ear, concluding the heavy knocking was likely the metal spring in something that would burst out when opened. As though defusing a bomb, she cringed, pulled at the ribbon, opened the top and dumped the chain, which she assumed was a decoy, onto the table. Ignoring it, instead poking at the wad of cotton inside, she tried to find the joke she believed it contained.

Finding no hint of humiliation, picking up the chain, much heavier than the plastic she believed it to be, she realized it was gold when she saw a small *18K* stamped on the clasp. She reasoned it had to be a mistake; he must have handed her the wrong box.

Regardless, she could not stop herself from going to the mirror to place it around her neck. It was the first necklace she ever wore not made of string and Fruit Loops. She loved the way it looked but more so the way it made her feel. Her fingers ran down the strand and pressed it into her flesh. A debutante, a rock star, a queen, she became all of them as she gazed at herself in the mirror. Her confusion melded into astonishment the day she returned to school and showed it to her friends.

"That is so beautiful!" June declared before double-checking the clasp and adding, "That had to be a hundred dollars!"

"I should give it back; he obviously didn't realize what was in the box."

"I don't think it was a mistake Anna," Dorothy began. "There's something you should know. He spoke to us before he gave it to you."

"Spoke? About what?" Anna asked.

"He wanted to give you a gift to send you the right message."

"He said he thinks of you as a hero," June interrupted. "He said you are the strongest person he has ever known. He called you amazing. He was asking us what gift he should give you to make that clear."

That was just the start of their lengthy retelling of what Ted had confessed to them.

"Ted? Ted Carrington? That Ted? The one hanging out over there with Tom?" she said, pointing toward him while he was standing two hundred feet away and at that moment being shaken down by Tom for his lunch money.

"Maybe he was joking with you when he said it?"

"Anna, look at what he gave you."

Anna paused for a moment as it sunk in. "My God, I was so mean to him! Why didn't you stop me?"

"We didn't...I mean...posts! He was supposed to get you posts!" June declared, throwing up her hands.

"I feel terrible. How am I supposed to let him know how much this means to me?"

"Go over and thank him," they said without understanding.

What she was told he had said far surpassed what was now deep appreciation for the gold chain. A thank-you? No, Anna didn't think that was anywhere near enough. Whatever it took she needed to show him. She knew the answer lay in her notebook, but just the thought of it made her shudder.

Gratitude

Present Day

Back in the office Ted hoped his victims were learning from all this. Things were about to unfold, and this preparation was important.

"Mr. Maze invested time in me. We met once a week for sessions after I had come to him that Christmas. He gave me all kinds of tips and techniques to deal with my emotions. Just recognizing you have them is eye opening.

"He taught things they don't teach in school but should. He told me one time that lack of failure is a form of failure in itself. Imagine that. It stuck with me. The man was brilliant.

"He pointed out things like the origins of anxiety and depression. Depression is repressed anger. Anxiety is unresolved fear. Once you know how those dragons draw their strength it becomes much easier to slay them. Reading, writing, math and all the subjects they teach are important but learning how to direct your emotional energy is a badly needed, missing component.

"I used to suffer from terrible anxiety. I told him I'd be up for hours worrying. He said something that practically made it all go away. He told me the things that can happen are always worse than what does happen. Reality is never as bad as the worst of what our imagination produces.

"Critically he taught me that when it comes to feelings there is no right or wrong. It is what it is. It is how you react to those feelings that matters. Learning to use them rather than be controlled by them I think is the single greatest variable in determining how one's life will turn out.

"I credit that man for saving my life. That is how influential a school guidance counselor can be and how significant what is missing from the school curriculum is."

Abilities

1979

"Pull it to the right," Chuck shouted.

"Bend it. It's not going to break. Wood has flexibility." Frank should know. His father was a master craftsman and they had been working together with power tools in their garage since he was five.

Ted considered himself lucky when he and Chuck teamed up with a classmate like Frank to complete another of the ridiculously involved social studies projects. The assignment was to build a completely self-sustaining model city.

They had to figure out everything needed, design a layout, create a three-dimensional model, and write a report on how the city functioned. Their classmates approached it using cardboard and oak tag.

"No way," Frank bellowed confidently, "we are building this out of wood."

This brought them to a lumber yard where they pooled money and purchased three four-by-eight sheets of plywood. Getting them onto a city bus for the trip home was perhaps the most challenging part.

"Turn it, turn it!"

"Are you pushing?"

"Stop! You have to wiggle it. I think it's getting stuck on the floor."

All three pushed, pulled, debated, and barked at each other trying to get it onto the bus. The driver, a burly man who was thoroughly tired of the holdup rose from his seat and as if unlocking a mystery of how easy it should have been gave it a hard shove. The board finally moved in far enough to clear the door.

"See, I told you it would fit," Frank said in vindication. "Now let's go get the other two pieces."

As the bus lumbered forward, the boys laid low, half hiding behind the boards to avoid their fellow passengers' dirty looks. Arriving at their stop the struggle recommenced in reverse. As they finally jostled the final board off, Ted, just before exiting, flashed a V sign with his fingers high above his head to all aboard. A sweet looking elderly woman responded with her middle finger.

They each dragged a piece to Frank's house, located in the Italian section of the neighborhood, denoted by statues of the Madonna on almost every lawn. One board would serve as the platform and the other two cut into smaller pieces.

Frank set to the task immediately while Chuck and Ted began listing all the buildings. Government center, courthouse, agricultural buildings, a church, stores, housing, tourist center, just some of the fifty-seven structures they had planned.

"Let's see it," Frank stated as he stacked all different shapes of wood and reviewed their list of buildings, silent, contemplating. He didn't notice the lack of a hospital but thought of something else. “It needs a whorehouse,” he observed matter-of-factly.

“What? Are you insane!” Chuck blurted out in disbelief.

“Yeah, it’s got to have a whorehouse. What city doesn’t have a whorehouse? It needs a whorehouse.” It seemed as though he was trying to see how many times he could say the word.

Chuck shook his head. “We are not putting in a whorehouse.”

“The assignment says the city has to include everything, that means it has to have a whorehouse. We’ll put the whorehouse next to the airport.”

“You’re nuts, let’s vote on it,” Chuck suggested. “Majority rules. Ted, what do you think?”

Ted had been busy trying to figure out what a whorehouse was. Did they mean warehouse and he had been mispronouncing it his whole life? Well, the answer was simple. Much as he hated to admit, Chuck was always right about everything. In fact, it was something that irked Ted to no end how the universe would seemingly bend the laws of physics just to make him right.

“As long as we have a place to store things, I don’t think we need a whorehouse.”

“No fair, he doesn’t even know what it is!” Frank shouted.

“Well, I win.” A subdued Chuck confirmed with a shade of green enveloping his face. “Guys,” he said seemingly trying to catch his breath, “I’m not feeling right.”

Just then his face contorted, his mouth fell open and a stream of projectile vomit launched to the other side of the room.

Following a chorus of "Ewwww" and "Yuck, Chuck" from his buddies, they acknowledged he was sick.

That was the first indication of the flu he was suffering. They never thought to ask one of their parents to drive him home. Instead, Ted walked with him, courteously pausing to allow him to throw up in the bushes along the way. Arriving at his home Chuck had only one request.

"Please, for the love of God, please don't start calling me Upchuck again!"

Ted and Frank kept the project going with Frank doing most of the building.

After giving Ted a few small tasks, it was determined the best thing he could do was stay out of the way. After a week they called Chuck to see if he was still alive and test his willingness to do the report.

"Just kill me, please kill me," he pleaded over the phone when asked about his condition.

"I guess I'll do it," Ted said, feeling guilty over how much work Frank had put in. Not sure he'd do a good job; in the end, it was impressive and a nice compliment to the incredible display Frank had built. All that was left to do was sign the report. That sent them to Chuck's house, where he greeted them in a bathrobe and slippers.

"I thought I was going to die but I'm feeling a lot better now. I'll be at school tomorrow when you bring it in. The least I could do is help you carry it."

"No, my dad and I are bringing it in before he goes to work. Can't wait for you to see it," Frank responded.

"I can't wait either, sounds incredible. Amazing report too, Ted. You write so well, I mean you are truly talented," he commented after looking it over.

"Good, if you're happy with it, sign it," Ted instructed.

"I can't sign it; I didn't have anything to do with it."

"Just sign it," Frank agreed wholeheartedly.

"That would be dishonest."

"If the tables were turned, would you do the same for us?" Ted questioned.

Chuck gave it thought then took the pen they offered and scribbled his name.

What they brought in the next morning, from its replica Guggenheim to the church's spire to the monorail, Ted's idea, made with fish tank tubing, which provided Citywide transportation, left the entire school administration speechless. Mrs. Butterman had a hard time accepting Ted and Frank had done the work rather than Chuck. It was such a marvel that it was put on display to the side of the school's entrance for weeks.

"Frank built it, Ted wrote the report, all I did was get the flu," Chuck insisted when questioned on his involvement. "Oh wait, I did close down the whorehouse."

Reconciliation

Had his mother not said, “Happy birthday,” Ted would have forgotten about it on his way to school. No sooner had he arrived, he was surrounded by his three companions. Suddenly remembering the infamous birthday ritual, he held up a hand.

“That’s okay. You don’t have to.”

Rip was first to fire off into his shoulder blade. Damn, that kid had a punch! Chuck and Itch followed in quick secession.

“Happy birthday, loser!” They declared in sarcastic unison while Ted rubbed his shoulder.

“Wait a second!” Itch declared before they broke off. “I forgot. You’re left-handed. We screwed this up. *Do over!*”

Technically Itch was correct. They had hit him at full force, which was appropriate if showing respect, but they had done it to the wrong shoulder. Proper etiquette dictated the non-dominant shoulder be struck so that the lucky birthday boy would still be able to write.

“No, that’s okay,” Ted insisted to no avail, moments later his right shoulder receiving three more punches.

Given it was his birthday one might have thought Itch would go easy on him as they played poker during lunch recess, held inside the classroom on account of rain. That wasn't to be. Itch, as always, was cleaning up, evidenced by the stack of chips piled in front of him, five times the size of Ted's.

"Mountain, seven o'clock, approaching fast," Itch quipped.

Ted looked over his shoulder to see Anna approaching, turned, and shot back a smirk. Anna stopped a few feet short, peered over Ted's shoulder, her face flushed, looking as uncomfortable as a cat in a cold bath. Ted glanced up, incorrectly giving the impression she wasn't interrupting.

"Pair of nines, I see," she blurted, trying to come up with anything to say.

"I see you and raise you fifty!" Itch cheered.

"Oh, come on!" Ted shouted, throwing down his cards in frustration.

"I was about to fold too," Itch gloated.

"Can I help you?" Ted asked Anna, his annoyance evident as Itch raked to himself the small pile of chips in the middle.

"Sorry about that, my stupid mouth. I came over to wish you a happy birthday."

Genuinely surprised, happily so, he put aside his loss. "Thanks. How did you know it was my birthday?"

"I saw the guys punching your arm this morning, so I figured."

"Well, thanks again."

"I, uh," she uttered as she shifted her weight nervously back and forth, "do you think we could talk, you know, just us?"

Suddenly filled with a sense of importance and waving his hand as though casting a spell, he looked to Itch. "Do you mind?"

"After beating you so badly, I need a good stretch," he said as he got up to leave the two to talk.

Her voice quivered a bit but was filled with a warmth that made it clear this was coming from the deepest place in her heart.

"I don't think I ever thanked you for the chain you gave me."

"I was hoping you liked it."

"It's beautiful. I love it. I'm wearing it right now." She leaned forward to pull a small section from under her collar for him to see. "You didn't have to do this."

"Oh, it was nothing," he started. "You want to know what happened? You see I had to buy it because the store was closing..."

"My friends told me what you said," she interrupted before Ted could embarrass himself.

A puppy-dog look, accompanied by the word *busted* that was all but written on his face.

"Well, that was the other reason."

"I need to ask you something. It's very important to me. Did you mean it? All those things you said?"

If only he had been born a turtle, just duck into his shell and leave the question unanswered. He huffed, or maybe it was a sigh. "Yeah," he croaked, looking off.

That wasn't right. So flat and uncommitted. He knew what he needed to do. Summoning courage is never easy. He looked straight into her eyes, a deep green. It struck him how beautiful they really were.

"Yes, every word, one hundred percent," he confirmed.

"Really?"

"Bring your friends over here and I'll say it again."

Hearing it from Ted, even though her friends swore it was true, was still shocking. In so many ways it reshaped a part of the world she believed she knew so well.

"I think about those beautiful things you said every time I put it on. Dorothy mentioned you wanted me to forgive you for something. Well, I want you to know, everything, anything, whatever it is, I forgive you."

He didn't think he cared anymore but her words brought a sense of relief that welled within. The sincerity was so pure he almost teared up. A weight lifted from his shoulders forced a rare genuine smile to his face.

"Thank you, Anna, what a wonderful birthday gift."

Now it was Anna who stared into his eyes. They were blue, not the black she was sure they were. She wondered if it were possible for a person to really change that much. It was in that moment her heart finalized a fateful decision.

"I actually have a real gift for you," she muttered, her voice weak but determined.

Her gift to him, in return for the exquisite chain, his beautiful heartfelt words and the horrible way she had responded, was at its core, trust. She was about to hand him the power to destroy her, if he chose, and in doing so put to the test this new hope of hers for humanity.

"I'll be right back."

Faith

Her legs shook as she walked what seemed a mile back to her desk. She believed there was a possibility she might collapse, which no doubt would bring on an endless stream of fat jokes. She pulled that special notebook she was always scribbling in and opened it to a page toward the end.

Shared with no one, her harbor in a storm, her security blanket, if the choice had been to show it to the world or die, no question it would have meant her funeral. She began carefully, meticulously folding the selected page back and forth, over and over, weakening it to the point it could be cleanly torn.

Ted was mystified. By the time she returned, she was shaking. Looking away, she placed the paper face down on his desk.

"Happy birthday, Ted. I made this for you," she whispered with what little courage was left inside.

Baffled by her tension, he turned it over. Pure amazement awaited! A sketch of his face with the detail so remarkable had it not been drawn in pencil, could otherwise be mistaken for a photograph. His eyes, scanning every inch of the unbelievable work, noticed something curious. While it looked almost impossibly real, she had omitted all imperfections. Blemishes, pimples, anything out of place was gone. She had changed his hairstyle too, adding a wave.

"Did you draw this?"

She nodded.

"Seriously? How long did this take?" Expecting hours to be her response.

"A couple of minutes," she replied to his and what would have been anyone's disbelief.

"My God, Anna, you are so talented."

"You think it's good?"

"Good? Oh, come on. You must hear it all the time."

There was a pause before the confession. "I actually never showed anyone before."

Ted was sure he misunderstood. "Really? You mean I'm the first person at school?"

She did not expect him to believe words she could hardly say.

"No. I've never shown anyone, not even my nana. You're the first person to see any of it, ever."

A conversation Ted initially believed as shallow as a pond suddenly proved itself deep as an ocean. Any ordinary kid might have passed it by, but Ted was different, special. His unique interpretation of the world allowed him to recognize the significance of this moment. He looked upon it with the same sense of awe a parent does a child walking for the first time. "First person ever," he repeated in his mind several times.

The hair on his neck stood straight; his stomach convulsed to half its size. He was angry fate would entrust to him a moment as crucial as this. Still, he recognized the incredible privilege bestowed upon him. He was the first to experience a wonder no less spectacular than the Grand Canyon, the pyramids, a sunrise!

Groping for his next action, his intellect revved to full power. Looking across his desk, he grabbed a pencil and held it up.

"You didn't sign it," he stated flatly.

"What do you mean?"

"You need to sign it for me. Great artists always sign their work."

She expelled a short, excited breath, then finished it with something no one had seen for a very long time. She gave him what he had hoped the chain would have delivered. Ear to ear, a most beautiful smile filled her face.

"You think I'm an artist?"

"No one would need to think about that. You are an artist, and the word to put before it is incredible."

Flustered, she backed away bumping into the desk behind her.

"Okay, well, I'm glad it's something you like. It's yours. Enjoy it."

"I definitely will," Ted replied, standing up holding it out to view the picture as though it were hanging on a wall. "I have a special shelf at home that I'm going to put it on."

Just then Rob passed and noticed.

"What is that?" he asked, moving in to get a closer look.

"One of the girls drew this for me for my birthday," he answered while moving his thumb to cover Anna's signature.

"Who?"

"One of the girls," Ted replied with a seriousness that bordered on threat.

Anna stood panicked at the end of the aisle wanting to rip the picture from his hand. Her eyes pleaded with Ted. Did he understand that she could not survive being ridiculed about this most intimate part of her existence?

Seeing he was hiding something Rob reached to grab the picture. "Who drew it?" he insisted.

"Anna," Ted relented.

"Big fat...." The world will never know what Rob intended to say. Using a move Rip taught him, Ted punched the center of his throat, ending the completion of his sentence.

Choking, Rob protested between coughs, "What gives?"

"Sorry" is all that was offered as he hid the picture between the pages of a textbook. There could be no compromise. This was Anna's moment, and Ted was willing to fight to the death to keep it protected.

She returned to her desk aglow, basking in the warmth of her glorious moment. Now Ted was about to have his.

Personalized

For some, the biggest day of their lives may be the day they get married, or the birth of a child. Up until now, for Ted, it was the day he was to get his tour of the New York Stock Exchange. Outside school, a half day on account of teacher conferences, the only thing he knew for sure is that he and Ashton were to wait for the car to pick them up.

Ted had prepared. Since the arrangements had been made, he had read books about the exchange, its history and how things operated. Hoping to meet a floor trader, he compiled a list of questions. With him was a snack and ten dollars for souvenirs. He was a well-armed fighter ready to step into battle.

His eyes scanned for the Town Car Ashton came to school in every day. That's why he paid no mind to the maroon Rolls-Royce Silver Shadow until the unmistakable Spirit of Ecstasy emblem adorning the hood rolled before him. His heart nearly stopped in disbelief when it wasn't the family's driver but rather Walter Burke himself who stepped out from behind the wheel. Stiff and serious, deliberately trying to imitate a chauffeur's actions, Walter hurried around to the passenger side and opened the back door.

"Ted first," he corrected as Ashton went to jump in.

"You excited?" he asked.

"You don't have to open the door for me."

"Today is your day, everything first class," he said. "You can close the door yourself," he added after Ashton climbed in.

The car moved, hardly noticeable, like a cloud along the roadway. The feel and sound, or lack thereof, was utterly different from the unrefined clunky Chevy Nova his father drove. He felt as though he had been whisked away into some secret underworld and feared at the end, he'd be given a potion that would force him to forget the whole thing.

While Walter drove, Ashton and Ted chatted incessantly, much of it pure silliness with them trying to impersonate the voices of various *Star Wars* characters.

"Let me get a word in," Mr. Burke interrupted as they crossed a bridge over the East River. "Ted, to be on the floor of the exchange, you have to wear a jacket. There are no exceptions. Our first stop will be at a store so we can take care of that."

He looked down and across his shoulders, wondering how a jacket might complement the shirt and tie he was already wearing. It didn't take long to find out. After a valet met them to park the car, they walked to a men's clothing store filled with fine suits.

"Walter, come in," the salesman exclaimed while holding open the door and shaking his hand. "Is this the young man?" he continued, patting Ted on the shoulder.

"Give him the royal treatment."

"We have a few jackets for him to try. The tailor is in the back, and he'll be right with you."

Ted stood on a platform in front of a three-sided mirror putting on each of the jackets.

"Let's get it a little larger than he needs and hem it, this way he can use it for a few years."

"Absolutely, sir," the tailor responded as he measured Ted and put marks on the jacket.

Ted had no idea how much it cost but the material was like nothing he ever owned. Thick, plush and soft as silk. Mr. Burke handed a wad of bills to the salesman, thanked him for the rush service and told him to keep the change. Fifteen minutes was all it took to put Ted in a fine jacket and pump his ego. A short walk to the exchange followed where they entered through a door on Wall Street beside the six iconic Corinthian columns of its front exterior.

Visitor check-in badges were already waiting. From the entrance it was onto an elevator to the seventh floor where Walter showed Ted around some meeting rooms. Beautiful paneling lined the walls throughout. Of particular beauty was a room called the Boardroom, with many parts of its walls decorated in gold leaf. In one corner stood a stone and silver urn, a gift from Czar Nicholas II in 1903.

On one wall hung a famous clock, the history of which Ted, from reading his books was familiar. Purchased in 1867, it resembled a wall mounted grandfather clock called the Wall Regulator Clock. It was used in the 1800s to time the allotment of five minutes of trading given to each individual stock.

The quiet atmosphere was in sharp contrast to the frenzied trading taking place below. To the elevator, down seven floors; next stop, the exchange itself.

The door to the elevator opened just outside the trading floor. If sound were heat it would have been like walking into a five-hundred-degree oven. To the side a man wearing a green jacket stood waiting. Introduced to Ted by Walter, he was one of the exchange's supervisors and would be conducting the tour.

"I want you to give him a great tour. Show him everything. Let him watch the closing bell, then send him up to the Luncheon Club, we'll meet him there," Walter shouted, competing with all the noise.

"Aren't you guys coming?" Ted asked, suddenly realizing Ashton didn't have a jacket.

"No, this is yours. Now enjoy and learn a lot."

It was two thirty, and the closing bell was at 4:00 p.m. What he had expected would be a tour of a few minutes was to be an hour and a half. They stepped through the door and into the maelstrom. All around people shouted and hurried about and they weren't even on the main trading floor yet. Everything his tour guide said had to be yelled. For over an hour, the exchange's inner workings, its personnel, and all the things the people did were explained.

"This room is called the Garage," his guide shouted as they entered the first room. "About 250 people work here, brokers, people taking orders. You have a group of reporters, the guys in the blue jackets over there. A lot of communication with the outside world takes place here because, believe it or not, it's quieter." Bustling and chaotic, it still was not like the iconic trading floor, which was next.

Up a ramp, out of the Garage he stepped onto the trading floor. Brighter than outside at midday, he looked straight up.

"How high is the ceiling?" Ted asked, staring at the floodlights beaming down into his eyes.

"Seventy-two feet. The trading floor itself is about twenty thousand. An interesting piece of trivia, the typical trader walks an average of twelve miles on these floors every day."

The people he was introduced to, and there were many, initially paid him little attention. That was until his guide added, "He's a special guest of Walter Burke." Hearing that they would stop, vigorously shake his hand and devote full attention to any questions asked.

Information, sights, sounds, shouts, and bright lights, for an hour it was like churning inside a washing machine atop a race car. A few minutes to 4:00 p.m., he was brought below the podium overlooking the exchange to observe the closing bell.

He joyfully endured its earsplitting fifteen-second ring. Almost immediately, things began to settle as many people headed for the exit. Within a couple of minutes, all was calm. It was as though the room itself exhaled.

His guide escorted him off the floor and up to the grandly decorated Luncheon Club to rejoin Ashton and Walter. Unlike before, Ashton was now in a jacket, as was the required dress code there too.

"Rub the horn for good luck, its tradition," Walter encouraged, pointing to a large bull-and-bear statue.

Ted took him up on the suggestion before erupting, "That was so exciting. I'm still shaking. Thank you so much!"

"My pleasure, Ted. I thought we'd have a bite before heading back. This restaurant is an iconic fixture here."

It certainly seemed it, and exclusive too. Leather chairs in the lounge, moose and elk heads mounted on the walls, chandeliers, quiet reserved atmosphere in such contrast to the trading floor. Walter and his guests were seated in a corner by themselves with a waiter assigned exclusively to their table.

There were so many things Ted wanted to talk about, but Ashton kept interrupting, mostly about school. For him it was the first real chance he had to sit with his dad and tell him about his teachers and the school year, even though it was more than half over.

When Ashton wasn't talking, the interruptions came from the restaurant manager who seemed to have nothing else to do but be sure everything was perfect at their table. At the end, Walter placed it on his tab, and they left. Once outside, onto the street just as rush hour was beginning, the chaotic bustle was nothing compared to what Ted had experienced.

On the way to retrieving the car they stopped at a jewelry store to pick up a diamond encrusted brooch Walter was buying his wife for their anniversary. Ted looked around for a souvenir to buy with his ten dollars. He knew there was nothing in the store he could afford but inquired for the sake of curiosity the cost of a thick gold tie clip, with the emblem of the clashing bull and bear, a small diamond in each animal's eye.

"That one, eleven hundred fifty," the man behind the counter told him.

"Ah," Ted replied, then joked, "might you have something a little more, well, you know, for a poor person?"

The man laughed. Ultimately, Ted wound up passing a kiosk on the street and purchased a Wall Street snow globe for $6.95. The day had been fantastic, but the best was yet to come.

Trade-Off

The Rolls was fetched, and the boys jumped in the back. Ashton laid against the plush seats and closed his eyes. Much as the seats invited him to sleep, Ted could not pass up the opportunity to talk with Mr. Burke. As people outside peered in to see who was inside such a car, Ted imagined Walter to be his personal chauffeur and himself a king, or perhaps a famous movie star, someone important.

The silence was punctuated by light snoring emanating from Ashton, signaling to Ted that the great Walter Burke was now all his. They chatted for a while about various things like the Burke mansion on the Amalfi Coast of Italy, Pompeii, a topic he discovered his host to be a veritable expert on, and finally, a question from Walter.

"So, Ted, anything you recommend in the market these days?"

He had been afraid he'd ask that. He was following a bunch of stocks but didn't have a definite opinion on any.

"I'm still doing research. I don't have any good recommendations right now, so I don't know."

"That is most impressive, Ted," Walter stated.

"Sorry to disappoint you."

"I hope you didn't think I was being sarcastic. I really am impressed. It takes courage to answer a question by saying you don't know. The truth is that is the correct answer for most people on most topics, but they never have the common sense to admit it. Everybody has an opinion on everything despite the fact they often don't have a clue."

"Yeah, well, it's not just the stocks themselves. I don't like the economy right now. We could have another oil crisis, interest rates are ridiculous, and that guy in the White House."

Walter adjusted his rearview mirror for a moment to take a glance of Ted.

"Everything okay?" Ted asked as he noticed.

"Yeah, I was just making sure I didn't have an old man back there by mistake. So, you think we're headed for the end of the world?"

"Oh, I'd never predict that. Even if I knew it for sure, I wouldn't make that prediction. You know why? Think about it. There is no upside. You see, if you are wrong, everyone will laugh at you, but just imagine if you are right! How in the world would you ever get credit? It's a no-win situation."

"You are a hoot, Ted, an absolute hoot," Walter proclaimed, letting go a chuckle. "So, tell me: Have you given much thought to what you want to be when you grow up?"

For years Ted had been fooling with the idea of pope but knew it was just a fantasy. Not knowing how else to phrase it he just blurted, "Honestly, when I grow up, I want to be you."

There was a long pause before Walter spoke.

"And why do you think you want that?"

Ted found it hard to believe the man would ask.

"Who wouldn't want to be you? You're...you know, you have everything. You're rich."

"You think I have everything? Ted, have you ever considered what goes along with it? The amount of stress, long hours, I never get to spend time with my family or do things I want. You just see the money and all you can buy with it. If I were sitting where you are right now, I think I would have done things very differently."

"But you see how everyone treats you. The people at the clothing store, the market, the restaurant, you are like a god."

"I'm a god? Wow, really. I know this is hard for you to understand, but do you think people treat me like that out of genuine admiration or because I have a powerful position and a lot of money? What you see is a courtesy they pay me. I don't even know if they like me. And you know what? I'll never know who truly does and doesn't, and that's just one of the many curses that comes with having money."

"Cars, homes, and all, don't get me wrong, it's wonderful, but there's a trade-off. With everything in life there always is. You can never have one thing without in some way giving up something else. I've given up a lot of important things for what I have, and you will never believe me when I tell you it's not worth it. So, Ted, I'm going to have to say you don't want to be me when you grow up, you only think you do."

"If you don't like it, then why don't you change? Stop all this and do the things you want."

"I would love a simple life, but there are obligations and commitments."

"You know what your problem is?" he interrupted. "You don't want to give up all this rich-guy stuff. It's easier to complain and make excuses than it is to do it all differently. You just said it yourself. You can't have one thing without giving up another. Much as you say it, you don't want to make the necessary sacrifices. Want to know something. Everyone suffers from some form of mental illness or other and I just found yours."

The car became quiet enough for the minimal road noise to become pronounced. Ted thought about what he'd just said and considered asking his host to pull to the side of the road so he could jump out.

"I'm sorry. Anyone who goes to school with me knows the stupid things I can say."

Ted viewed this as another example of his inept idiocy. Mr. Burke had differing thoughts.

"What you lack in tact, you make up for in honesty. Don't apologize. I think everyone could use someone like you around them. Someone without fear who says what they see. You nailed it Ted, I'm not willing to give up what I have for the things I claim I want. My advice to you is to look in a direction other than money. I worry about Ashton, it's so easy for him to fall into the same trap."

"Oh, you don't have to worry about him. He's got to be the most popular kid in school. Everyone likes him, except Itch maybe, but Itch is a moron. And the girls. Oh man, are they nuts about him too. If he were to fart, they would all run from their desks to smell it."

After Mr. Burke finished laughing, he asked, "Is that because of the person he is or because everyone knows he comes from money?"

"Money? Nobody thinks that at all. I'd bet half the kids don't even know he's rich. He's got a great personality, he's nice to everyone, funny too. Money has nothing to do with any of it."

"Well, I have to tell you, that is most reassuring. Ted, do you know what karma is?"

"Not really," he replied after giving it thought.

"What karma means is when you do something for someone, it tends to come back to you. What goes around comes around. You said I made this day special for you, but what you just said made my day too."

"The Bible says that. When you give to someone it comes back tenfold."

"And I have seen it come back eight hundred fifty-fold."

As they turned the corner to his house, Ted thanked him once again.

"Thank you so much for everything. The tour, the jacket, lunch, it was too much."

"What was your favorite part?"

"It was all great, but"—he paused—"I don't want to sound like I didn't appreciate everything, but honestly, the best part about today was getting to talk with you."

"You are full of surprises, Ted," he commented as he stopped the car by his house, then held out a small box. "I'd like you to have this, a souvenir from today."

Ted popped open the top, the contents causing him to stop right in the middle of his thank-you. It was the bull-and-bear tie clip he had been admiring at the store. Everything he had been taught about a situation like this told him he should make at least one halfhearted attempt to hand it back, but that wasn't going to happen.

"Don't wear it to school," Walter instructed.

"Yeah, I could lose it."

"True, but that isn't the reason. Your friends don't have tie clips like that. I learned the hard way that you should never do anything that makes your friends jealous."

"This is too much already, but I'm going to ask, do you have any last advice for me?"

"Yes," Walter responded, "I hope you see how amazing you are. You need to look in the mirror more."

Ted nodded, wishing there was some kind of container that would allow him to scoop up and take with him a helping of the wisdom this man seemed to have. Once inside he took the advice and ran to the half mirror in the hall. He looked himself over trying to see what Walter had been talking about.

"How did it go, Teddy?" his mother inquired. "Did you get to see Walter at all?"

"Mom! He drove us there himself. I got to talk with him and everything! He canceled his whole schedule to spend the day with me. Can you believe that? With me!"

Ensnared

It was an impatient crowd, the pushing barely contained. The fanfare surrounding the upcoming altar boy assignments hung as usual outside the principal's office, but the excitement was unprecedented. It was the mass of the century. The century and a half to be more precise. It was to celebrate the 150th anniversary of the parish and was to be the grandest of spectacles. Set midday during school hours, it eclipsed in importance any of the upcoming previously over the top Easter mass assignments. All the boys desperately wanted to be chosen, but all left disappointed. To avoid fighting and jealousy, the four lucky assignees were told privately.

The draw for the boys was twofold. The press would be there and that offered a remote possibility of having their picture in the paper. But the real opportunity was to show off to every girl in their class. Only the best of the best altar boys was selected for this special mass which is why Ted received what all of the others wanted.

The extent of the display in the church was extreme. Floral arrangements adorned all areas and crept up the walls. The entrance to every pew had a white bow and the lectern was draped in purple bunting. A red carpet lay the entire length of the center aisle. There was a section cordoned off for local dignitaries and honored guests. A reporter from the local paper, complete with cameraman, was already stationed to the side of the altar.

The altar boys were supposed to arrive a half hour early, but at such a time Ted found himself alone. He scrambled to get everything in place. At ten minutes to the hour, they still hadn't shown. The priest had a request as he joined Ted in the back, waiting for all the classes to assemble. The Archdiocese was phoning in a special message from the Archbishop of New York, His Eminence Cardinal Terence Cooke, to be read during the mass.

"What an honor it is to read the holy words sent to us by this great man," the priest reflected somewhat rhetorically, while Ted was instructed to hurry down to the principal's office to retrieve it.

"Eight minutes," he shouted to Ted nervously as he tapped his watch to emphasize the need to rush.

Looking at the pews, only the first few grades had assembled. There is no way this mass was starting on time, but he hurried anyway. Sister Howard was jotting the last words just as he arrived. She carefully folded it, put it in an envelope and sealed it, as if Ted would care to read it and if he did, it might somehow diminish its holiness. She made a sign of the cross and handed it to him.

"This is the holy word of God, and you have the privilege of being His messenger."

Ted barely refrained from saying the words, "Give me a break."

Heading back to the church brought him past a stairway where the students from his grade were assembled one floor above. He could hear girls talking. Slowing, then stopping, he looked up the stairwell to see if he could get a peek up any of their skirts. No one was in sight, but he could clearly overhear one of the conversations. They were playing that game where they try to describe someone using one word, only this time applying it to boys in their class. Ted stood spellbound as he eavesdropped.

There was no time for this, but he reasoned that as long as the class wasn't in church the mass would not start. Regardless, God would have to wait, nothing was going to pry him from listening in on this exchange.

They had gone through two boys when Ashton's name came up. The words *Adonis*, *dreamy*, and *wonderful* were offered, with *Adonis* winning. Ciro was next. "Vulgar," "Obnoxious," "Eww, just Eww," the last girl said.

"I vote for Eww."

"Me too."

"All right, so Ciro is best described as Eww."

"How about Ted?"

A floor below there was a boy whose blood drained from his head. On tip toes, he strained to hear, afraid some noise, distraction or maybe even the detonation of a nuclear bomb nearby would, by fate, cause him to miss what they were about to say. He held his breath and made every effort to keep his heart from beating.

"Smart."

"Funny."

"Adorable."

"My vote is for adorable."

"He is absolutely adorable," one of the others confirmed.

"For Ted, it's adorable."

The adorable Ted jumped with an enthusiasm that almost took his head to the floor above. He ran full speed toward the church, his heart pounding, every few steps containing a leap.

Just as he was in full revel he came to a dead stop as it hit him, he had no idea which girls had said it. For a moment he toyed with the idea of going back but he was already five minutes late. He knew this would drive him crazy, but he resumed his dash to the church.

Coming in the back breathless, he handed the message to the priest then moved to the small side room to join the other altar boys, assuming they had showed. There was a moment of shock. Pure shock. The expression on his face mimicked someone driving at seventy-five miles per hour playing with the radio and looking up to see a brick wall ten feet in front of their car. Joy morphed into terror.

Demolished

"Hello, Theodore," Ciro chirped ominously, Steve standing next to him.

"Guys, don't do anything, okay?" he pleaded, still catching his breath.

"What's that supposed to mean?" Ciro grumbled.

"Who, moi?" Steve said, pointing at his chest.

"I'm insulted you'd think I'd do anything," Ciro added. "This day is for the glory of our Lord and Savior Jesus Christ."

The devious grin they wore was as foreboding as the specter of death.

"I thought we were four. Where's the other guy?"

"We had a talk. He agreed we didn't need him," Ciro explained.

Lightheaded, feeling like a man about to be strapped into an electric chair, Ted sighed. There was no time to protest. The signal was given, and Ted hoisted a crucifix set at the end of a pole high into the air. Ted at point, Ciro and Steve in tow, and the priest behind holding an ornate Bible high above his head walked the red carpet down the center aisle. Ted genuflected and moved left to sit behind the priest. Ciro and Steve went right to take seats on the opposite side.

Most of the work fell on the altar boys behind the priest, which for this mass was just himself. All the other two had to do was sit, stand, and kneel at the appropriate moments, then prepare for communion in the sacristy during the Gospel reading.

A lot was running through the young man's mind. A bit was on his responsibilities. More was spent wondering what these two delinquents facing him were up to. By far, though, his primary focus was staring out into the congregation trying to figure out which of the girls had said he was adorable.

His partners sat throughout the first two readings, whispering to each other and looking him over like cats eyeing a canary. An increasing nausea filled Ted's stomach. Repeatedly, he wiped the sweat from his brow and then, before they had done anything, started with the giggle he couldn't control whenever nervous.

At the appropriate moment, Ciro and Steve got up, bowed most respectfully, and exited into the sacristy to prepare for communion. Now the only people up on the altar were the priest and Ted.

The choir in the balcony belted out all verses from "Hallelujah," accompanied by the pipe organ's overwhelming blast. Cameras clicked incessantly from photographers, public and private. The church, massive as it was, had every seat filled and people standing in the back.

The priest went through the Gospel without a peep from the two predators in the sacristy. It was when the homily began that the door opened.

Standing back about five feet, far enough so it was only Ted who could see, Ciro put his hand to his lips and began blowing kisses. Behind him was Steve in the background doing some strange amateur version of a hula dance. Ted knew he should look away, but curiosity forced him to keep his eyes fixed on the scene.

Steve moved up and pressed against Ciro's back, reached around, and started massaging Ciro's breasts. No longer in control, Ted threw his hand up to his mouth to keep from bellowing. The door quietly closed. A muffled cackle now emanated from the altar as the priest spoke of the beauty contained in today's reading. Hearing the giggling and supremely annoyed, he turned to succinctly admonish Ted.

"Knock it off," he scolded, then added. "You need to leave?"

"No, Father," Ted mouthed back silently.

That took enough wind from his sails to stop. Ciro had gotten him good, and this was bad. The priest would tell Father Tom. Given it was such a significant mass it wasn't beyond comprehension it could be his last. He'd have to formulate some excuse as ratting out his tormentors simply wasn't an option.

Attack over his eyes scanned the girls from his class and he studied every face. He looked for some telling sign for the girls who had the conversation about him.

The sacristy door opened once again. Peeled back by Steve, who remained out of view, Ciro was in the center of the room. He was staggering around with a half-full wine bottle pretending to be drunk. Lifting the bottle, he took a slug, deliberately allowing a burst to gush across his face. Steve then appeared from the side, playing into the act as if trying to keep him upright while Ciro pretended to vomit on him.

Ted covered his eyes but made the mistake, as would most, of peeking. One look and he started to lose it again, this time far worse. Pushing back at laughter is like trying to hold back the cork in a shaken bottle of champagne, it becomes explosive! Ciro was just warming up.

Meanwhile the priest continued, "I have something wonderful to share. His Eminence Cardinal Cooke has sent us a special and most blessed message for this occasion." Now realizing it was sealed, he began to pull at the envelope and mused, "I feel like I'm opening a prize."

That was met by the muffled sympathetic laughter one finds exclusively in a church. Behind him Ted began to cackle. For a moment those in the church thought it was an exaggerated response to the priest's pitiful attempt at humor.

Ted would later recall the priest never got past the first few words of the cardinal's letter. "It is with great joy...."

In the sacristy, Ciro, still acting drunk, lifted his cassock to reveal that except for shoes and socks, he had removed all other clothing, then turned around and bent over. Ted was facing a full moon. Right there in the middle of this most glorious celebration, unseen by all but their victim, there was a big red smiley face drawn on Ciro's rear end, complete with rosy cheeks and a buck tooth smile.

Ted began laughing so hard he was having trouble breathing. Ciro was by no means finished.

If being demented was a subject at school Ciro would have earned an A+. How he ever managed to stuff his boy parts into a half-full bottle of wine and get it to hang there is known only to himself, Steve, and God.

Setting the moon, he stood straight, turned around with cassock still raised he revealed the bottle of wine dangling between his legs. He began swinging his hips to make it smack against his thighs. It was the most bizarre site witnessed in a church in two thousand years of Christianity.

Ted was past the point of no return. Like staring into an atomic explosion, he could close his eyes, but the image remained burned into his brain. He burst into a full belly laugh, loud enough to bring everything to a halt. His attempts at stopping only resulted in wheezing that made him sound like a goose being strangled.

Nine hundred souls, all silent, focused in disbelief at Ted, his bellows amplified by the church's echo effect. The priest shot a look of rage unbecoming a man of the cloth while Ted pulled his cassock's sleeves to hide his face and attempt to stand.

Just then the bottle hanging between Ciro's legs slipped off and crashed to the floor. The sound of shattering glass only momentarily distracted the audience from Ted to the door of the sacristy. The two clowns inside panicked, their eyes bulging as it happened. Steve ran to close the door, running into Ciro, causing him to step on a piece of glass and, with arms flailing desperately, fall into a puddle of wine.

Despite water filling his eyes, Ted witnessed the entire thing. His knees gave out, and he doubled over howling.

"This is unbelievable," Rip whispered to Itch. "He's turning purple, I can see the veins in his neck from here."

"When his head explodes, it's going to make a mess of the altar," Itch replied. "Too bad we didn't have a chance to say goodbye."

With considerable effort, Ted fought to get back to his feet. Blinded by tears he groped around the altar like a man on fire, searching for the way out. Aiming toward the side room that led outside, he bounced off the doorframe in his first attempt. He passed through on the next try, threw off his robes, blasted out the side door, down a small flight of stairs and face planted into the finely manicured lawn to the side of the church.

Incredibly, the hundreds of chatterboxes they called students made not a sound. Mass on hold, everyone could still hear Ted hysterically laughing from outside through the stained glass windows.

Two teachers retrieved the wreck and practically needed a wheelbarrow to transport him to the principal's office. There he sat with his face hung toward the floor and dared not look up. Every time he did, he started giggling in spasms again. The nuns, who soon filled the office, were not amused.

"You are an abomination! How do you look at yourself in the mirror? How do you hold yourself in front of God?" Sister Bethany scolded.

"He should be ashamed of himself, but he sits here laughing! Obviously, he doesn't take any of this seriously," someone else added.

"This is what happens when we accept a bastard into our school," Sister Howard proclaimed in a voice a bit more pronounced than the rest.

That comment did for him what thus far he had been unable to accomplish. Any trace of a smile dropped from his face as the words spread their poison. He closed his eyes and wished he could do the same with his ears as he waited for his mother to retrieve him.

Minutes later she burst into the room, wildly slapping Ted's head. It was Sister Bethany who moved between them to put an end to the assault. They disappeared into the secret, forbidden office on the side.

The look on his mom's face when she emerged made words unnecessary.

"I'm sorry," he whispered to the nuns as he left.

"We will pray for you," Sister Bethany responded.

Ted knew it was especially bad when his mother, infamous for yelling at everything, sat next to him in silence without starting the car. She just stared at him derisively, fishing for words that would cut him the deepest. She found them.

"I can understand now why your mother didn't want you."

He emptied his lungs, slumped in the seat, and stared at the floor. Emotionally he had just hit the bottom of the Marianas trench.

"They are having a meeting tomorrow," she said in the calmest voice he ever heard from her. "Sister Bethany said they are going to talk about throwing you out. I hope they do so we can stop wasting all this on you."

While it might seem harsh, Ted wasn't surprised. This was a strict Catholic school and he'd seen kids expelled for less. The meeting the next day was among the trustees. His fate would not be determined then, but it would go a long way toward starting the process.

Once home his mother didn't lace into him. She said nothing and he went to his room to sit on his bed and stare at the wall. Then he heard the phone ring. He didn't think it possible but when he overheard who it was his heart sank even further.

Mrs. Burke had been in the church and witnessed the entire debacle. She was calling to see if Ted was okay. His mom did nothing to defend him, just barked on and on about the possibility of him being expelled and how much he deserved it. Ted closed his watery eyes and laid flat on his bed, wishing it would swallow him up and never allow him to see the light of day again.

His mind grappled with so many issues. Would he ever return to school? Was his career in the Catholic Church over? Would Mr. Burke realize just how wrong his assessment of him had been? What were all the kids saying about him? Concerning above all else were the three girls, whoever they are, that most likely no longer considered him adorable.

Prejudged

The trustees met at noon the next day. After formalities, accepting the prior meeting's minutes they moved to the agenda. Ted was the first item. Sister Bethany was the only one in the room who would have been able to pick him out in a crowd. Their knowledge of Ted was limited to hearsay of the incident and what was in his file.

There was a rehash of the event which was mostly accurate as concerned Ted but incomplete as far as the actual circumstances. Ciro and Steve did not even receive so much as a cameo.

True to any politicized environment, there was brisk competition to demonstrate which of them was the most appalled. Following the bulldoze of politically correct statements, they turned to his school records. The Vice Chairman made the first comment before they all piled on.

"We have first graders who can't count as high as the number of detentions he has had."

"There is no place for him here."

"We can't allow the others to think they can get away with this. We need to make an example."

"One bad apple spoils the bunch."

"Sister?" The secretary from the office interrupted sheepishly opening the door. "Walter Burke is on the phone."

"Tell him I'm in a meeting. Can I call him back?"

"He said it's urgent, he's calling from Asia."

The room fell silent. A philanthropist of his magnitude is not put off, especially when calling from halfway around the world. Sister Bethany excused herself to take the call as the rest speculated what could be so important.

After a greeting that was polite but brief, Walter communicated the reason for the call succinctly.

"My wife was in the church, and I think I have been adequately appraised of the situation. I've had the opportunity to get to know Ted. I can personally vouch for his character. My guess is you don't have all the facts. Even if you do, kids make mistakes at thirteen. You need to consider that. I know you're talking about expelling him or suspending him or whatever it is you're trying to decide. I'm calling because I won't sit idle while this extraordinary young man gets railroaded by some kangaroo court you've put together. I'm not telling you what to do, but my advice is to avoid taking this one step further."

The look on Sister Bethany's face as she rejoined the meeting communicated the conversation in advance of her words.

"For whatever reason Walter is putting his full support behind Ted. We can be as appalled as we want but let's be honest, we already know what we'll decide."

The phone rang in Ted's home that afternoon with the unexpected news that he could return to school on Monday. His mother inquired about further punishment, but Sister Bethany deliberately cut the conversation short, only adding that Father Tom canceled his mass schedule. He would meet with him Monday afternoon after school to discuss what happened.

Relieved to be going back to school, Ted still sat with his face in his hands worried about being thrown out of the altar boys wondering how he could possibly endure such a disgrace.

Anticipation

The schoolyard wasn't easy to tolerate that Monday morning, being the first time anyone from his class had seen him since the incident. He tucked himself in with his three friends but could hear laughter aimed at him from multiple directions.

Itch shook his head, lamenting in sympathy. "Man, that was so bad I'm going to lay off making fun of you today."

Just then Ted saw Ciro approaching, apparently wanting to seize the opportunity to do a victory dance on his head.

"I demolished you! Deemolished!" Ciro said, gloating amidst three of his cronies.

"I so freaking got you!"

Ted was in no mood and willing to take the chance Ciro might beat him up.

"Yeah, you got me to laugh. You know what I was laughing at Ciro? You really want to know?" Ted held up his thumb and index finger, spread a half inch apart. "I was laughing at the fact you were able to get your thing in a bottle opening that small."

"Ohhhhh!" one of his cronies chortled as he punched Ciro in the arm. "Looks like he got you."

"And to think there was still enough room for it to fall off!" Ted added, accelerating the deflation of his victory gloat.

Hearing more than enough he turned to leave but Ted shouted after him.

"Tell me something, Ciro? How is it someone with such a small wiener can be such a big dick?"

With Ciro now off his back, his real dread was for the meeting he had with Father Tom at the end of the day.

It all seemed to be coming to a head as he entered the principal's office to await his fate. He bounced both legs nervously and gripped the arms of the chair as if he might somehow fall out. Sister Bethany remained silent but held an expression as though she wanted to throw her cup of coffee into his face.

He thought the worst part was the anticipation, but that turned out untrue. As Father Tom entered, he could feel bile rise into his throat before settling back, leaving behind a burning sensation. His fate had just walked through the door.

Confession

"You may have supporters in high places, but you should know my connections go far higher," Father Tom proclaimed. Having no clue of the Burke conversation, Ted didn't understand. "We will do this in the rectory."

Walking across the street to a separate building, they settled into a small sparsely decorated room several minutes later, its main feature being two chairs facing each other. It eerily reminded him of the place where he planned to meet himself when he turned fifty.

"Ted," Father Tom began, "I've always been a big supporter of yours but you're making it difficult. You need to explain what happened."

Ted shook his head. "I don't think I can."

"Listen, Ted, I don't know if I want to smack you or throw you out the window. This is your one chance to tell me your side."

"I'm sorry I've disappointed you. I'm sorry to God. I'm sorry about the whole thing. I'm sorry I ever became an altar boy," Ted stated, as somber as though he were at a funeral.

"Why did you become an altar boy?"

"I wanted to serve God." Ted said, providing a coined answer.

"No, seriously, why did you join?"

He was surprised Father Tom rejected it. What was he supposed to say? He thought, then volunteered what he thought had been the reason.

"I suppose it isn't that. I have plans you see. Being an altar boy, well, that's the first part of the plan. At least, it was."

"And what are these plans?"

"The plan is to become a priest. But that's not the only part. You see, I'll rise in the church and one day, well, I thought maybe I could become pope."

"And why would you want that?"

"What do you mean? I'd be the most powerful person in the world. I'd have fame, fortune, everything I could ever want. Everyone would have to show me respect. If they didn't, I could destroy them."

"So, what you are telling me is by becoming pope you can have lots of respect, money and power."

"Yeah," Ted confirmed with a deep almost devious tone.

"For yourself. You want to obtain the holiest position so you can have all these things for yourself. Is that right?"

The glimmer of enthusiasm faded from his eyes. He slumped back into the chair.

"Well, Ted, there are a lot of reasons I can give you why you will never become pope, but you just gave me a great reason why you should never be pope."

Ted released a breath to empty his lungs and refrained from refilling them as long as he could. The sheer embarrassment from his display of selfishness overwhelmed him.

Barely able to conjure the energy to say the words, he admitted something out loud he always knew.

"Father, I know I'm never going to be pope, I've always known it. But sometimes I create dreams in my head just to get by. It's stupid, but I think I can tell you now why I became an altar boy." It was the first time he consciously processed it.

"Okay, do tell."

Ashamed, surrender in his tone, he confessed as if it were a crime.

"It's something all the cool kids do, and I was hoping it would make me a little more popular. And I thought maybe it would be a way to get noticed by girls."

"Now that I can believe. That said, how about you tell me what happened on Thursday."

"Father, the other kids will hang me."

"Well, you need to tell me."

Remembering the sanctity of confession, an idea flashed into his mind. He made the sign of the cross.

"Bless me, Father, for I have sinned. I'd like to confess everything."

"So, you are ready to tell me now?"

"I'm asking for confession please. I want to tell God."

"Okay, you know how to begin."

He stated how long it had been since his last confession, then confirmed the most important part. "This has to stay between you and me? Right?"

"And God."

"Yeah, of course, God. Okay. Well, I was so excited to do this mass, but I didn't know you also assigned Ciro and Steve."

"The best altar boys I have."

"Serious? Are you serious!?! The only reason Steve isn't the greatest jackass to ever put on a cassock is because Ciro has such a firm grip on the title. Those two dirtbags always act so respectful when they're being watched but put them out of sight and I'm telling you, Ciro is just like his dad except he's not in jail. Yet."

Father Tom wondered if and how his perception could be so off. But Ted spared no detail. As horrifying as the story was, Father Tom had trouble fighting back a few chuckles as he described what took place in vivid detail.

"Is that everything?" Father Tom asked as the story concluded up to the events in the principal's office.

"No, Father, it isn't. I have left out the most important part. I told you why I became an altar boy, but I haven't told you why I continued being one. I have come to realize many things about myself. I'm not smart or creative or athletic. I can't play an instrument, sing or draw. I have no coordination. I've never won an award or a trophy, for anything. I've racked my brain to identify a single talent that I have. My grades aren't good, and I used to tell myself it was because I didn't try, but that is just another lie. No matter how you look at me there is nothing special about me. There really is no reason I can tell for me to exist. I'm like a piece of dust."

"But being an altar boy, this was the one thing I wanted to do better than anyone. It meant everything to me to be the best you ever had. I put my entire heart and soul into it. What happened in the church Thursday was me trying to do my absolute best. What it proves is that no matter how hard I try, no matter how much I put into something, I will always amount to nothing."

"My sin, Father? I'll tell you what it is. I ruined what was the most important mass in the school's history. I let you down and made a fool of everyone who's ever stood up for me. I'm sorry about it all, but you know what's so messed up about me? The thing that bothers me most, and it just won't leave my head, is how I made a complete idiot of myself in front of all the girls. I know that's not what you want to hear, but it's the truth."

"When my mother, I'm adopted if you didn't know. When my adoptive mother heard about this, she said she understood why my birthmother didn't want me. It's not that she didn't want me. She was just smart. She knew to get as far away from me as she could the day I was born. You asked me for the truth father and I'm going to give it to you. The world would be a better place if she had gone and had an abortion."

Father Tom tried to refrain from interrupting this pouring of his heart but couldn't let that stand. "Don't you *ever* say anything like that again."

Ted shook his head reflectively and closed his eyes. When they opened, they were watery and held a look as though pleading.

"God never answers my prayers, but if I could get him to do one thing for me, just one, it would be to make me into anyone other than who I am."

Father Tom's expression became pained as he lowered his head onto one hand leading to a silence that settled into the room for an uncomfortably long time. Ted readied himself to leave with the quiet still undisturbed, but as he began to rise Father Tom motioned with a finger for him to sit back down.

"How do you think Jesus would respond if you said to him everything you just told me?"

"He would punish me."

"No Ted, absolutely not. Jesus, the Son of God, would summon all his power to show you how much He loves you. All your imperfections, all the mistakes you have ever made, everything about you, He loves you.

"I don't know what you think you need to be or what you are hoping one day to become, but Jesus isn't waiting for that day. He loves you right now just the way you are. But I'll tell you this, no one, not even God can love the person you are not. It has to be you. The real you, and you don't have to be anything more.

"Now for your penance, Ted, I want you to think about what I just said. Really take some time and try to understand it.

"I now absolve you of your sins in the name of the Father, Son and Holy Ghost. Give thanks to the Lord for He is good."

"For His mercy endures forever," Ted responded with the standard reply.

Following a sign of the cross he stood, not knowing and too afraid to ask as to his status as an altar boy.

"So how was your day? Was there any trouble? How did the meeting go with Father Tom?" His mother inquired as he walked through the door.

He was close to saying "Fine," but a different thought rolled reflectively from his tongue. "Some days are better than others and when it's happening you can never know for sure which is which."

The new altar boy schedule was hanging in the hall next to the principal's office the next day. Since Easter was the following week, all hoped for masses with the highest attendance, Good Friday 3:00 p.m., Holy Saturday 8:00 p.m., and greatest of all, noon Easter Sunday. Ted could not conjure enough nerve to look while anyone else was there. The embarrassment of no longer being part of the roster was too much to bear in front of others.

Waiting until the afternoon, then using the excuse of needing to go to the bathroom, Ted left his class and sneaked downstairs. With the hallway empty he decided to go for it. Scanning the morning slots his heart sank, noting the absence of his name. There was relief at least in knowing. He hung his head, closed his eyes, and took the moment necessary to accept Father Tom's decision.

He looked up again to see who was given those most coveted slots. Stunned, it was far more than he could believe. There it was, his name assigned not to one, but all three. So unbelievably placed, he hadn't bothered looking there on his first inspection. Becoming choked up he offered a prayer and reflected with a chest filled with gratitude for the faith Father Tom was showing toward him.

He looked back up to see if there was anything he missed and only then noticed just how many of the detested 7:00 a.m. masses had been assigned to Ciro and Steve. Returning to class he pushed back against a smile that refused to leave his face. That was until he began to stare at the dark hair covering Ciro's head, sitting two desks forward.

There were great life lessons to be had from this experience but that wasn't his focus. Perhaps he should have been working on the penance Father Tom had assigned but he wasn't considering it. He wasn't thinking of schoolwork, or altar service, or amazingly, even girls. The look on his face became hard as stone, eyes cold as ice, taking on a psychotic glow. Every thought flowing through his mind, every cell in his body, every fiber of his being now focused on one thing only. Revenge.

Carnival

Easter Sunday, capped off by Ted's flawless altar boy performances, the very definition of perfection, was also the unofficial beginning of spring. The weather was beginning to change, ushering in April and with it the early hints of the upcoming summer vacation. It was close enough, but too early to start thinking about obsessively.

Traditionally, it also kicked off the annual fundraiser. A project run by Mrs. Butterman and assigned to the seventh grade; it provided free labor under the premise of building leadership skills.

Billed as food, fun and games for the entire parish, it was a hodgepodge of different ways for the school to raise money. Bean bag tosses, silent auctions, lotteries, darts, hoops, hot dogs, and popcorn, typical take for a successful night was $2,500. While participation was mandatory, Ted of course was plotting his way to get out of doing any of it.

"I'm an idea creator for the event," he boasted to Itch, "I've got an idea for a great game. It will raise hundreds of dollars. You see, I will tell Butterman my idea and that will be my contribution, voila! I'm done."

"You see no flaw in this plan?" Itch shot back skeptically.

"Watch and learn my friend, watch and learn."

Ted did have a good idea. His suggestion was to set up a strength tester. He explained it to Mrs. Butterman in grand fashion how a rubber hammer is used on a lever to drive a small puck up to ring a large bell on top. Every carnival has one.

Mrs. Butterman loved the idea. The part he didn't expect was when she insisted that now he go and build it. Saddled with this new task he returned sulking to Itch.

"Did she go for it?" he asked impatiently.

"She loved it. Then she told me to put it together. I'm supposed to build it."

"Build it? You can't nail two pieces of wood together."

"She said she expected me to rise to the challenge, I am completely screwed."

"Okay, let me get this right. You seriously did not see this coming? Oh my God, you are stupid!"

"Wait!" he exclaimed, snapping his finger, "I'll bet Frank and his dad could help me put this together. Hey, Frank!" he called from two rows over.

It turned out Frank was in a quandary about what to contribute and was happy to jump on it.

"Come over Saturday early, maybe, say, eight thirty. We'll get it done in one shot. This is going to be a blast!"

Ted loved his enthusiasm but unfortunately shared little of it. His usual Saturday morning activity was sleeping late, and this was no exception. Showing at Frank's house three hours into the project, it was already nearing completion. All that was needed was for it to be painted. Frank and his dad were going inside for a break.

"Let me at least start painting it," Ted insisted, too embarrassed to take the break with them.

That was a mistake.

"What the hell are you doing? It's ruined! It looks like a zebra laid down and died on it," Frank exclaimed.

Ted stood back and had to agree.

"I thought the black-and-white stripes would look different."

"What is that glob in the middle supposed to be?"

"It was a rainbow. The colors got mixed."

"All right let's not panic," his dad said, before determining what to do. "Just let it dry, then we'll sand it and start over. That's all. No harm. Nice try, Ted. I know you were just trying to go for that carnival look."

Staircase

With much on his mind, Ted once again forgot to bring lunch money for Tom to extort. Usually met with a punch rather than the blank look this time, Ted wondered what might be going on.

As was more often the case Ted was staying after school for detention. His transgression this time was unintentional. What landed him in hot water was a discussion regarding the pope.

"If you could ask the pope anything, what would it be?" This question was floated to all the students.

Ted's answer was sincere but abysmally worded and taken as blasphemous.

"I would ask him how many starving people could be fed if he sold all the rings he had on his fingers."

That answer earned him a full week.

Finishing up an hour past dismissal, alone, standing atop one of the stairwells fumbling to get the zipper of his coat closed there was a sudden shove from behind. He flew clean over the first two steps before reflexively grabbing the banister. He swung entirely around, falling headfirst and backward down the stairs, coming to rest in a twisted pile two stairs above the mid landing. The book bag strapped to his back was the only thing that prevented serious injury.

"Forget again and I'll kill you!" he heard from above recognizing Tom's voice.

Heart pounding, he waited without moving as if being still might somehow keep Tom from seeing him. A full minute passed. Slowly he started to wiggle a finger here, move a leg there, assessing if anything might be broken. His wrist bothered him most.

Already swelling and in pain he hoped for the best and headed for Rip's house.

In the basement with Rip, they chatted about Tom's reign of terror. Isabel came down with her usual pitcher of water and latched onto Ted to find out what had happened.

"You're hurt! Let me see," she exclaimed, grabbing his hand.

She gently squeezed his wrist and palm, then worked her way up each of his fingers. While a bit of what she did hurt the sensation of her squeezing his hand and fingers was so incredibly pleasant he wished he'd said both hands had been injured.

"Nope, don't think it's broken," she declared, as though she had x-ray eyes before darting upstairs.

She returned with a pot filled with ice water to submerge his wrist.

"I should have thought of that," Rip commented.

"Well, you aren't going to be the fabulous nurse she is going to be one day," Ted replied, aware becoming a nurse was Isabel's dream.

"Well, yeah, I'm okay at it, I guess. It's just common sense really. Soak it, if all the ice melts let me know and I'll get more."

She then turned and ran up the stairs.

The cold water felt good, and Ted leaned back attempting to calm down.

"You know Rip, I don't know why I'm doing this. I'm supposed to be getting stronger but Tom is always going to be able to beat me up."

"I couldn't take him either, remember, and he's bigger now. He isn't right in the head. Seriously, there's something wrong with him, but don't let it get to you. If you quit, he wins."

"And if he kills me, he wins too, I'm so depressed."

"Don't be. You have many great things going on."

"Like what? Bad grades, no girls, no friends."

"No friends? What am I supposed to be?"

"I meant like being popular."

"Would you trade me for being popular? And there are girls into you."

"Yeah, right."

"I'm serious. The other day when we were playing shirts versus skins, I swear to you there were a bunch of girls watching you take your shirt off."

"I didn't see it."

"Of course you didn't, guys stare and drool. Girls take peeks. They're like leprechauns. They never let you see them. It was obvious from my angle of view."

"That is such bull, name one girl who likes me."

Rip sat stone faced, eyes piercing through Ted. He had at least one obvious answer. It was just one he didn't want to give.

"See, you can't even name one."

"My sister," he blurted, "my sister likes you."

"Who, Isabel?"

"You don't think so? That pitcher of water she brings down for us every day, you think she's doing that for me?"

"Just thought she was being nice."

"My sister is the biggest pain in the ass, but I'm telling you, whenever you are around, she gets all goofy. But just don't go out with her, please. It would be weird. There are plenty of other girls you can get."

"I won't. Besides she's only in fifth."

"Yeah, but she'll get older, and one day..."

"I won't. I'm still depressed, though."

"All right, I was saving this for just such an occasion, I'm going to make you laugh."

"I doubt that."

"No, I will. I have a confession to make. You know how I told you I got my nickname Rip?"

"Yeah, it was your street gang, because of all the people you killed."

"Well, I kind of exaggerated that. I used to tag around with a street gang when I was eight, but I was more like their mascot than a member. The reason they called me Rip? Well, it's because I used to fart a lot."

Ted went into hysterics.

"It's not that funny. If you ever tell anyone..."

"I won't. I promise. But it is funny."

"Let's call it a day. Take care of your wrist. Maybe you should get it checked out, my sister is not exactly a doctor."

A trip to the hospital, this time nothing was broken. Some ice, rest, he would be fine. Ted told his mom he fell on his way home because of an untied shoelace. It all seemed better until he tried to go to sleep. Worried about Tom, nothing could get his eyes to stay shut or his heart rate to slow.

Then he thought of a conversation he and Mr. Maze had during one of their sessions.

Mr. Maze had told him whenever he was feeling anxious, he'd feel better if he wrote down his problems. It was worth a try. At his desk under the faint light of a small headlamp, he began writing.

I'm failing social studies.

Tom pushed me down the stairs.

Butterman hates me and I'm going to summer school.

I won't get into the same high school with my friends.

Tom is going to beat me up.

Tom is going to kill me.

Tom is going to throw me down the stairs again.

I'm a dead man.

He folded the paper and tucked it deep in his drawer under an old coloring book.

Returning to bed, he put one hand on his chest to feel if maybe his heart rate had slowed. Then he remembered another piece of advice. If you can't stop worrying about your life, think about ways you can help others. Ted decided to try this too. His mind drifted from person to person before settling upon Anna.

As he fell asleep, his mind launched into high gear.

Phoenix

That's it! It's brilliant! he thought as his eyes flew open just a few minutes before his alarm would have awoken him anyway. Rising from bed like a phoenix, throwing on his clothes, thoughts of Tom were banished. All he could do was pace while shoveling down breakfast, planning the execution of his idea which seemed so simple. He would serve mass and when he hung his cassock in the classroom after, he'd confirm his theory.

Arriving at Anna's desk he looked for that special notebook. To his surprise he found several tucked at the bottom of the cubbyhole. He planned a quick peek, but it fell apart when he opened it.

On the first page was an image of a girl in their class, brilliantly drawn, and yet with the hair restyled. Turning the page there was a different girl, than another. She made each of them beautiful, gently restyling their hair, omitting anything that might detract from their radiance.

The next page was poetic. There she was standing under a rainbow, hearts fluttering around, holding hands with Ashton. Every girl in the class had a crush on him, why would she be different?

The page after took his breath away. It was the kind where one hesitates to exhale for fear of contaminating the work of art. The sketch, spread over two pages, was from a basketball game, several of the boys in a run. The action was palpable, the strain on their faces clear, as one of them moved to make a shot.

"*How dare you!*" Anna screamed, causing Ted to jump and throw the book into the air. "I'm getting Mrs. Butterman."

Ted had forgotten she came in early on Tuesdays for extra help. Anna stormed from the room while Ted retrieved the notebook and opened it to the basketball scene. The only thing left to do was wait and wonder how many detentions this would cost him.

Butterman was yelling the moment she set foot in the room, Anna trailing behind. He weathered it like a ship facing a giant wave and waited for her to take a breath so he could counter.

"You don't understand, look at this! Anna is amazing! These pictures are incredible!"

"Did you go into her things?"

"Look at this picture! Look at these!" he said now turning the page to others.

"We have our own Rembrandt! This is what you do, set up a booth at the fair and have Anna do sketches of people. Put them in a frame, you'll make a fortune!"

"So, you went into her personal things, without permission?"

"Anna is amazing! Anna is beyond amazing!"

"Wait," Anna interrupted. "I think there was a misunderstanding. I told Ted awhile back he could look. I didn't mean by himself, but I could see how he got confused. I totally forgot."

Anna's entire statement, end to end, was false.

"Is that what happened, Ted?" Rita asked.

"Yeah, Anna said I could. Mrs. Butterman, she is the most amazing person ever. You have to let her do the booth. She will blow the entire fair away."

"That's up to Anna. We'll talk about this later. Both of you finish up in here and get going."

"I'm sorry about that," Anna began as soon as Mrs. Butterman left. "When I saw you looking in my notebook I freaked. You really think my drawings are amazing?"

"No, you misunderstood. Your drawings are incredible, they really are, but *amazing* was the word I was using to describe you."

"Why do you keep saying these things about me? I'm not special."

"Anna, now that I looked, I see it more than ever. There are pictures of girls in that book, girls who have tortured you for years. They made every day of your life here miserable. If it were me, I'd put horns on their heads, but you draw them as if they were Goddesses, how can you do that with people who have been so mean to you?"

"Well, it's easy. There is good in everyone. That is the only part I look to see and the only part I draw."

Ted threw his hands to his face wishing words would come. In his head the only thought that crossed his mind was "What am I supposed to say that would have any meaning to a being so superior to all of us here?"

"You have to do it! Do the fair! Set up a booth and draw people. Show the world who you are! Anna you're going to blow them away!"

"Oh no. No, I can't do that. No. No."

"Anna!" he shouted as he lunged toward her. "You can never accomplish anything great until you let go of your fear!"

With that he placed both hands on her shoulders and gave her a shake. A look of repulsive horror filled her face and she took her hands to peel off his as though they were a pair of tarantulas. She shuddered and stepped back.

"You are not allowed to touch me without permission!" she shouted then ran from the room.

"I'm sorry Anna, what did I do?" He called after her. "What did I do?" he said again, this time to the empty room.

Alarm

Ted's mother was pacing by the front door as he came home from school.

"What is this?" she demanded, holding up the piece of paper with his notes on it from the night before.

"Tom is going to kill you?"

How the hell did she find that? he thought in panic. *That woman must go through my stuff top to bottom every damn day.*

"Oh, it's nothing," he replied in a futile attempt to downplay it.

"It wasn't a shoelace! He pushed you down the stairs! He's going to kill you! We have a meeting in the school office with Tom and his father at 8:00 a.m. tomorrow."

"Oh! My! God! Please tell me you didn't do that."

"They want you to tell them what happened."

Ted looked at the clock. 8:00 a.m.. That gave him seventeen hours to figure out some plausible excuse to let Tom off the hook. Ultimately what he came up with wasn't convincing.

"It was an accident, he bumped into me, that's all." Ted contributed as he stood before the principal with his mom on one side and Tom and his seven-foot, one-inch mutant-sized former baseball coach on the other.

"Oh, so after it happened, he ran down the stairs to help you up and see if you were okay?" the principal retorted.

Ted's long hesitation as he tried to figure how to address that was the only answer she needed. All the adults in the room disappeared into her private office, leaving Tom and Ted alone.

"I tried Tom," Ted whispered. "Can you just forget this? Please. Can we be friends?"

"Ted is dead. Ted is dead. Ted is dead." Tom grumbled.

When they emerged from the room the principal was adamant as she shook a finger at Tom. It wasn't the first time he had done things like this.

"Ten-day suspension. One more incident like this, one more, I don't care if you are a day away from graduation, we will expel you. Understand?"

"Tom isn't going to give anyone any trouble, I guarantee it," Mr. Chenko responded while gripping Tom tightly by the back of the neck.

Following the meeting Ted joined Itch in the schoolyard.

"Itch, I have two weeks to plan my funeral arrangements. That is when Tom is back." Ted said.

Itch was focused on something else.

"Hey, there's Tom and his father by the fence. He's waving. Our old coach. Let's go say hi."

When in range, Mr. Chenko pointed to Itch. "Just Ted," he barked.

"He probably wants to yell at you some more for blowing that series game the other year," Itch joked.

"I didn't blow it."

"You did nothing to help."

Ted figured, if he were lucky, Tom would wrap his hands around his throat and do it quickly.

"Ted, Tom has something he wants to say to you."

Tom sneered from over the fence separating them, like an ill fed caged animal at the zoo.

"Go ahead," Mr. Chenko prompted.

Tom said nothing.

From behind Mr. Chenko drew his arm far back. It was a surprise when he whacked Tom in the back of the head so hard his entire upper body lurched over the fence. Ted had never seen anyone take a hit like that. Half of him wanted to run in fear, the other to step forward and see if Tom was okay.

All he did was freeze in terror.

Tom slowly looked up and when he did, all the toughness had left his eyes. He spoke mechanically.

"I'm sorry, I'm not going to give you any trouble." He then turned to his father, face pale, voice trembling. "Was that okay?" he asked.

Mr. Chenko motioned for Ted to come close to the fence. With knees shaking, he obliged.

"Here, put this in your pocket. That's my phone number. I don't want to see Tom thrown out. If he gives you trouble, anything at all, you call me. You don't have to tell the school. Call me and I'll take care of it. What I'll do to Tom is far worse than anything they'll do to him here. You got it?"

Ted glanced at the number and memorized it.

"I got that dumb gorilla by his big ugly monkey balls," Ted boasted to his clutch later that day. "He's never going to bother me again."

"I wouldn't get cocky, Ted. He's got you in his crosshairs, and that can be fatal," Chuck countered.

Ted paid no mind, carelessly forgetting his own understanding of the Universe that Chuck was never wrong.

Imagery

The day of the fair Ted met Frank and his dad outside the school to carry in the strength meter together. Mrs. Butterman gushed over it.

"A plus," she said to Frank and Ted, even though it wasn't being graded. "I'm putting you right by the door. This is going to be a *hit*," she said, emphasizing the final word to make a pun that rolled the eyes of both boys.

"Leave it in the cafeteria and finish setting it up after school. Either of you have any problem staying after school?"

"I'm pretty used to it," Ted answered.

Following an uneventful day, made delightfully so by Tom's absence, Ted went down to the cafeteria to set up the booth. They finished and stepped back to admire their handiwork just when June came through the door struggling with a large box.

"Let me give her a hand," Ted said to Frank.

"You can't do that," Frank whispered to him, pulling him by the arm. "You can't just walk up to her."

"Why the heck not?" Ted scoffed.

"Why the heck not? Have you looked at her? She's gorgeous. You got to prepare for something like that."

Ted turned and looked at June. *Mr. Ed?* he thought, remembering the old nickname he had for her and having looked at her a hundred times and never changing his perception.

"I got this."

"Let me help you with that," he said, walking up and putting his hands under the opposite end of the box.

"Thanks," June responded, but thinking he was taking it altogether, let it go. Not expecting that, it crashed to the floor.

"Ah sh—" He stopped himself.

"I could have done that myself. Notice anything different by the way?" she said, flashing a broad smile toward him.

"Am I supposed to?"

"Got my braces off. What do you think?"

Ted stared at her face. A new image emerged and overtook the former.

Beautiful deep green eyes were looking into his, golden hair bouncing off her shoulders, a perfect smile. Frank had it right—she was gorgeous. His heart began to pound. Suddenly, it felt as though his tongue had swelled to twice its size. His mind veered off the road and crashed into a tree.

"It definitely doesn't look as bad," he fumbled in a confused response.

The smile dropped from her face.

"I think I can take it from here," she responded.

He returned to Frank with a groan. "I completely messed that up."

"Don't complain to me. By the way, did you break what was in the box, dumbass?"

"I don't know. Hey, June," he called over, "what was in the box? Did I break anything?"

"It's okay. It's just wooden parts for an easel."

Ted paused, considering what it implied.

"What booth are you doing?"

"Anna is going to sketch people. I'm going to do the frames."

It was proven that day that people's heads do not easily come off their shoulders.

"Yes! Yes! Yes!" He screamed as loud as his throat could fire, pumping both fists into the air.

He didn't care that everyone's attention was on him, and their conclusion was he had gone crazy. He grabbed Frank by the shoulders and shook him violently.

Dropping to his knees and throwing his face to the ceiling, raising both arms in victory, he cried, "Thank you! *Yes!*"

"What? What happened?" Frank asked.

"A miracle Frank, that's what is happening," he said shaking his fists and jumping up and down like a five-year-old. "I cannot wait until tonight!"

Frank, completely confused, was ready to leave anyway.

"We're done here. I still have to finish up that assignment. I might not be here right at seven."

Ted made the mistake of paying no mind to the comment. With all that was going on he'd forgotten another social studies project was due first thing the next day. It was scheduled the day after the fair to give them the challenge of multitasking. They had to select how a major historical issue was passed from one President to the next. He was one assignment away from getting a zero and a sentence to summer school.

Karma

Returning early, he paced, finding it all but impossible to sit still or keep his mind from wondering. His thoughts drifted across topics—Anna, Tom, Ciro, how the night might go, and then to something he hadn't thought of in a long time.

The fair had been well publicized. Everyone knew the seventh grade was hosting it. He thought it was a long shot, but maybe, just maybe, his birthmother would take this opportunity to see him and secretly show up. She would be discreet, but he was confident he could spot her. What child would not somehow recognize his own mother?

Those thoughts were interrupted as Anna and June arrived. They walked over to their booth, opposite Ted's, put down some more boxes before June hurried off to get more.

"So, Anna, *wow!* Here you are. All set?" He was so ecstatic, long sentences were beyond his capability.

"Yeah, I'm so nervous though. My hands are shaking. If I can't get them to stop, I don't know what I'm going to do."

"Why be nervous? You should do this for a living."

"Oh no, this is just a hobby. I want to be a beautician. I love to make people pretty."

"Well, you could do this instead if you wanted to. So, what are you charging?"

"Twenty, and more for the frames"

"Pretty steep, worth it though. Glad I got mine when they were free."

"Yours will always be free Ted."

"That's good to know. When they sell for millions, I'm going to take you up on it."

Anna looked down, almost blushing. "I know you're a big fan, you really think I'm that good?"

"Anna stop this, don't question yourself. Just be you and see what happens."

"Thanks, I kind of needed that. Look! My hands have stopped shaking!"

"Just in time, it's almost seven. I saw Butterman walk in," Ted said.

"Well, I'm ready. By the way, which President did you pick for her project this month?"

"I don't know yet. It's going to kill my whole Saturday."

"No, Ted, it's due tomorrow."

"No, wait, what?"

"Due tomorrow, 9:00 a.m."

"Why would she do that? She knows we have this tonight?"

"Ted, we had a month to get it done."

He thought, his memory now recalling several things she'd said while he was half daydreaming.

"I didn't do it. I'm a dead man. Wait! Do you know what time the library closes?"

"Six, it's closed. Maybe she'll let you slide?"

"It comes down to simple math. If I take the zero she gives me, add in my sixty-eight average, then multiply it by her hatred of me, it equals a guaranteed place in summer school. I'm dead, Anna, screwed beyond dead!"

His head held so high moments before, now deflated, he returned to Frank.

"Why so glum?"

"I didn't do that social studies assignment."

"Oh, that sucks, you know you'll get a zero."

Ted would have liked to wallow in self-pity but had way too much going on.

People were arriving and a line began to form in front of their booth. One eye watched the door to see if he could spot his birthmother and the other on Anna's booth.

At fifty cents for three tries of the strength meter, the money began to pour in. Across the aisle, Anna and June sat waiting, no one willing to shell out twenty dollars for a sketch, even for charity. Anna tried to appear unconcerned, but she was already starting to bite her nails.

"Hey," Ted called over, "put out a sample. You know, do June."

They faced each other in amazement that neither had thought of that.

"Hey, I'm supposed to be the smart one. You are crowding my turf," June shot back with a smile.

In just a few minutes, a framed sketch of June sat next to the sign that said twenty dollars. The response was immediate. People stopped in their tracks, looked at the drawing, and then at June. One person stepped up while others watched Anna's masterful hand flutter across the page as though she were dusting it.

"This girl has real talent," one man watching said to his wife.

"Wow," her first customer uttered, a middle-aged woman who then commented about how Anna had drawn her perfectly but changed the hairstyle. "I'm going to have them do it like this at the beauty parlor."

She held it out to show others, and the line quickly grew. That was just the beginning. Ted lost count, getting too busy at his own booth, and suddenly getting distracted with the arrival of someone he recognized. It was Ciro's father! There he was, obviously sprung from prison and walking in with his wife and daughter.

Even though Ted had seen his picture in the newspaper years before, he'd always imagined him wearing a fancy suit and acting like Marlon Brando in *The Godfather*. Nothing could have been further from reality. A fat, sloppy loudmouth, wearing an old undershirt with a cigarette burn hole, it was easy to see where Ciro got his miserable personality.

Almost every sentence from his mouth began with a bark. "Get me..." "Ay..." or "You, get over here!"

Ted turned to see how Anna was doing, but that was no longer possible. A crowd five deep surrounded the booth to watch her transform a blank canvas into stunning art in mere minutes. Ted only knew she had finished another from the periodic bursts of applause. From people coming off the line he overheard someone saying, "Look how she did my hair. I have to get it styled that way."

Mrs. Butterman asked only once if she wanted a break.

"No way," she yelled without stopping.

Although barely able to keep up, Ted still had his eyes scanning all around. When not focused on the door evaluating every woman that walked in to see if she might be his birthmother, he was trying to get a glimpse of Anna's booth.

Then something else caught his attention. There at the end of his line was Ciro's dad with his daughter. Ted's eyes fixed on them, and an idea began to form. Sinister, evil, devious, conniving thoughts filled his head. He worked on it, kneading them into shape like a radioactive ball of clay. Revenge is a dish best served cold. He had just concocted one straight from the freezer.

Justification

On a break, Ciro couldn't help himself but to have two hot dogs in one hand while forcing a third down his gullet. He noticed the demented look covering Ted's face as he stared.

"What are you looking at?"

"What you're having for your last meal."

Ted loved to drop clues. Mumbling to himself while managing the line of people, he practiced his words repeatedly until the moment Ciro's father was standing before him.

"Hey, Frank, did you hear they let Ciro's dad out? Ciro said he's coming tonight."

"Okay," Frank replied, too busy to be interested.

"I want to get a look at this guy. I wonder if he carries a gun?"

That comment got more of Frank's attention.

"Why do you say that?"

"It's because of what Ciro said. I don't know if it's true, but he's been telling everyone his dad kills people for a living. Then he drives the bodies out to the docks and dumps them in the river. Ciro said he's done it fourteen times. I think he's bragging, but who knows?"

Not a word of what Ted said came from Ciro, or anyone, but by the time he turned around, the man was gone. Had Ted been more attentive to events near the door, he would have noticed Ciro being pulled from the hall minutes later like a misbehaved dog. The first punches from his father landed as soon as they were in the car. A short drive home was all that remained between Ciro and hell.

Justice

When it ended Ted left Frank to total the receipts. He was consumed with curiosity about how the booth across the aisle had fared. They even had to keep the fair open late just so Anna could finish doing those who had waited online half the night. Anna, exhausted, but with a smile that wouldn't leave, had just finished her last sketch.

"This has been the greatest night of my life," Ted overheard her say as she gave June a hug before walking off to the bathroom to wash her thoroughly blackened hands.

Too tired to care that June was gorgeous he asked, "You need any help cleaning up?"

"No, we're good, outstanding, actually!"

"Just how good did you do?"

"You won't believe it. Over a thousand dollars!"

"Geez, I bet you raised more money than anyone. Anna's incredible."

"You could say that again. You know the best part about tonight?" June observed. "Watching classmates of ours who made her life miserable having to wait all night in line and then pay twenty bucks just to sit in front of her. I don't think Anna's ever going to be the same. How did you guys do?"

"Not like you. Maybe two hundred dollars."

"That's great. You should get some of the credit for ours, Anna told me this was all your idea."

"I have to do something to earn my keep in this school."

"She also told me you needed help with the social studies assignment."

"Oh yeah, with so much going on tonight I kind of put it out of my mind."

"Well, you don't have to worry now. This is for you," she continued, holding out pages of loose-leaf.

"What is this?" he asked, taking the pages from her.

"It's the assignment, just rewrite it in your own words."

Ted wasn't sure if he heard right.

"This is the assignment?" he stated in disbelief, glancing it over. Stunned, he was stuttering. "When did you? How did you? Why did you do this for me?"

"Why? That should be obvious. And when? I had time between sketches."

"I can't believe this. You don't understand how much this means to me. Thank you so, so much! One question though. Why did you pick James Buchanan? Who would pick him?"

"Civil War. Understand? He passed all the issues to Lincoln. I picked him because I know you're into the Civil War and you'll be okay if she thinks maybe you didn't write it and quizzes you."

"Oh, that's genius, but how did you know I'm into the Civil War?"

"Books aren't my only interest, Ted."

"Well, I owe you my whole summer. Thanks again and I'm so glad you guys did well tonight."

Yin and yang, karma, for every action there is an equal and opposite reaction. As spectacular a night it had been for Anna, it was correspondingly dreadful for Ciro. It didn't matter it was his own son. Once Vinny "No Show" got into a blind rage, all control left his body. If it weren't for the padding Ciro's fat provided, his father would have broken many of his bones.

"I swear, Dad! I'll never tell anyone again!" Ciro screamed as his father punched him up the stairs. He would have admitted to the murder of Jimmy Hoffa if that was what he demanded. It is known only to God and possibly a few of his dad's cohorts if a single word of what Ted claimed was right. Still, he couldn't take any chances his son was spreading rumors, especially something like that.

Dimensions

If there was ever evidence of an alternate universe, an up-and-coming doctoral candidate could write their thesis about the world Anna had just entered. Her talents in drawing, makeup and hairstyling ferociously unleashed, her incredible ability to transform any ugly duckling into a radiant swan, every girl in the grade now wanted a piece of her. Ironically, there was hardly enough Anna to go around.

Without a single invitation to a party for years, suddenly, she had overlapping invites with classmates begging her to come to theirs.

"Please, you *must* come to my party, and bring your makeup kit," they would implore.

Many were willing to pay for her skills and for the first time, her pockets began to contain money.

Her former nickname, now strictly forbidden, was affectionately replaced with "Belle." Mornings in the schoolyard she would find herself surrounded by a gaggle of the school's popular crowd vying for her attention. She could silence them all by simply raising her hand. Far from the pariah she had been, it was now downright cool to be friends with her.

Ted's universe had improved too. He had a break from Tom because of the suspension and Ciro, absent on account of needing two weeks for the bruises from his father's beating to disappear.

When Ciro finally did return, an uneasy truce formed. Ted's fingerprints were all over what had happened, but it was too risky to retaliate until Ciro knew for sure what Ted had done.

Circumstances surrounding Tom were different. All Ted had to do was say the first three digits of the phone number his father had given him. It was enough to make Tom as gentle as a pussy cat. Coming in from recess a few days after he returned from suspension, Ted found him harassing Itch for his homework.

"Do we have a 724 problem here?" Ted asked from behind.

Looking like a lion at the zoo being harassed from outside the bars, "No, there's no problem," he said as he pushed his shoulder into Itch but walked off after that.

"I got that ape under control," he said to Itch.

"How did you do that?"

"He's terrified of his dad, and I got his number. I'm going to make his life here miserable from now on."

"I wouldn't push that, Ted. He'll kill you first, then worry about his father later."

"I know what I'm doing."

"No, you don't. As your friend, Ted, I'm telling you to be careful. If he attacks you there is nothing I can do to help and trust me no one else is going to."

"I'm not worried."

Ted had a foolish side.

Shading

The news was depressing. Itch and Chuck had aced the high school entrance exams. Ted's score, well, he wasn't getting into any school where his friends would be attending. Most likely it would be public education. There awaited a whole new crop of kids, all in already well-formed cliques that would be lining up to beat on him. He wasn't paying attention as he meandered around the schoolyard and, staring at his feet, walked right into the back of Tom.

Instinctively, he reacted.

"Let's not have a 724 problem."

There was no threat of violence, no reaction at all. Ted peered around to his other side to discover the unbelievable, tears were rolling down his cheeks.

"Something wrong?" Ted inquired, feigning concern.

Desperate for some comfort, uncharacteristically he reached out, even if it was to Ted.

"I can't take it anymore."

"Can't take what?"

"It's my mom. She wasn't conscious when I left this morning."

"Well," Ted fished for words, "did you call an ambulance?"

"It's not that, she can't control it, she drinks. It's every day and I just can't take it anymore. I never know the day it will happen. I'll come home, and she'll be lying somewhere dead."

He pulled his sleeve across his face and attempted to compose himself.

Ted had long viewed Tom as the devil incarnate and was quite comfortable with that perspective. Seeing him as evil made it simple, but real life is never so straightforward. All it took was this small moment, this tiny peek into Tom's life, to conjure a measure of pity. The color of anything depends upon how it is illuminated. The hat on Tom's head he was sure was black, now appeared gray.

Ted was a master at composing the most poignant thing to say in a situation like this. What followed was not a good example. Instead, he took a swan dive into a one-foot-deep swimming pool.

"I'm sorry, Tom. I didn't realize your mom's a drunk."

From the look across Tom's entire face, he instantly realized his mistake.

Black hat firmly back in place, Tom exclaimed, "I'm going to rip you in half!"

Figuring confusion offered the best escape, he pointed his finger into the air. "Before you do that, I have just one thing to say." Then he ran as though on fire before finishing the thought.

Stunning

Ted couldn't believe it when he opened the letter. Incredibly, he was invited to David's birthday party. With a guest list limited to twenty, that invitation was more coveted than golden tickets to Willy Wonka's Chocolate Factory! The truth was that he was the last person David wanted to waste an invitation on.

With the threat of expulsion, real or perceived, David put him on the guest list. It was too much of a risk to possibly be accused by the school administration of Ted's mistreatment.

Ted had things other than the party on his mind. The two weeks before the end of school he spent every waking minute studying. He needed high grades on all his finals to avoid summer school.

"See me after class," was the note he received instead of his returned final for social studies.

"Here it is Itch, she has been salivating for this moment all year. She is going to fail me!"

"Hey, you did it to yourself, you should have studied."

"I did study, I studied like mad, I had the entire textbook memorized. There's no way I failed. Unless she rigged it!"

Ted spent the remaining ten minutes fuming. When the recess bell rang, he remained at his desk.

"You want to come up?" she asked as the class cleared out.

"No," Ted responded, refusing to move from his desk, seething.

This was the OK Corral, and he was going to make her come to him for this gunfight. She came over to the desk next to his and began, "You want to explain this?"

Placing his test in front of him. The score was ninety-eight.

"I didn't cheat if that is what you are going to accuse me of."

"I never thought that. You got the highest grade in the class by six points. You only needed a ninety to get a C. What I haven't been able to figure out is why you went for the extra eight points," she began with the appropriate sarcasm.

"So, I passed?"

"Yes, but that isn't why I wanted to talk with you. You accomplished a lot this year. It wasn't grades. I can go into many things but let's focus on just one, Anna. I know all about the chain you gave her this year, and the poem too. That suggestion for her to draw pictures at the fair was brilliant. You had it all figured out. You knew exactly what would happen that night."

"Ted, you transformed another person. Do you understand how special a talent that is? You are quite unique."

"Actually, I'm just an ordinary snake," he interjected.

"Excuse me?"

"I am what God made me. There isn't anything I can do about it. I'm a snake, and if you don't believe me, you just don't know me well enough."

“Is that what you think? Well, if it’s true then you have some pretty powerful magic in your venom. But let’s get to why I want to talk.”

As she continued, the confused look never left his face. This demonic woman who Ted was sure hated him and frothed at the mouth with delight from the thought of sending him to summer school, was giving him an A. He barely processed what she said as his mind could not decide about which to be more astonished, getting the A, or the fact his perception of her had been so wrong.

“Listen, Ted, no matter where you go to school, I know you can get straight As but you will get straight Cs. That is just who you are. I figure you may as well do that in a top school. But there is a bigger picture here. I know I am not telling you anything you don’t know when I say you aren’t popular. But you have something most of the popular kids don’t. You have close friends. True friends. And you want to know why that is? Popular kids conform. They have to do what is necessary to remain popular. You, Ted, you don’t care. Maybe it’s on purpose or maybe you can’t help it, but with you what you are is what you get. The friends you have are because of that.

“It would be devastating if you didn’t continue to go to school with them. A boost in your grades will help you get into the school you want. I hope that goes a long way toward you becoming whatever God means for you to be. I have high hopes for you, Ted. I spoke with your other teachers. I don’t know what they are going to do, but I do know Mrs. Delray is giving you an A in religion because of what you did for Anna.”

Out in the schoolyard, Ted looked dismayed.

“That bad?” Itch questioned. “What happened?”

"She showed me a few things. I'm an idiot, she's a saint, and I got an A."

Despite all his opinions to the contrary, he had long ago won over Rita Butterman. She believed in him before he believed in himself. While he was amazed by the grade, what he didn't know was far more shocking.

Leveraging her excellent reputation within the school system, she wrote an impassioned letter of recommendation on his behalf. She had it signed by every teacher who taught him through the years along with the majority of the school's administration, then hand delivered it while meeting with the principals of the three high schools where he had applied.

Recognition

That last week before summer vacation, Ted sought out Anna. They hadn't spoken since the fair, and he had so many things to say. All of it was personal and he needed to talk to her privately. Now the center of so much attention, it was impossible to find her alone.

Running out of time he was forced to approach her in the schoolyard the last morning before summer recess. She stood in the center of a group some called the Sisters of Stuck Up because of their attitudes.

If nothing else, Ted figured it was a rare opportunity to at least breathe the same air as they did. They did not make it easy. Standing in a tight circle, he was all but refused entry. As he tried to wiggle in, their eyes landed on him, this invader of their space, and moved from the top of his head to his shoes and back, as if erasers, trying to remove his presence. Anna was finishing a conversation with someone in the group.

"The bridesmaids were told they have to be at the church an hour earlier, so can you do my sister's hair at ten instead of eleven on Saturday? She said she would pay you extra," a girl was asking.

"I'll be there whenever you need me and the money is enough," Anna replied.

Noticing Ted standing awkwardly and out of place in the back, she raised her hand to silence the chatter of her new court.

"Hold up, everyone. Be quiet! Yes, Ted?" she called over now, doubling the evil eyes he had already been receiving.

Ted had so much he wanted to tell her. He longed to say how proud he was of her and how it filled his heart to see how much things had changed. It wasn't until that moment he realized how ridiculous it would be to share such feelings in front of that crowd.

Realizing his mistake, he awkwardly traded it for something trivial. "I hope you have a great summer."

"Thanks, Ted, I hope you have a nice summer too."

He was a good ten paces away when he heard her shout his name. Putting her thumb under her collar, she pulled the gold chain from beneath. Her tone, warm and appreciative, was complimented by a full smile. The simple few words she spoke encompassed everything he had wanted to say.

"It's been a really good year."

Cake

David's birthday party, occurring on the first Saturday after the school year ended, for those invited, was the official start of summer. Ted still wondered if his invitation was a mistake. To avoid embarrassment, he decided to show up an hour early to test the waters. Attempting to smooth things over, he blew all of what little money he had on a skateboard he knew David wanted.

There was a sign on the door that said "Go around back," but Ted misunderstood and thought that meant through the house rather than the side gate. As he passed through the living room, he paused to gaze enviously at an enormous display cabinet filled beyond capacity with trophies David had won. So many, some weren't even standing, laying on their sides and stacked like books. Four entire shelves, each of them larger than the single trophy shelf he had in his room that currently contained nothing but mementos.

Into the backyard, placing his wrapped gift on the table, he was greeted by an unenthusiastic wave from Dave but a much warmer greeting from his father when he offered to help with the setup. This allowed him to pry into what special event lay in store. Mariachi bands, professional baseball teams showing up for autographs, David's parties were legendary.

“Well, in addition to the pool we have a cake you are going to have to see to believe,” his father eluded. “Everyone can take some home.”

With the temperature in the nineties, Ted was already sweating when other guests began to arrive. He had worn his bathing suit under his clothes to avoid the possibility of having to change in front of anyone, and the steaming sun made the wait to get into the cool blue tinted water unbearable. Still, Ted figured proper etiquette was to wait until at least some other guests arrived.

Tom was first and cannon balled in as soon as he completed the formality of saying happy birthday and turning over his present. Now he was resting in the deep end, taunting Ted to get in.

“Ted, come on in and let me give you a tour of the bottom of the pool.”

Tom, Steve, Rob, Ciro, just a few of the sharks that soon were lurking in the pool ready to turn it into a death trap. Much as he wanted to go in, he realized it was off limits and wondered how he’d manage to stay out. Just then a classmate named Peter arrived. What glorious good fortune Ted thought, noting a long leg cast as he hobbled in on crutches, the result of a bicycling accident two days earlier.

“He shouldn’t have to be the only one to stay out. I’ll keep him company,” Ted offered gleefully.

They found other things to do, the main activity was sitting at a table by the pool playing poker, using M&Ms as money. Throughout the afternoon Ted was bombarded with compliments from David’s relatives who had come for the day. They marveled about how wonderful Ted was to sacrifice his time in the pool to keep Peter company. Ted embellished with feigned modesty.

"You are such a special young man. You should go in, though. I'll keep him company."

"No, if he can't go in, I'm not going in either. It's just a pool anyway."

Sun soaked and nearing heat stroke, the sweltering day finally began to turn into evening and the pool evacuated. Dinner was barbecue fare, consisting of cheeseburgers and hot dogs, served at a long table in the middle of the backyard. Rumors about the "most amazing cake ever" were already spreading. Dramatic tension built as the dinner dishes were cleared.

Cameras flashed, adults applauded, and everyone's mouth gaped open. In honor of his thirteenth birthday, thirteen different cakes were layered one on top of the other. Underneath, almost invisible, was a structure of connected metal plates on which each separate cake sat. The plates swung out, allowing each to be cut individually. Standing over seven feet high, it was cake-a-neering at its finest.

Getting it right, starting from the bottom and working upward, included were a chocolate frosted blackout cake, a vanilla ice cream cake, chocolate lava cake, napoleon, cheesecake, pound cake, rainbow layer cake, red velvet cake, banana cake, sponge cake, Boston cream pie, and carrot cake. Finally, it was topped off with a croquembouche studded with thirteen candles.

With the bottom cake two and a half feet in diameter, the others tapering only slightly from bottom to top, it took three men to carefully place it on the table. David required a step ladder to reach the top. He found himself serenaded to various insulting versions of the happy birthday song as he blew out the candles.

David's father took the croquembouche back into the house for the adults, leaving all the others for the boys to decide which they wanted. Fate chose to seat Ted next to Geo, who, not satisfied with the red velvet cake on his plate, decided instead to swipe his finger through the chocolate icing from the bottom of the first cake. Sucking it off his finger with a deliberate slurping he returned it to the cake, doing it again.

"That's disgusting!" Ted proclaimed.

Geo looked at Ted with a smug smile, then, with a lump of frosting on its tip, jammed his finger into Ted's ear. The wet saliva tainted chocolate mess pushed deep into his ear canal. Without needing to consult the rule book that governs the behavior of thirteen-year-old males, Ted knew this required an immediate response.

He picked up his own plate with a barely touched piece of cake and smashed it into Geo's face. Geo hesitated in shock for an eye blink before tossing his cake at Ted. Missing, the kid next to him was hit and returned fire with his own cake, striking someone else. In a chain reaction, within moments, everyone had badly misused their piece of cake.

All stood motionless amidst a tense standoff. One by one their eyes moved to gaze upon the cake tower before them. Each knew what the others were contemplating but no one dared be the first. It's lost to history who initiated the fateful move.

Like a lamb surrounded by lions, the giant cake was under attack from all sides. Fingers plunged to rip off mounds for use as projectiles. Everyone pushed and shoved for their share of ammunition. Tom, not content to throw a fistful at a time picked up the entire cheesecake, raised it above his head, and as if from a scene in a King Kong movie, smashed it down onto David's head. It sent multiple participants to the ground coated in sticky globs of delicious creamy cheesecake.

David's father and a few others ran from the house at full speed to stop the out-of-control mob. If they were running to save any of the cake that horse had long left the stable. Finally, after a sharp whistle, some threats and yelling, the fight was over.

All stood dripping various amounts of cake, separating them into three distinct categories. A very few were clean enough to wash up in the bathroom. Incredibly, although at the epicenter when it started, this small group included Ted. Other kids could be salvaged by use of the garden hose. Finally, the largest group, and they knew without needing to be told, were so far gone they decided to jump into the pool.

Like staggering zombies, they moved to the side and, with the appropriate resignation, threw themselves in. All this while, David's father screamed, *"Don't go in the pool like that!"*

The beautiful pool, its ornate Romanesque statues looking on, became the final resting place for a good portion of the magnificent cake. Larger chunks floated on top but most of it disintegrated, turning the water a murky brown.

Ted was able to grab one of the upstairs bathrooms, wash his face and hands, and even find a Q-Tip to get the frosting out of his ear. His mother arrived to pick him up just as he was coming down the stairs.

“Got to go!” he shouted to his mom while grabbing her hand and pulling her out the front door.

“Bye, David, happy birthday!” Ted shouted toward the backyard from outside the fence during his rush to evacuate.

The next day his heart nearly stopped when his mother announced David was on the phone. *Did he know he had started it?* Ted thought, preparing to deny any role. Instead, he had just called to thank him for the skateboard.

“It was a great party David, thanks again for inviting me. I had a great time. Too bad it ended on a bit of a sour note.”

“A sour note!” David exclaimed. “A sour note? Someone tried to kill me with a cheesecake. I’m grounded for a week. And the pool! Holy Moses. It’s a disaster. We have to drain it and replace the entire filtration system. My dad said it’s going to cost $2,000. He said I’m never having another party again.”

Ted was glad David couldn’t see him through the phone standing, eyes closed, teeth clenched and hand on his forehead.

“Well, I’m sorry about that. Did anyone figure out who started it?”

“Nah, it’s a mystery.”

Ted breathed a sigh of relief and hung up abruptly as he realized the stupidity of his final line.

“Guess we’ll never know. And, David, that cake was amazing. Too bad there wasn’t any left to take home with us.”

Flirtation

Up until the end of the summer, David's call was the only time the phone rang for Ted. Then, just three days before the end of summer vacation, the unthinkable happened.

"Teddy!" his mother screamed. "There's a girl on the phone! It's a girl! Oh, here we go! It's starting! The girls are calling!"

Ted dropped everything and ran for the phone, horrified that whomever it was could hear his mother's blathering.

"Would you shut up!"

"Oh, it's cute. The girls are calling!"

"She can hear you! Can you shut your mouth!"

"Oh, I'm just teasing you. Go to hell if you can't take a joke."

"Why don't you go to hell for a change? Die and go to hell," he fired back.

"Hello?"

"Don't talk to your mother like that!"

The deceptively young sounding voice was that of Sister Ann. In the last days of the previous year, Ted and Chuck had joined the school safety patrol and volunteered for crossing guard duty. She was calling to confirm his post and for him to come in the day before school opened for training.

Freedom

Eighth grade is marked by more challenging work but laxed discipline. As one might expect when opportunities are given, liberties are taken. A favorite class of everyone was math. It had nothing to do with the subject but who, in theory, taught it.

She was an old nun nearly deaf and blind. Coke-bottle glasses and hearing aids did little to improve anything. She could hardly see a few inches past her face and could not tell what the kids were saying or doing. The students called her Sister Helen Keller.

"What is the longest side of a right triangle, opposite the right angle?" she questioned and pointed to a raised hand.

"The hippopotamus," Steve replied.

"That's correct!" she confirmed amidst giggles.

Kids loved her class; it was like having a free period.

Ruse

On the first day back from summer vacation, everyone was excited to see their friends again. Ted paired with Itch and was of course immediately tortured with his adventures at summer camp.

Itch won first place in a crossbow contest. He caught so many fish on the lake he had to start throwing them back or they might sink his canoe. This year their cabins had TVs with Nintendo.

"Someday I'm going to be too old to go," Itch lamented.

That was more than enough to set Ted off.

"Come on, Itch, what about the girls?"

"Sorry, can't say anything. I'm sworn to secrecy."

Frustrated, Ted begged and begged, then begged some more.

Finally Itch relented and confided some secrets. There was one rather promiscuous one who had a real crush on him. She wasn't his type though, or so Itch explained. Instead, he became close with a big-chested blonde named Gwendolyn who loved to make out. Itch confessed they went to second base and on the last night, went to third. It was left to Ted's wondering what that meant.

Itch tortured him for days. Boys would paddle in the middle of the night over to the girl's side to meet them. The sparse details of what they would do filled Ted's imagination. His face went flush as Itch dropped vague additional information. He swore he could taste envy on his tongue.

He would spend weeks cursing his lot in life and fantasizing about details even more salacious than what Itch had told him. At points there was a blurring of what he had been told and his own fantasies. He resented having to worship a God who would throw such favor at a troll like Itch rather than him. These are the kinds of obsessions and creators of self-doubt that lead to thoughts of suicide.

Then Itch made the mistake of telling Ted he was meeting up with some of his scouting buddies from the camp after school. This was Ted's opening to hang with this adventurous gang. Hours into his whining Itch finally relented and invited him to tag along.

"Don't talk about camp. We're all sworn to secrecy. I shouldn't have told you any of it," Itch warned.

"Don't worry. I'll keep my mouth shut. This is going to be the best afternoon ever."

Why was it Ted always got these things so wrong?

Belonging

Ted showed up twenty minutes early to Itch's house and immediately became annoying. On his bicycle, off, then on again, he couldn't decide which would seem the cooler of the poses for when the other kids arrived. He finally opted for on and then sat impatiently bouncing his leg on one of the pedals.

After a few more minutes and intolerable annoyance, Ted could see four figures riding toward them from down the block. They pedaled in zig-zag formation from one side of the street to the other, seeming to demonstrate their ownership of the road. Ted imagined powerful motorcycle engines revving as they approached. Itch wasted no time making introductions.

"Everyone, this is Ted. Ted, that's Ghost," he said, pointing to a kid who was so pale it looked as though he'd never been in the sun. "That's Viper over there. Bugger's next to him. We call him Viper because he's mean, and Bugger, well, just look at him, and that's Red."

Red, the oldest at fifteen, topped with a head of thick, red hair, had a mean grin and was taller than the rest.

"I guess they call you Red because you have red hair," Ted exclaimed, trying to fill the void as they sized him up.

"No, they call me that because of the color of my piss," he replied with derision. "Scraping the bottom of the barrel, huh, Itch? Is he following you around because you owe him money or something?"

Itch held Ted back a moment as the others began to pedal off, their destination some marshland a few blocks away.

"For God's sake, Ted, don't be yourself," Itch implored before the two caught up.

Once off the road, past some trees, beyond reeds standing eight feet tall, there was a clearing that revealed a sandy trail curving off toward the shoreline of Long Island Sound and some bluffs. It ended at a cliff with a nearly vertical ten-foot drop and each dared the others to drive off it.

Ted thought it pure insanity. Lacking both courage and a dirt bike, he hung back.

Each went over several times before Bugger flew over his handlebars on one of the attempts. Scraped but otherwise okay, they decided to cease tempting fate and settle in for something else, lighting a campfire! The call went out to get firewood. They all scrambled into the woods, each coming back with an armful of twigs, branches, and whatever else they thought might burn. Red instead returned with a six pack of beer.

Ted watched in awe as Ghost started the fire using nothing but a flint he was carrying and a small rock, while Red passed out his quarry. With six beers, the math worked out well, and they each took a can. Ted initially waved it away, but Red insisted.

"We don't allow girls here. You need to drink it!"

Ted was leery. The can was hot, its hiding spot apparently exposed to the sun.

He took a breath and opened it with the others, faking a smile over his apprehension, then showing off, took an impressive slug. The vile 110-degree beverage assaulted his tongue, and while instinct prompted him to spit it out, he closed his mouth tight preventing that from happening. The mouthful sloshed to the back of his throat, but that closed too. With no place for the carbonation to go it erupted through his nose with beer spraying out in a gush. Dropping the can, the precious golden liquid drained into the sand while he choked as if drowning.

"Who invited this guy?" Red yelled.

"Listen, Red, everyone has at least one token friend to make fun of, and he's mine," Itch answered.

Ted slunk back a bit from the others and hoped the fire would absorb the attention away from himself. For an hour, the boys talked about nothing but sports, eliminating any and all possibility of him joining in. Wood was added to the fire until one of them blurted it was six thirty.

A chorus of "Yikes" and "I have got to get home" erupted from all around.

They needed to douse the fire, and Red suggested they do it the traditional way.

"Beer can only be borrowed. We have to return to the gods what is rightfully theirs."

A cold sweat filled Ted as all the others stood and lowered their zippers.

"You know I think I got sand in the gears of my bike. I don't want to hold you guys up so let me go clean them now," Ted exclaimed, then rushed off to address his made-up concern.

"This has happened before, let me see if I can knock it out," he continued, now away from the circle of boys who were occupied turning the fire into a pile of saturated ash.

"Come on, you have to clean up too," one of them called to Ted as they finished then inspected the area to remove any trace they had been there.

As Ted rejoined, a small flame broke out among the ashes.

"Hey, Ted, you're the only one with ammunition left, put it out," Itch requested.

"Can't you step on it?" Ted responded.

"You know how gross that pile is? I'm not stepping on it!" Itch responded. "You step on it."

Red interrupted, "Hey! Put the freaking fire out the right way! Do it! Do it *now*!"

Ted looked over at Ghost and knew their faces matched. Walking up to the fire he stared with hate at the little dancing flame laughing at him. The other boys seemed busy hunting for trash, so he focused his eyes down. Ignoring them he fixed himself in place and aimed at the flame, mentally trying to convince himself his exposure was nothing.

And that is precisely what happened. Nothing, nothing came out. And as nothing continued to happen, panic set in.

"Okay, just relax, I have to imagine," he told himself then closed his eyes. He placed himself on a barren mountaintop. Wait, better yet, he was running along the shoreline of some distant beach all alone in a short sleeve shirt. It was cool. No, icy cold, and the spray from the waves almost froze to his skin. It might have worked had Itch not opened his big mouth.

"Holy shillelagh! Ted's been hit by the puberty fairy!"

Had Ted's hands not been otherwise occupied, he would have reached out and strangled him.

"Yeah, he got clobbered," another joked.

Still with his eyes closed, listening to the laughter, his cheeks instantly felt as though they were on fire.

"Why is it retards always have big ones?" Red commented.

"That's 'cause all the blood goes there, and they have nothing left to think with," another voice added amidst more laughter.

Bugger stepped forward to the fire.

"This is pathetic, you guys owe me," he insisted, then stamped until the flame was out.

Ted couldn't figure out if he was supposed to say thanks or just zip up and shut up. The next thing he remembered, he was standing back with Red glaring at him, offering a deadly serious suggestion.

"I got an idea. Let's beat him up and trash his bike."

To that point, Itch saw all of what was going on as harmless ribbing, but Red was putting it out as an actual suggestion, and that crossed a line. He straightened and moved to stand next to Ted.

"You lay one finger on my friend or his bike, and I'll put a crack in your head that will match the one in your ass."

"Relax, Itch. I'm only kidding," Red protested.

"I'm not."

A few minutes later, Ted was walking his bike toward home, ironically, desperately needing to go to the bathroom.

In a trance, almost oblivious to his surroundings, he didn't consider how much quicker the trip would have been had he rode instead. All his jumbled and embarrassed thoughts were focused on Itch, praying he wouldn't use this to make fun of him at school.

For years, he had agonized over his decision to not join the Scouts. To his surprise, he discovered he didn't even like them and unless he was willing to pretend to be someone different, they didn't like him either.

Not a moment's peace, his mother laid right into him when he walked into the front hall.

"You're late! You don't call me, nothing. I don't know why I bother. I made pork chops. Your father is working late so these were just for you, but they are all dried out now. You don't care, you are never grateful. Well, they are ruined, and you are going to eat them anyway.

"What is that smell? Have you been smoking? You smell like a campfire! It's that Itch kid, isn't it? I don't like him at all. You are going to have to stop being friends with him."

Pulled by his mother to the dinner table, Ted gave a thousand-yard stare to the kitchen wall. His mother piled on a pork chop, applesauce, mixed vegetables, and a supersize serving of mashed potatoes. All the while her droning never ceased.

"Well, what do you have to say for yourself? Huh? Huh?"

Ted leaned forward, paused to contemplate what he might be facing at school the next day and dropped his face straight into the center of the food.

Judgment

Ted's approach to school was cautious as he took his place with Chuck at the crossing guard post. He studied the faces of his classmates all morning. Not the slightest hint of a leak appeared. It wasn't until after he talked with Itch, who seemed unable to recall anything from the previous day worth blabbing to anyone, that he relaxed.

No one is perfect. Itch was a world-class pain in the ass but knew when to step up as a friend. When we have friends, real friends, we must weigh the value of their qualities against our willingness to accept their faults. This is a necessary part of every long-lasting relationship. It was moments like this that Itch tipped the scale in his favor.

Quality

Ted had a talent for writing but rarely put it to use. Being assigned essays at school was just another form of punishment. Initially greeted by his usual disdain, he began to change his mind regarding the most recent assignment after considering it a bit. The essay was how people view each other. More precisely the task was to have each student ask two friends and one family member what they thought was their best quality, then write if they agreed and why.

Other than the two-page length, he thought it would be easy. Turning to Itch moments after it had been given, they simultaneously gave each other answers.

Based on what had happened the day before, Ted didn't have to think twice about Itch's.

"You are a pain in the ass, but at the end of the day, you're a loyal friend."

Itch would use the entire statement verbatim in his report.

"You're the only one who gets my sense of humor," Itch replied.

That didn't seem like much of a quality, but it was one down. Someone else and then his mother. That was all there was to it.

He asked Chuck as they stood at their crossing guard post.

"Easy, you are absolutely brilliant," Chuck responded.

Ted rolled his eyes, "Come on, be serious."

"I am. You are absolutely brilliant."

"You are talking about yourself. You're the one who is brilliant."

"No, Ted, I'm smart. I can memorize facts in a book. You, Ted, don't need to read the book. You just figure things out yourself."

"That's a ridiculous answer."

"Then write you disagree. That's my answer. You are brilliant, I'm not changing it."

Even though he disagreed that made two. Now for his mother.

"Mom, for something at school I need you to tell me what you think is my best quality?"

"What do you mean? Like being helpful around the house?"

"It's supposed to be the very best thing about me?"

"Okay, Teddy, that's easy, I enjoy having you around."

"And what does that mean?"

"You know, you have a nice personality. I like having you around."

"That's it?"

"What else do you want me to say?"

What did he want her to say? "That's the best my own mother could come up with," he considered in stunned surprise. The more he thought about it, the more heartbroken he became. Addressing the situation but not the feelings, he slunk to his room to try and make up something better and claim she said it.

As minutes passed, he became increasingly frustrated, his mind as blank as the page before him. With the paper still untouched he clawed at it, tore it to pieces and let it fall to the floor, disgusted in the fact he could not come up with anything better than what she said.

He moved to collapse on top of his bed when a different idea dawned on him. His friends, his mother, none of them had any real answers. Maybe if he asked people who didn't like him and they could come up with just one thing, that would have to be it. But who to ask?

Surprise

When the assignment had been given, all students had been advised to take it seriously. Naively, he believed that would mean something.

"I thought I'd ask you, Ciro, I know you can come up with a hundred of my faults, but you have to be able to come up with one quality I have, right?"

Ciro stood next to Steve, both carrying expressions of pure amusement.

"Oh! Oh! Oh! Let me answer!" Steve shouted to Ciro throwing his hand up as though he were in class.

"No, I got this. Okay, your best quality is that you have a face that makes people laugh."

"I was going to say he makes a good punching bag," Steve added, then turned to Ted. "Or, no wait, I got a better quality, you could be the poster child for birth control."

"You make everyone around you seem smart," Ciro continued. "Don't go away. You have so many. I was just getting started."

He walked off almost scrapping the whole idea but then caught sight of Ashley. Her incredible beauty both inside and out made her truly special. Perhaps if she saw one quality within him that would have to be it.

Just looking in her direction gave him butterflies. It took him half the day to summon the courage to go up to her desk in a rare moment she was alone. Busily writing an overdue homework assignment, she wasn't looking to be disturbed.

Throat dry, palms sweaty, heart pounding three times normal, he approached, hoping the worst he might do was stutter. The little courage he had was cut in half before he finished the eight short steps it took to put him at her desk.

"Ashley," he began, "you know that assignment about asking people about their best quality?"

Her eyes darted up then back to her paper, taking just a second to confirm who the voice belonged to and more than a little annoyed for being distracted.

"Yeah," she replied without missing a moment of writing.

"I was kind of thinking," he continued, "that it might be better if I asked people who don't like me rather than friends."

"Okay, so?"

"Well, I know you are someone who doesn't like me."

Finally devoting a minimum of attention, she lifted her pen, looked up, and asked, "You don't think I like you?"

"Well, yeah, you know we've had..." He stopped, not wanting to raise that most unpleasant topic of the time she beat him up.

She resumed her writing and, without looking, replied, "Just because you don't talk with someone doesn't mean you don't like them."

"I suppose that could be true. It's just we, well, never mind. Could you tell me what you think is my best quality?" he blurted, suppressing the urge to vomit immediately following the statement.

"I don't think so, I don't know you well enough. I mean, would you be able to answer that question about me?"

"Absolutely," he replied, then awkwardly stood, wondering if he should volunteer the answer.

She ran her hand over her hair. Pulling it back over her ear and asking coyly, but still not giving the courtesy of looking at him, "I think I already know, but what would you say is mine?"

Ted was without doubt. "Your compassion."

Her head jerked back in surprise, as if she had been poked in the eye. She stopped writing, fiddled with her pen while she thought, then paid her full attention to Ted.

"I asked that question to a bunch of my friends, and they all said my best quality is that I am beautiful. I hate that answer. I hate, hate, hate it. There is so much more to me than just being pretty. Sometimes I hate being beautiful. Everyone judges my looks and stops right there. Compassion, that's so refreshing."

Wanting the conversation to continue he grabbed the one thing that had him confused.

"Why don't you like being beautiful? Girls would kill to look like you."

"They think they want to be like me, but they don't realize how it is. People don't take me seriously. I get comments all the time, 'Oh, she's so beautiful.'"

With sarcasm in her voice, she said, "Not that I'm in the honor society. Oh no. Not that I won the soccer league playoffs with no help from my team. I play the piano and the violin. I'm better than anyone in this school at both. No one talks about that. No, it's always I'm so pretty. That's what I get and it's frustrating. You know the worst part? Whenever I go out with boys all they want to do is get their hands up my blouse."

Gesturing one hand in frustration, she continued, "I never know why a guy asks me out. I always hope it's for more than my looks, but it never is. It would be so much easier if I were ugly. When an ugly girl gets asked out, she knows it's for what's inside. She's lucky. Me? I don't want to be like my mom, divorced at forty-five because she couldn't remain the prettiest in the room forever. That's the lousy prize you really get when you win the beauty contest. Still sounds like fun?"

"Yeah," he said, "No, I mean, it doesn't sound fun at all."

Her question, although rhetorical, woke him up. He'd almost missed her whole point. From the moment she made the comment about the boys wanting to get their hands in her blouse, all he could do was stare at her shirt and push back at an irrepressible desire to run his hands all over her well-stacked chest.

She looked at her watch. "Well, I have got to finish my homework, but you surprised me, in a really good way, and you know what? I'd like to answer what I think is your best quality. You are very insightful."

"I'll take that," Ted replied with a smile.

As he started to walk away, she put a finishing touch to the conversation by calling out, "You really made my day."

Awakening

When a boy has a conversation with a girl that goes well, he'll replay it in his mind a thousand times. Ted spent the next hours analyzing every word and concluded there was a hidden message in what Ashley had said. The more he thought about it, especially the comment about asking her out for the right reason, the more he realized it was a hint that she wanted him to do it.

He devised the perfect plan. He would frame it as an innocent lunch to get to know each other. It would appear as friends but would really be a date. It was foolproof. Ted scraped together all the money he had, which amounted to nine dollars. If they went to a diner and he ordered nothing he'd have enough.

The next day, in the same class, Ashley was there but this time engaged in a conversation with her newest best friend, Audrey. There was no chance getting her alone like the day before. The two of them could talk until the room ran out of air.

Like the day before, he stood, this time his heart pounding twice as hard. His ears seemed to have a ringing in them and his head a feeling like it might float off his shoulders. He moved in, determined to get this done before he passed out.

Forgiving himself for being a little rude, he interrupted their conversation. His mouth was so dry he could hardly keep his tongue from sticking to the roof as he uttered his words.

"Um, Ashley, I wanted to ask you something. You said yesterday you didn't really know me that well, and I thought that with Saturday coming, maybe we could get together and have lunch or something. You know, so we could get to know each other better."

Ashley abruptly stopped her conversation. "Are you asking me out?"

Ted wanted to explain how it was just as friends but couldn't unravel the complexity of the intention, threw his plan away and replied, "Yeah."

Audrey rolled her eyes, then put one hand up to her brow to partly block the amused expression on her face. Ted could not tell if the embarrassed look the gesture portrayed was for Ashley, himself, or both.

"The guys I date are in high school!" Ashley exclaimed as if it should have been obvious. "Why would you ever think I would want to go out with you?"

"I know. It's because he's got brain damage," Audrey whispered between giggles.

Much as Ted hoped the conversation was over, the question had not been rhetorical.

"No, I got to hear this, whatever made you think that?"

"Well, we had a terrific conversation yesterday."

As Ashley bulged her eyes and shook her head, Ted could sense all his blood pooling in his feet, making them feel like lead weights. A faint feeling filled his head as she aimed her gaze at Audrey.

"I swear, with God as my witness, Audrey, nothing I said should have made him think I was that desperate. If I ever go out with someone like him, don't even ask—just go ahead and kill me."

Audrey, one hand still on her forehead, looking down to hide her expression, tried to contain her laughter.

Ted snapped back. "You know, Ashley, you should try going out with guys who appreciate you for your inner beauty."

Ashley retorted forcefully, "You know, Ted, you should try asking out girls who are in your league."

Audrey pulled her hand from her forehead and threw it to her mouth in an unsuccessful attempt to contain a burst of laughter.

Ted didn't know what expression was on his face but didn't want to give either of them the satisfaction of seeing it and turned. He returned to his desk an inch shorter and slumped in his chair with one hand covering his face. He could hear the two of them cackling from across the room.

Whenever he felt down, Mr. Maze had implored him to dig deep and identify the feeling. One might think it was obviously humiliation, but there was more to it. Something much more profound and tragic.

Up to that moment, Ashley had been a person he deeply admired. She had possessed a beauty that could not be seen in a mirror. That beautiful girl so filled with compassion two years before was gone. It was that quality that made her special. Now she had become nothing more than another countless pretty face with an attitude.

There had been no wake, no obituary, no place in the ground for her to be visited, but at some time between then and now, unannounced, and unrealized by anyone, the very essence of her beauty had died. A blanket of sadness enveloped him as he grieved over her loss. How terrible that the most beautiful and precious orchid in her garden had been choked out by weeds of conceit.

With a heavy sigh, Ted paid his last respects to the girl he knew and filled the chasm with an obsessive need to complete his essay. He wrote on and on, not from desire but necessity. Blood from the wound she had inflicted ran down his arm, into the pen and onto the page. As he wrote, it became apparent. He finally realized his most outstanding quality.

He finished and turned in the essay right then without so much as a proofread. Itch asked him at dismissal how his day went.

"You won't believe it. I asked out Ashley."

Itch's mouth dropped.

"Well, what did she say?" he countered following a long pause.

"Remember where she kicked me a few years ago?"

"Yeah," he said cautiously, scrunching his face.

"She did it to me again."

Slamming his locker shut, he had already determined his next move. Ashley had opened his eyes. Just like all the other guys, he became ensnared by her looks. Feeling stupid for even having considered her, he once again summoned his courage, deciding this time to ask out a girl of unquestionable beauty.

Legacy

His essay was an eight-page masterpiece. Halfway through her first of many reviews, his English teacher paused to stare at the back wall of the classroom in stunned disbelief that this had come from one of her students. She circulated copies among other teachers and the office staff. Father Tom read it and borrowed parts for his Sunday homily. Anyone who did not know Ted doubted it could have been written by an eighth grader.

He began with a definition. Talents we are born with, skills we develop, traits we do out of habit, but qualities emanate from our heart. They define who we are, what we stand for, and ultimately determine the value we bring to this world.

Things we achieve, build, create, degrees we earn, competitions we win, all those things we get to keep, but our qualities require constant nurturing. They can be improved but just as fast fade into oblivion and carry with them the definition of who we are.

He disagreed with everything identified in him by others as his finest. He may have a quirky sense of humor. He might possess hidden intelligence or be tolerable to have around. He might be able to make people laugh and see what others do not. However, none of these were his finest.

They were all wrong. Ted's finest quality was his never-ceasing struggle to improve.

He could see all around him people who knew what they needed to do but never lifted a finger to make it happen. People like Ashley who clearly saw the train coming but refused to step off the tracks. People like Walter Burke who lamented their lot in life but refused to embrace any other. When Ted determined he needed to change, his superpower was that he did it.

Day after day, little by little, over time, it did and would continue to compound, making him an unstoppable force. All these kids who believed they were better, that they would always beat him at everything, stood no chance. And the more he thought about it, the more he began to see that this quality could one day propel him to far exceed even his idol, Walter Burke.

Girlfriend

He had practiced what he planned to say, but the moment he saw Anna his thoughts scrambled like bumper cars. It was the same strategy as it had been with Ashley. He'd innocently suggest a get together and the fact it was an actual date could be realized later.

Anna was also impossible to get alone these days. But when he asked, amidst the gaggle that surrounded her, if they could speak privately, there was no hesitation. She'd always make time for Ted. He could feel his heart suddenly pounding as they walked off together. Secretly in his mind he thought about what it would feel like to hold her hand. He started to compose a list of things they might talk about on their date. He was a bundle of nerves yet everything about this seemed right.

"I've been reading good reviews about the Starlight Diner, and you know, I was planning on checking it out for lunch on Saturday, or something, and I thought maybe you might like to check it out with me."

He swallowed as he awaited her reply. She was too stunned to say anything for a few moments. The idea of a boy asking her out was as unexpected as stepping on a scale and having it read sixty pounds.

"Are you asking me out?" she blurted in shock.

Ted wanted to explain his master plan but just like the day before, his tongue suddenly lacked the ability to go through with the whole idea.

"Yes," he admitted.

Anna shook her head, "I'm sorry, no, I can't."

"You can't? You mean no, as in you don't want to."

"No, Ted, I can't. You're a really nice guy, but I just can't."

"Is it your folks?"

"Heck, no, not at all. My nana would love to see me go out. I can't tell you why, but I just can't go out with you."

"You're serious, you don't want to go out with me?" Ted said, unable to comprehend. "What's so wrong with me?"

"It's not you, Ted, I'm sure there is someone else who would love to go out with you, I hope you understand."

"Perfectly," he said forcefully, wondering why he put himself through this a second time in two days.

"I want you to know," she said as he began his march of humiliation back to his friends, "you are already in the deepest place in my heart."

He walked off despondent, wondering what on earth it was about himself that could be so vile. He was in no mood for Tom to pounce as he felt five fingers dig into the back of his neck.

Bravado

"I need one more," Tom snapped. "What's my quality? Can't be that I'm strong, I got that one already."

"That assignment's due today. You didn't do it yet?"

"Just give me what it is. I need one more opinion."

Ted hesitated. He had an opinion. He just worried about sharing it.

"Okay then. Okay, your best quality. What it is...your best."

"Come on!"

"All right, how do I put this? I would have to say it is how well you hide your fear."

If Tom hadn't been so confused, he would have punched him outright.

"What the freak is that supposed to mean?"

"Well, what I mean by that is it must be hard for you to go home every day. To leave school and not know if your mother is going to be dead or alive. Maybe she's lying on the floor in a pool of her own slop. It's got to be impossible to live like that and you hold it all inside. That's why you are so mean to everyone. You know Mr. Maze..."

Tom plowed his fist full force into Ted's shoulder, forcing him to reel back. Right at the arm socket, it felt dislocated and hurt like hell. Ted put on his best act, avoided rubbing it so as not to confirm he was in pain, and stood straight. After what happened with Anna he was in no mood.

"I'm going to let that one slide, but that's the last time you ever hit me. Do you understand me you stupid ape? Never again."

"What are you going to do, rat me out, Teddy Bear?"

Tom drew back his fist again but held it as Ted spoke. The words were like nothing Tom had heard before.

"No, I'm not going to tell anyone. Not the school. Not your father. If you ever lay another hand on me, you better be ready to kill me because I'm going to come at you with everything I've got. I'm not going to stop until one of us is dead. You'll kill me, but I'll rip your face off in the process."

Heart pounding, brain disconnected and everyone within a twenty-foot radius stopping to watch this reckless act of insanity, he moved up close on his toes getting into Tom's face. Through gritted teeth he added, "Even you can get it through your...*thick*...*brainless*...*skull*...that isn't a good idea."

Even Ciro would not have dared do something like that. All eyes were fixed on the kid who had just committed suicide. No one within earshot appeared to breathe. It was like a movie where time stops and everything hangs motionless.

Ted expected at any moment to be knocked to the ground but when it didn't happen, slowly began to take steps backward. Still facing Tom, he knew better than to turn his back on such an animal. The bell rang and all gathered to assemble for class. Whispers of what happened scattered around with eyes falling on Ted, all curious to get glimpses of this dead man walking.

Once in class, several rows from Ted, Tom slammed his fist down on his desk, generating a loud bang. Ted responded to the primitive demonstration by taking a textbook and slamming it flat side down to the floor, causing an equally loud bang. Even Sister Helen Keller heard and turned to quiet the class, which, following the display, had already silenced itself. They all wanted to get a look at Ted one last time before his wake and funeral.

Ted appeared calm and collected, as though none of this bothered him in the least. He even managed to maintain his trademark fake dull smile on his face. Inside, underneath the veneer of a thin layer of skin, he was all but rattling apart. Regretting what he'd just done, he plotted the safest route home.

Whether one's actions are judged as brave or foolhardy is most often determined by the outcome.

Alanon

The library was Ted's go to place for answers. On most visits he'd select an arm full of books, take them home and never read any of them. While on the checkout line something caught his eye. It was a stack of bookmarks for the group Al-Anon. "People Who Have Family Members with a Drinking Problem" was the description.

Tom! he thought as he grabbed a bunch with an idea filling his head. The next day he visited Mr. Maze's office to get enough business cards to staple one to each. The idea was simple—place them around where Tom would find them.

Whether he was doing it for the sense of power it gave him in driving Tom bonkers trying to figure out who was doing it or because he wanted him to get help was up for debate. Truth was that his motivation was a bit of both.

Unseen, he carefully planted the bookmarks where Tom alone would find them. Coat pockets, lockers, in his lunch bag. For two weeks, this went on. Then luck ran out. Shoving one in the cubby underneath his desk, he felt a large hand grip his head as though it were a melon. He knew it was Tom. He was the only one with a hand that big.

Why isn't my life flashing before me? he thought, with his heart in his throat, expecting to die. His head seemed to empty of all blood as he waited for the squeeze that would crack his skull.

"I got the message. Knock it off," is all he said before releasing him. Ted, already crouching, collapsed the short distance to the floor. He spent most of the remaining day in a sullen funk, doing all he could to stay out of Tom's sight. That was until later in the afternoon when their most outstanding quality essays were returned.

The A+ he received, circled and underlined for emphasis, snapped him out of it. He was less than enthusiastic about the comment though, seeing how the universe once again bent over backward to declare Chuck right. It read, "This is amazing. We need to talk. You are absolutely brilliant!"

He went for that talk after class. It was requested he do the unthinkable, read it aloud to his entire grade at assembly.

By reading that essay she was asking him to admit, in front of all, that he felt isolated, inferior, vulnerable, and flawed. Yet the essay went on to say that it was not only okay, but normal. That every one of them, much as they might try to hide and deny it, all of them felt the same, at least sometimes.

His first instinct was to jump out the window, but, after her gushing about everything, plucking lines from it and going on and on, "Why not?" We all have to die sometime, and he felt lucky to know when, where and how. For him it would be the following week, in the assembly hall and basically from embarrassment.

Admission

He approached the podium, pages in hand. He had reviewed the material so many times he barely needed to reference it. There before him was his entire class. It felt unfair so many eyes fixed on him, and he had only two to stare back.

His unsteady voice meekly chirped out its opening lines. Then, like wind coming into a sail, his confidence started to build. Soon his words became like cannon fire and the entire room was riveted.

"When I recognize a fault in myself, which is more frequent than I would want you to know, I refuse to leave it be. I refuse to sit back and let my problems and shortcomings determine my fate. I refuse to let a day go by without becoming more of the person I want to be!"

In the middle he tossed it to the floor. No longer reading he covered the concepts globally. At points he pounded the podium with his open hand as he yelled, his voice barely needing the microphone. Moments later he'd have to pause as his voice cracked with emotion.

"I'll make a bet there is one area where I can beat every last one of you. It is in the number of faults that I have, and fears too. There are so many times I feel that I can't measure up. I'm afraid I will grow up and become nothing. There are times I can't understand why anyone would want to be friends with me—"

He took a long pause as his next words truly tapped something deep inside that he was so hesitant to share, "—or why any girl would ever want to go out with me."

"But you know that already. And you know how I know? I know it by the way you treat me. I see it in the way you look at me. I hear it when you speak to me."

"So here, I have been honest in front of all of you. I've made this admission. But if you are being honest along with yourselves, you will admit that you have faults and fears too. And this brings us to where we might be different. I do not have the fear of facing any of it. I accept my faults for what they are and then fix them. Or at least I try. I will never wallow in my shortcomings, those things I can change. I can't stop myself from doing it. That is my finest quality. Every day I struggle to be a better person when I go to sleep than I was when I woke up.

"I have a suggestion for all of you. A call to arms if you will. A dare! Develop that quality. Every day improve something about yourself. Also allow me to give you a warning. Those of you who do this, our kind, will one day leave the rest of you in the dust. And far worse, you will have squandered the opportunity to become the person God meant for you to be."

The only reason applause was withheld was because everyone was waiting in anticipation for what might be next. The class had never seen this side of Ted. That former image they all held was now a smoldering crater. Anna had been at the edge of her seat and was the first to spring up and applaud, realizing Ted was done when he started obsessively adjusting his tie. The standing ovation that followed was for both the content and delivery. Even Ciro got out of his chair.

All throughout Ted stood humbly staring at his feet, as though what he had said was so obvious it didn't deserve the fuss it was receiving.

He hated the attention and was not about to put up with it any longer. He was supposed to take an unoccupied chair in the front row. Instead, as the applause faded, he abruptly turned and walked out, desperately needing the comfort of his empty classroom. There he patiently waited for the day to return to normal.

Ashley had listened spellbound to his presentation until realizing halfway through that she had most likely been its inspiration. She spent the second half slunk low in her seat in a pall of unshared humiliation. Her eyes never left Ted until he exited the room. One finger mindlessly twirled a strand of hair as she contemplated a most startling truth.

Ted had proven her right when she said they were in different leagues, but he had just made it clear to her it wasn't in the way she had assumed.

Selfishness

It was a cold November morning that it dawned on Ted why there had been no competition for the crossing guard assignment. When the days were warm and sunny it was the best assignment to have. On a day like today, with light drizzle falling, it had potential to be masochism at its best. Temperature hovering near freezing with a steady wind of twenty miles per hour, gusts almost double, there with Chuck, on the opposite side of the street, they lamented their mistake.

The mist from the sky was just a teaser. Foolishly, Chuck reached for an umbrella in his backpack hoping it would offer some protection. The wind quickly tore it to shreds.

Without warning, the drizzle became a downpour. The sound of the rain hitting the pavement, the trees, and the nearby parked cars drowned out all else. No matter how thick their coats were, the boys stood little chance against a freezing rain that fell nearly sideways.

"My books!" Chuck shouted. "The rain is going right through my bookbag. This thing is useless. Well, that's it, I'm going to fail. I'm never getting into Johns Hopkins now."

"You are so dramatic Chuck, go, get out of here. I got this," Ted shouted, just loud enough to overcome the rain.

Chuck didn't have to be asked twice. He grabbed his backpack, pressed it tightly to his chest and raced for the school entrance.

"Never saw a girl run so fast!" Ted shouted as Chuck passed him.

Now he stood alone against the relentless deluge. His coat came with a hood but wanting to seem less of a dork, he had detached it at the start of the season. No matter how much he tried to hold his collar closed, the ice water infiltrated inside. In a matter of minutes his underclothes were saturated, and he stood shivering uncontrollably.

His eyes, fighting the sting of the wind driven rain scanned the streets for anyone who might be crossing. Cars passed and pulled in front of the building, the young occupants leaving their warmth and dryness to scramble at full speed to get inside the building.

Holding his shaking hand over his watch to protect it, he checked the time. In just ten minutes the morning bell would ring and five minutes later he could go inside. Teeth chattering, shivering, clothes soaked as if he were standing in an ice-cold shower, the rain and wind refused to show mercy. He no longer had the will or the strength to fight, stretched his arms out wide, aimed his face to the sky and allowed mother nature to assault him unchallenged.

"Get inside! Get inside! What is the matter with you?"

The voice was Sister Ann's. She'd run from the school office the moment she noticed him. Both hands were firmly clutching her habit to keep it from being ripped from her body.

"I've got twelve more minutes," he retorted pointing to his watch.

"You are out of your mind. Get inside now. That's an order."

Ted grabbed his school bag and joined her in a mad dash inside the building.

She pulled the door behind them to keep the wind from seizing it and made sure it clicked shut. She was about to ask Ted why he chose to stand in a puddle before realizing he had just created it.

"Oh goodness, you are a mess. Let's get you inside the office," she said as she led him in pushing him toward the radiator.

To Ted it felt so unusual to be in the principal's office without being in trouble.

Sister Howard, stunned for a moment at the sight of Ted, then stood and exclaimed, "Good Lord what happened to you?"

"I couldn't leave my post. Today of all days, the kids need to be crossed," Ted said, shivering so much his words were staggered.

"I'll call his home, hopefully someone can pick him up," Sister Howard interjected.

"Ted, no one is walking today. Only a fool would be out in this weather," Sister Ann commented, before adding, "and I didn't mean you."

No one at his home answered.

"We'll try again in a few minutes," Sister Howard advised.

She then rose from her seat, took hold of a shawl hanging from her chair, and placed it around Ted's shoulders. It was not lost on him this was the first act of kindness she had ever shown toward him.

Sister Bethany entered and stopped midsentence when she saw him. "What happened to you?"

"I got caught in the rain," Ted answered.

"No," Sister Howard interrupted, "he was worried about the children and refused to leave his crossing guard post."

"What happened to Chuck?" Sister Bethany inquired.

"I sent him inside before it got awful."

"You know that no one is walking today. Didn't you realize that?"

"Yeah, I know. I know. I figured it out now."

"Well, it appears no one is home," Sister Howard informed the room after calling a second time. "Why don't you go up to the convent and put his clothes in one of the dryers?" she suggested to Sister Ann.

"That's a good idea," she replied.

Ted's face went pale. Did they really expect him to undress in front of Sister Ann? He'd have to stand there naked for what could be a half hour! While it was his worst nightmare, his teeth were chattering way too much to protest.

Being as disheveled as he was, Sister Ann took him the back way through the church to minimize the chance of any of his classmates seeing him. More than once, Ted considered running off. He liked Sister Anne. In fact, she was his favorite nun by far, but that didn't mean he would be okay stripping with her standing right there.

Once at the convent she led him to one of the bathrooms. Placing a plush white robe on the counter, she instructed him to leave his wet clothes outside the door. He exhaled a deep sigh of relief as she closed the door to give him privacy and the perceived return of his dignity.

Ted locked the door and gingerly undressed from clothes that were beyond saturated. He was even able to wring water out of his socks in the sink. Just before placing his clothes outside, he tucked his underwear into his shirt sleeve so she wouldn't see them.

Through the closed door, Sister Ann asked if he would like to wait outside but he declined. A short while later she slid a *Mad Magazine* under the door that she had confiscated from someone a few years before.

He hadn't finished reading it before there was a knock at the door signaling his thoroughly warm, dry clothes were outside. He waited for the sound of her footsteps to fade before cracking it open and peeking out to be sure the coast was clear. Right in front were his clothes, all neatly folded, with his jockeys sitting right on top.

Oh my God, she touched them! he wrestled with the thought. *Not bad enough she saw them, but actually placed her fingers on them.* Ted wondered if and how, with such knowledge, he might continue living. The concern was quickly driven away as he put his clothes on, the splendid dryer warmth present and transferring to his still seemingly semi frozen skin.

He hung the robe on a hook behind the door and emerged reenergized, ready to return to class.

"Don't go back just yet. I made you some hot chocolate. Let's warm you up inside too," she called as he passed the kitchen.

With that invitation, he sat and attempted a sip, too hot to drink just yet. It was made from real chocolate syrup and whole milk.

"Ah, this is the good stuff," he said as she sat at the table across from him.

Relaxing, waiting for it to cool, he never recalled being alone with a nun before. At least not at any time he hadn't been dragged by his earlobe. He loved Sister Anne and felt comfortable around her. Hesitating at first, he wondered if he might ask her something. The inquisitive look on his face gave his desire away.

"Is there something you want to ask me?"

"Yeah, actually, but you might think it's personal. Can I ask it anyway?"

"I may not answer it but sure, go ahead."

"Well, I was kind of wondering something. You know, I mean there's a reason I'm asking. You are not like the other nuns."

"How do you mean?"

"Well"—Ted surely didn't want to come across as insulting, but he genuinely wanted to know—"other nuns all seem mean and crusty. They walk around like they are mad at the world or something. Like they made a mistake and now they hate who they are and want to take it out on everybody else."

"I wouldn't say that at all. You see I know them better…"

"That's not my point," Ted blurted before catching himself. "I'm sorry for interrupting. I'll shut up now."

"No, you wanted to ask me something. Did I miss it?"

"Well, you see, you aren't like any of them. You are really good at being a nun. Everyone thinks so. I look at you and want to be a better Catholic."

Without realizing it Ted had paid her what she felt was the highest compliment.

"My question is what made you decide to become a nun? Was it a calling from God?"

"I love God. I serve him, and I am devoted to this life. There are a lot of great reasons to do good deeds, but in my opinion the best reason, the one that makes it most true and genuine, is when you do it for yourself. I became a nun because this is who I am, and the order is everything I want people to see in me. I could tell you it was to sacrifice, or worship the Lord, and all that is part of it, but at the end of the day, I became a nun for myself."

Seeing him confused, she asked, "Does any of that make sense to you?"

"Not sure I fully understand, but I'll think about it."

"See if this helps. Why did you stay out there this morning? Why did you send Chuck in while you got soaked? I'm going to tell you. It was a selfish reason. You were concerned that one of the kids might get hurt. You thought someone might need you. You had a sense of responsibility. You stood out there because that is who you are and the person you want to be. This morning you defined what it is to be you. You did it because it meant something to you. Ted, you will get the best results when you do good for reasons of selfishness."

He thought and, now with the clarification, understood more so why she was such a wonderful nun and how he could apply such a principle to himself. He raised the cup to his lips, blew on it, and took a sip. Remaining silent, he felt anything he might add would detract from the beauty of what she had just shared.

Payback

Debts can take the form of money due, work owed, a favor needing to be returned, an apology. One thing they have in common is all should be repaid. While it is most commonly repaid through places like a bank, this day it took place in the boy's bathroom.

By eighth grade there was no lining up to return to class. The bell would ring, recess was over and they would come drifting back in small groups. As was typical, Ted and Itch would dally, making it almost a point of pride to be the last to return. Itch would stop off at the usually empty bathroom and take all the time he wanted while Ted dutifully waited outside as everyone else meandered to class.

"Get out of my way, peasant. Royalty is coming through," Ciro barked as he gave Ted the usual shoulder bump as he was entering.

It wasn't long before he heard Itch call out from inside.

"You ass!"

Ciro had thrown a cupped handful of water onto Itch's crotch.

"Pissed yourself. Come on, get to class. It's late!" he gloated as he stood admiring his handiwork. With his back to the door, he failed to notice Ted enter.

If Ciro had done it to him, he would have done nothing. But this was Itch, and unknown to Ciro, there was a vow to be kept.

Everyone must die sometime Ted assured himself before doing the unthinkable—attacking! Breaking protocol and all gentlemanly rules that governed their fighting, he put Ciro in a headlock from behind. Brilliantly capturing the element of surprise, Ted bent him down, pressed forward and rammed his head into one of the urinals. Pushing his face into the trough, he flushed, causing the ensuing waterfall to gush liberally over Ciro's head, across his face and even enter his mouth and nose!

Ciro broke free and came up swinging but found himself unable to connect.

Each punch was met with a step out of the way or a block. Itch shoved Ciro from the side causing him to throw up his hands in protest.

"No fair! Two on one! This isn't a fair fight!"

"This is my fight, Itch! *Back off!*" Ted screamed.

"As you wish," Itch proclaimed, bowed then moved to lean against the sink and watch.

"Oh, this is going to be great," Ciro gloated. "You can't even...like that time with Ashley."

Ted knew what he was fishing for and finished it for him.

"Yeah, Ciro, I got beat up by a girl, and you can't even land a punch on me. What do you think that says about you?"

Ciro's face contorted in anger as he swung wildly. Ted moved out of the way and then stepped in closer, forcing Ciro to step back. He repeated the move twice, just the way

Rip had taught him. On the final attempt, Ciro's elbow hit the wall behind him, allowing Ted to make his move unchallenged.

A forceful right hook landed with a loud crack. Eight years of hate spread across four knuckles smashed into Ciro's jaw. His head hit the wall behind him so hard Itch looked to see if the tile was broken. Ciro spun. Had the sink not been there to grab, he would have been on the floor.

Itch's mouth hung open, Ciro was in disbelief, but neither was more stunned than Ted. They all paused as it appeared the fight was over. Ciro inspected his injuries, putting a finger in his mouth to feel his loosened teeth and a hand on the back of his head to check for blood.

Pulling his hand around, Ciro completed his inspection with his head slowly rising, eyes glaring.

"Do you realize who my father is?"

"Yeah, he's an even bigger asshole than you are!" Ted screamed in reply.

That was it. Ciro snapped out of it.

"You don't insult my family!" he yelled as he lunged forward, put Ted in a bear hug, and slammed him against the stalls.

Ted, still standing, rained punches across Ciro's neck, the sides of his face, and boxed his ears. Ciro tried to counter with hits to Ted's ribs, but for each one given, five or more were received. Unable to bear the punishment, Ciro collapsed to his knees, then rolled into a fetal position. Ted pounced on top of him. If possible, Ted would have ripped a pipe from the wall and beat it into Ciro's skull until all signs of life left his eyes.

This was no longer a fight. Ted was now determined to commit murder. He wrapped both hands around Ciro's throat and applied full force. With foam beginning to form around Ciro's mouth, Itch pulled to get Ted off.

"Get off! He's had enough!" Itch insisted.

"He'll have enough when he's dead!"

"Hey! Hey!" Itch yelled before slapping Ted across the face. "*Wake up!*"

Enough sanity returned to allow Ted to respect Itch's wishes. Ciro took the opportunity to gasp at life-giving air and then wiggle out from under him.

Both boys scrambled to their feet. It was only Itch standing between them that kept Ted at bay.

"Friends!" Ciro exclaimed panting, holding out his hand.

The nerve, what incredible nerve. Having lost, it wasn't even his to offer.

"Go to hell!" Ted responded.

"Ted, I swear on my mother's life, friends from now on."

"I'm coming in!" It was the voice of Sister Ann. She gave the standard several second warning before entering the boys room for the stowing of any outside baggage.

Itch nodded. "Do it."

That was the only reason he accepted. That, and because of the trouble he knew he was in.

"Friends," Ted replied, allowing Ciro to shake his limp hand.

Sister Anne caught the tail end of the exchange and knew immediately they had just reconciled from whatever had been going on. Given the looks on their faces, the noise from the ruckus and disheveled clothes, it was apparent they had been fighting. She wanted to hear it from them.

"What is going on in here? Why is your hair all wet!" she exclaimed pointing at Ciro.

"Uh, uh, uh," Ciro uttered with long pauses in between as he tried to catch his breath. "Uh, you see. Um, I got some gum stuck in my hair, and uh, well, Ted was trying to help me get it out and we started horsing around a little."

She rolled her eyes and turned to Itch. "What happened?"

"I didn't see anything."

Frustrated, she turned to Ted. "Well, Ted, at least, I know you'll be honest with me."

She was right. He couldn't lie to her.

"In all honesty, I don't think I can make up a better story than Ciro just did."

"We're friends now, Sister Ann," Ciro said, putting his arm around Ted's shoulder, then adding a broad smile.

The goal of the school wasn't to punish. That was the means to encourage the kids to behave. Sister Ann had the good sense to know this goal had already been achieved. Suspensions, expulsions, Ted might not last another round.

"I want all of you back in class now, and if I ever see any of you behave like this again, there will be no mercy. You understand?"

"Yes, Sister," they replied in unison.

"Dry your hair first!" she barked at Ciro, then left.

Itch and Ted left while Ciro held back to pull paper towels from the dispenser.

"Sorry I hit you back there," Itch whispered as they walked.

"Sorry I didn't kill him," Ted responded as they hurried back to class. Before entering, Ted noted Ciro emerging with a handful of paper towels and pressing them to his hair.

Itch entered first. In all the excitement, neither had noticed or remembered that Itch's pants still had a noticeable wet spot. A big circle right at the crotch with a streak running the full length of his leg. The class burst into laughter.

Sister Helen Keller turned to see who it was, squinted, and near as anyone could tell, only knew they were boys. She motioned for the two to sit. Embarrassed, Itch meekly took his seat with Ted following. Steve didn't waste the opportunity to say something snide.

"What do you two gay guys do when you are together?"

Ted looked at his now humiliated friend and remembered something. To end one controversy just create a bigger one.

"I took a piss on Ciro's head," he replied, louder than necessary, stunning everyone within earshot.

"What!" Steve questioned.

Ted realized how this was about to unfold and repeated himself, this time loud enough for the entire class, minus Sister Helen Keller to hear.

"You heard me. I said I took a piss on Ciro's head!"

Just then Ciro walked in still pressing paper towels to his hair. The room filled with a collective, very audible gasp.

"Oh my God!" one of the girls screamed.

"Ciro, what happened?" Steve uttered as he sat in the chair the next row over.

"Oh man, you don't want to know."

"What did that little dirtbag do?"

"Hey!" Ciro interrupted. "Don't say anything about Ted. Me and him, from now on, we're cool, got it?"

Steve's head spun to Ted, who rolled his tongue across his lips seductively, then puckered them in a kiss and finished it with a wink. The last thing Steve wanted to do was mentally process whatever might have just been implied. Facing forward, eyes focused on the blackboard, he did everything possible to erase any thoughts from his mind.

The class looked at Ted as though he were crazy. All except Itch, who, stunned beyond his wildest expectations, knew full well, in addition to the fight, what Ted had just done for him.

Ciro believed he had dodged a bullet, and no one would find out Ted beat him up. The obnoxious fool had left one crucial detail unaddressed.

Friendship

"Extra! Extra! Read all about it! Blimp-sized bully gets the cannoli beaten out of him by my best friend!" Itch came in the next day with a flier he'd created to resemble a newspaper headline and had a hundred copies made. "Go ahead. Ask him about the red mark on his chin," he said as he passed them out to everyone in sight.

"That's what happened yesterday. I was laughing so hard watching Ciro get his ass kicked that I peed myself."

Shocked, stunned, embarrassed, panicked, there was no describing the look on Ciro's face as he realized what was going on. He rushed to Itch, confidence so shaken from the day before, most uncharacteristically, he tried a tack other than immediate violence.

"Hey, what you got there? Let me see. Well, joke's over, you going to stop?"

Itch continued as if Ciro wasn't even there.

Ciro got close to his ear and whispered, "All right, how about I give you a hundred dollars?"

"Sell out my best friend?" Itch shouted. "Not going to happen."

"I'll beat the crap out of you!"

"You? Really? You're going to beat the crap out of me? Watch out or maybe I'll get Ashley over here and she'll beat the crap out of *you* this time! I'd do it, but you seem so obsessed by the time it happened with Ted, you'd probably enjoy it, you sick moose."

Point made Itch tossed the remaining fliers high into the air, leaving Ciro scrambling to gather the falling cascade.

"There's the guy you respect so much," Itch said to the crowd of Ciro's cronies as he deliberately pushed through the middle of them.

Careers

"The whole place was talking about it," Rip exclaimed excitedly as they met to work out after school. "Ciro sure had a bad day, he went home before lunch."

"I was wondering what happened to him."

"Why couldn't you have had it out with him in the schoolyard? Then we all could have seen it."

"It just kind of happened, it was spontaneous. I used all the stuff you taught me. I owe you so much. You know if it weren't for you—"

"Don't get mushy on me. I hate that. You're the one who did what you had to do. That's all there is to it. Tell you what, let's celebrate. I was going to give you something for your birthday next week but let's do it after this."

"What is it? What did you get me?"

Ted's best guess was sparring gear.

"It's a surprise, something special. If I give it to you now you won't be able to work out."

That blew sparring gear as the most likely item. Rip didn't have any money so what the heck could it be? It was on his mind the entire workout. Then the mystery deepened.

They went up to his room. There was nothing unusual in that until he closed and locked the door. Neither said a word as Rip opened his closet and emerged with a bunch of karate books. The second time he emerged with an armful of weightlifting magazines. For the final trip he disappeared for an extended period and could be heard moving things around. When he came out, he had a healthy stack of Penthouse magazines. Ted's mouth dropped, and his eyes bulged. Before the days of easy access to smut on the internet, such things to a teenage boy were worth more than a solid bar of gold!

"How did you get your hands on those?" Ted asked in amazement.

"My dad, he doesn't think anyone knows. He gets them, and when he's done, he throws them out and always puts them at the very bottom of the trash. Well, it's my job to take out the trash!"

"It looks like you never miss a copy."

"Don't think I have. I've been doing it for like two years now. Okay, here's the deal," Rip explained, interrupting the many fantasies already going on inside Ted's head. "You get to pick one from any of these. Magazines, books, any one you want."

No offer of thanks. No recognition at all. As if in a trance, Ted stepped up to the Penthouses and perused the covers. He didn't dare open any of them, wanting some privacy before inspecting the surprise that awaited inside.

"You know this is one of the best books ever written on jujitsu," Rip noted, picking one of the book selections. He was more than a bit insulted Ted wasn't even remotely considering anything else.

"This one," Ted said, selecting a *Penthouse* with a pretty blonde on the cover dressed in frilly white lingerie.

"You sure?"

"Oh yeah, I think it's time for me to get going. Thanks for the gift. I'm late for home anyway."

"It's only four thirty. We haven't gone for the run yet."

"Got to go."

As he raced home so he could enjoy his birthday gift, he'd already figured out an excellent hiding spot. Thinking himself clever, he'd put it in the box beneath the game Trouble. His mom was a world-class snoop and went through his drawers regularly but seldom the games in his closet.

Passing his mom as he stormed through the door, he barked he had a very complicated homework assignment and not to bother him in his room. He locked the door, tested it twice to be sure no one could walk in, and then pulled out the magazine. Anyone venturing a guess as to what he did next would be correct.

He emerged some fifty minutes later, breathless, and sweaty, hair askew, having reached a life-altering decision. He was definitely not going into the priesthood. While he had known it for quite some time, the decision was now final. He was happy to have made it but disappointed in himself over how it had come about.

It was supposed to be something beautiful. He envisioned the answer coming in a vision while deep in prayer. Jesus himself would hover above on a cloud with a bright halo over his head, beams of sunlight encompassing them both. Words spoken softly would direct how he was to spend the rest of his life.

Instead, it was made while staring between the legs of a naked blonde, the image convincing him there were some sacrifices he was just not willing to make. There could not possibly have been a worse, more guilt-laden way to reach this decision. In any case, he was relieved to have come to it, the method used only convincing him further that such a life was not good for him, or rather, he was not good enough for it.

Exorcism

On this day, his fourteenth birthday, Ted was ready for birthday punches. He approached the schoolyard with bravado, bracing for the inevitable from his friends. He didn't expect it so soon and was surprised when Dave passed and took the first shot. Ashton, Rob, half a dozen others followed in quick succession. He plodded on, becoming a living punching bag. Ciro seemed to enjoy it the most. Tom, who amazingly asked for permission first, was definitely the most painful. When it was done his eyes were watery, arm useless, but pain had never felt so good.

Anna caught up to wish him a happy birthday and apologized for not having his gift right there. It was something extra special she said. Anna's gift sat covered in brown paper, safely in Mr. Maze's office. Waiting until the end of the day, she retrieved it giving him a warning as she handed it to him.

"Here you go. Happy birthday. Please though, you have to take it home and open it there. Do not let anyone else see it until you do."

"This is gigantic. I assume it's a picture?" It felt like an enormous frame, which was thirty-by-forty inches. "I bet this wasn't done in a couple of minutes."

"I've been working on this every day for almost ten months. I wanted to do something special for you ever since the school fair last year and this is it. It's my first oil painting."

"I can't take this if it's your first oil painting."

"You have to. I made it specifically for you. It's about you."

"About me? Now I really want to look at it."

"Not here! Take it home and look. Make sure no one is with you."

"I guess it's not a sketch of my face. Why can't I see it now?"

"Well," she sighed, "it's personal. Look very carefully at the details. You might not like it. It's okay if you don't. I can paint something else."

"I'm sure I'll love it."

"Okay, well, happy birthday. And again—"

"I know. I have to be alone when I open it."

Given the size of the picture the walk home was long and torturous. His mind drifted into what could be so personal. He had an idea though. This was probably a nude. He cringed at the thought of her painting him unclothed but couldn't help but wonder how generous she might have been with her imagination when it came to his parts. Oh no! Perhaps it was a nude of her, or maybe them both!

In a stroke of luck his mother was doing laundry and he snuck to his room without her noticing his coming home. She would have been all over that package. This was it. He'd do it in one swipe. He grabbed a corner and with one motion of his arm, tore off the cover.

An absolutely horrid sight assaulted his eyes. There in the picture was an image of him, brutally slain. A broken body, fragments really, fingers of one hand severed and laying about. One eye had been gouged and bowels eviscerated. A second image of him was bathed in a bright light standing over the broken body, a blood-soaked sword in his hand. Turning away he sat in shock, trying to comprehend why Anna would have created this.

He had to summon courage before taking a second look. Her instructions were to look at it closely. Just like everything in life, meaning is found in the small details. Ignoring the picture as a whole, he put his face close, examining each brushstroke for some clue. There it was. Barely visible, yet legible, an inscription had been etched onto the sword. With just one additional piece of information, his entire perspective changed.

Later in life he would own original works by masters such as Rembrandt, Picasso, and Van Gogh. Yet it was this picture by Anna that was the crown jewel in his collection. Hung on the wall behind his desk in his office, he loved the utter shock on people's faces, wondering what kind of sick depraved man would display such a thing.

No one could see the tiny inscription that ran the length of the sword. It read:

"It Was Here I Fought Inside Myself To Slay My Demons And Changed To Become A New Person."

Realignment

Whoever thought Ted would stay after school voluntarily? It was all part of a master plan he had put together when he learned about a new peer tutoring program. A recent addition to the school, a student with an A average would volunteer to tutor a classmate who needed help. For math the tutor was Elle, his crush from the third grade. The girl who had shown him the birds and bees. He immediately signed up hoping something between them could be reignited.

He stood outside the class fixing his tie for two solid minutes, attempting to get it perfect, then spent another five building his nerve to go in. All the while she looked at her watch wondering where he was. He entered with high hopes, but disappointingly, the lesson began cold and impersonal.

"Let's start on page fifty-eight, the Pythagorean theorem. What it is saying is A squared plus B squared equals C squared."

Ted wasn't listening. His eyes rolled over her tightly tied strawberry-blond hair, her angelic face, her beautiful, perfect complexion, her lips. His mind was far from all this math nonsense. There he was next to her gazing over a field.

Maybe it was corn that had been standing tall just a few weeks before. It had been freshly cut, leaving stumps, like razor stubble on the face of the earth. The sun was rising with its subtle warm beams of light embracing them both. Just like in third grade they giggled over nothing. They took each other by the hand and began to run, or more like dance across the field. They stopped to gaze into each other's eyes. The sun positioned behind her head gave the effect of a halo. With one hand he grasped her by the arm, with the other he began to unbutton her shirt.

"What are you doing?" she asked sharply, clearly annoyed.

It was just then Ted realized he was stroking her arm. Completely oblivious but now aware and mortified, he snapped his hand back and excused himself to the bathroom. He stopped at the fountain instead and splashed water across his face. It was nowhere near cold enough to extinguish the burning desire that radiated throughout his body. Liquid nitrogen would not have been cold enough. Too embarrassed to return, he abandoned the otherwise useless lesson.

He unloaded on Itch the next day.

"I was actually feeling up her arm. I had no idea I was doing it. Thank God it was only her arm I grabbed."

"That little strawberry cupcake would never go for you," Itch argued.

"That's what you think. She and I, well, we have a special connection."

"Yeah, like what?"

"Well, I shouldn't tell you this. You have to swear on your life you will never tell."

"Yeah, I swear, what is it?"

"Well, back in the third grade, we used to talk a lot and share secrets. There was one secret more special than all the others combined. You see, this one day she had me excuse myself to go to the bathroom."

"Let me guess. She took you into the girl's room for her version of show and not tell."

Ted's face went pale.

"You look shocked. She did that to all the boys."

"*All!*" Ted exclaimed with the same emphasis on the word a millionaire might use when finding out he lost *all* his money.

"Well, I don't know about all. Me, Tom, Ashton, Rob. What, you thought you were special?"

"That...that...that harlot! She used me!"

"Oh, get over yourself."

Ted suddenly wasn't feeling well. Begin with a fond memory of a girl, add a generous helping of misinterpretation, throw in Itch's special spices of derision. Now bake it until everything in the memory is ruined and you have a recipe for mental illness.

"She got busted with Geo," Itch blurted.

"Geo! What the hell, how did you find that out?"

"He told me."

"That kid is the biggest blabbermouth in the school. So, what happened to them?"

"That part he didn't tell me. Suspended I guess."

"Where was I when you were finding all this out?"

"I don't know. Maybe you were in one of those comas you spend six months at a time in."

"And you never thought to ask if she had done it to me?"

"I just assumed she had better taste."

Ted covered his face with his hands and groaned.

"I made an idiot of myself yesterday."

"Only yesterday?"

"Could you lay off for just five minutes?"

"No, I can't. Dude, a lion roars, a frog jumps, and you should know this one best, a snake bites. We do it for the same reason, it's our nature."

Vows

That afternoon, Itch and Ted were out riding bikes. They stopped at a park not far from their homes to take a breather. Off the bikes, Ted placed his ten-speed against a bench and turned to Itch, who had just dismounted his. The look on his face was odd.

Just then, Ted noticed the stranger standing before them both. A teen, maybe sixteen or seventeen, just standing there. He and Itch facing off.

"Give me the chain," he demanded of Itch.

Ted looked down to see a gun aimed at Itch's midsection.

Itch reached behind his neck to feel for the clasp, but panic had already set in. Hands shaking, he could not get it to open.

"This is a gift from my grandmother. She gave it to me a week before she died."

"No bullshit, man, you got three seconds."

"I can't. It's not opening! Don't be pissed at me just because you're too stupid and lazy to make honest money."

Itch could not believe he'd just said that. Such was his personality that the words had been automatic. The gunman raised the gun to his head.

"I'm trying! I'm trying!" Itch stuttered.

"You f——," the gunman retorted.

Nothing is remembered as certain in times of extreme stress, but Ted would have sworn on a stack of Bibles that he saw the gun's trigger and hammer start to move. Choices, both great and trivial, can have huge effects. Choosing left over right, extending a conversation a little longer, traveling home a different way can hold life-or-death consequences that we will never know. Unaltered, the book of Itch's life was writing its last chapter. But fate was changed by Ted's next move.

"I have money!" Ted exclaimed as he stepped forward squeezing himself in between the two, pushing Itch two steps back in the process. A gun that had been mere feet from Itch's face was now aimed straight into Ted's right eye.

Focusing on the blackness of the barrel, it felt as though ice water were being pumped through his veins. He contemplated if the trigger was pulled, would the thickness of his head be enough to keep the bullet from hitting Itch.

"You can have all my money. I'm going to reach into my pocket to get it. Is that okay?"

Ted shoved his hand deep, pretending there was a wad of bills he was trying to wiggle out. He had all of three dollars and crumpled it so it would look like more. Lightheaded, too scared to look anywhere but the gun, he handed it over. One bill escaped the exchange and fluttered to the ground.

That was the moment of opportunity! The assailant bent over to pick it up. With the gunman's neck exposed, Ted believed he could use his weight and break it with his elbow. He had practiced such a move with Rip. While it stirred in his head, his muscles did nothing. He froze. Not even a flinch. He watched, frustratingly, as the bill was snatched, and the gun returned to position.

By this time, Itch had unclasped the chain, reached over Ted's shoulder, and handed it over.

"I'm taking the speed," the gunman said, referring to Ted's beautiful ten-speed bike.

"It's a great bike. Take it. It's yours now," Ted offered.

"Follow me and I'll kill you," he asserted as he mounted the bike.

The two boys, feet cemented to the ground, watched him ride off.

"We'll go to my house! Its closer!" Itch yelled, mounting his own bike and riding off before Ted had a chance to say anything.

On foot, Ted ran as fast as he could to Itch's house, arriving three minutes after.

The front door was open, but Ted stood outside patiently knocking. When no one came, he sheepishly went in and called out to acknowledge his presence.

"Come in. We are in the kitchen," Itch's mother called. "He just got robbed!"

Itch hadn't told her much of the story yet. Ted, breathing heavily from the run, otherwise stood so emotionless it seemed inconceivable he was mugged too.

"He was there with me. He got robbed too. They stole his bike," Itch reported.

"And three dollars," Ted added.

"Oh, heavens, Ted, come in. Please sit. Sit."

She handed each a glass of water and called 911.

Focused on the items lost, and more than a little shaken, neither thought to mention the gun. They were instructed to go to the precinct to file a report. While Itch couldn't steady the glass of water in his hand, Ted seemed aloof, passionately disinterested, staring stoically at the kitchen wall as though watching a boring TV show. One hand reached repeatedly to his neck to fix a tie that was not there.

"You should call home. Do you want me to do it for you?"

Ted groaned. "No, I'll do it." Good God, breaking this news to his mother would be worse than the mugging.

"Hi, Mom," he began, trying to keep from sounding stressed.

"Dinner's just about ready. Where are you?"

"I'm at Itch's house."

"You were supposed to be home ten minutes ago. I made swordfish. It will be ruined by the time you get here!"

"Mom, I have to tell you something."

"I'm going to throw it in the garbage. I don't care. You want to know why? Because you don't care. You don't care about anyone but yourself."

"Would you listen for a second? My bike got stolen."

"What! The one we bought for Christmas! Do you know how much that cost?"

"I know. I'm sorry."

"Well, let me tell you, Mister, that is the last bike you are ever going to have."

Following that, the line went dead.

Ted pretended he was still talking.

"I'm okay. Everything is fine. I will. I will. Love you too, very much."

When Itch's mom waved to him, wanting to speak with her, Ted returned the phone to the receiver.

"I wanted to talk with her. What did she say?"

"She doesn't need to speak with you. She told me she loved me, and I should come home."

"Yes, let's get you home. I'll drive you."

"Can I stay here just a little while. Please?"

He was in no condition to deal with his mom. He stalled as long as he could so his dad could be home when he got there. It wasn't until he filed a report at the precinct that they realized a gun had been involved.

Albums filled with mugshots were presented and even a sketch artist was called. When she was finished all Ted could think was how much better a job Anna would have done. The whole process took hours. All the while, his mother fumed and paced awaiting his return. She was under the impression that he had carelessly left his bike and someone walked off with it. Upon learning of the gun, she became hysterical, "You could have been killed!" It took Ted and his dad two hours to console her.

Ted went off to sleep that night very disturbed, mostly about himself rather than the mugging. He believed he could have taken the guy. The moment the mugger bent over, it was right there, but he did nothing. This was proof he was a coward. And now that cowardice had cost Itch a precious chain. He wondered if Itch would ever speak to him again.

Misinterpretation

The incident made the neighborhood crime watch on page thirty-seven in the newspaper. The details were pathetic. It merely said two teens were robbed of jewelry and a bike. There was no mention of a gun. Their classmates, painting the picture that they had just zealously handed over their possessions awarded them "The Two Most Likely to Surrender."

The same as with everything, it was misreported and misinterpreted. Their parents knew some details, the police report contained lots of facts, but the exact specifics were known only to those present. Even then their interpretations varied tremendously.

Itch seemed oddly distant the morning of their first day back together. During a break in the late morning, after avoiding Ted as much as possible, Itch planted himself into an empty desk directly behind him.

"Don't turn around. Just face forward and keep your eyes on the blackboard. If you don't see me, I can deny it was me who said what I'm about to."

"Okay," Ted agreed, baffled.

"I owe you some money." He passed forward a five-dollar bill.

"What's this for? I only lost three dollars."

"Nothing to do with that. I owe you this, and a lot more. I'll give it to you when I have it."

"Huh?"

"It's about cards. There's something I need to tell you. You know how I win all the time? It's because all these years I've been cheating."

"Cheating? What do you mean? How?"

"We've been playing with a marked deck. I can't believe you never figured that out. I'm going to pay you back, every nickel, with interest. And another thing, it's about that summer camp I always brag about."

"Yeah, what about it."

"Well, I've been lying about that too."

"What do you mean? Late-night beer? Scantily clad Girl Scouts? Gwendolyn?"

"The whole thing, all of it. There is no Girl Scout camp on the other side of the lake, no late-night beer runs. I made it all up. I mean, the place does exist, and my parents force me to go, but it isn't at all like I told you. There's a garbage dump two miles down the road. I'm not kidding, it's a real dump. You can hear the trucks going by all the time. Day and night. It never stops, and when the wind blows the wrong direction, it smells like rotting corpses.

"Worse than that is the food. The Styrofoam it comes in is more appealing. And the bugs! Oh my God, the bugs! There have to be a thousand types in those woods that science has yet to discover."

"The girls, all that kissing, third base?"

"All made up."

"Why would you do that?"

"'Cause the only fun I got out of that camp is the look on your face from the stories I'd tell you."

"Itch, do you have any idea how jealous I was over what I was missing."

"I was jealous you got to stay home."

"So why are you telling me this now?"

"Why? Because that's no way to treat someone who saves your life."

"What are you talking about?"

"You know, Ted. Don't make me say it."

"I really don't."

"The gun, Ted. You stepped in front of the gun. That guy was going to kill me. I could see it in his eyes. My life was flashing before me. I was remembering things from when I was a toddler. It stopped the moment you stepped in front of me. That was the bravest thing I've ever witnessed, and I'm including TV and in movies. I don't have words to describe it."

"It wasn't brave. You're my best friend. I did it without thinking."

Itch threw his hands up to cover his face. He erupted into a groan that lasted until his lungs emptied.

"Why did you say that! Good God, you didn't even have to think about it! That makes it ten times worse!"

"It's not a big deal. You would have done the same for me."

Itch replied with his eyes, and they weren't reassuring.

"You would have done the same for me, right, Itch?"

"I can't lie to you. Not about this. I had that gun aimed at my face, so I know how it feels. I would have wanted to. I really mean that. But I don't have the kind of guts you do."

"No, you would have."

"No, Ted, let's be clear. You are a better man than I am."

Ted was stunned. If Itch had been replaced by an imposter, other than the words flowing from his mouth, the resemblance would have been remarkable.

"I will never forget this. Never. I'm still going to razz you. It's an automatic reflex that I can't turn off. But no matter what happens, whatever I might say, I will never forget what you did and never allow you to forget it either."

"Well, whew! It feels good to come clean on all this. I'm done. I'll give you more money when I have it. I figure I owe you something like $200."

Ted didn't know what to make of it but there was one additional thing he didn't know. The next time he felt his life threatened it would be by someone he knew.

CIRCLE

Present Day

Ted turned to the people in the office recollecting a story that took place toward the end of eighth grade.

"Tom walked up to me in the schoolyard. His setup was simple. He asked me if I was doing anything Saturday afternoon. I should have known to ignore it. Instead, I told him I was free. Big mistake. All he said, and it was more like a grunt, was "My house, be there, 1:00 p.m." I knew what it was, he was intent on murdering me. He'd get me down in the basement and I'd never be seen again. What could I do though? When Tom demanded something, you had to do it."

"So, did you go?" Robert inquired.

"Just a moment," Ted instructed as Karen gave him a nod.

"Well, Theresa, here is the part of the ride where you get off. The car is here."

She had been distracting herself by listening to his recollections. This woke her up to the reality she faced.

"Please," she mouthed to him taking one last shot at mercy. The cold dark eyes of a viper stared back.

"Remember our deal," Ted snapped.

She managed to keep most of the hatred off her face. She stood and silently walked out the door.

"That was strange. Where is she going?" Robert observed, commenting on how she left.

"She won't be back today. Things appear strange only when you don't have all the information. Speaking of which, I have something interesting to show you on Theresa's desk."

This was it. Karen, John, Devon all watched intently knowing things were about to unfold swiftly.

"But let's address Robert first, shall we? Recently I set up a foundation. Its purpose is to enhance the educational system. Work directly with children, find the very best educational methods, and then roll them out across the country."

"That sounds great. If you would like me to help in some way," Robert offered.

"Love your understatements. I specifically want to apply your methodologies. I'm asking you to Chair the Committee."

Confusion and horror mixed within Robert's mind. He believed anyone who found out about his past would never have him working with children.

"I couldn't Ted, I was thinking of getting a second job anyway. I wouldn't have time."

"This is a paid Chairmanship. We would revolve it around your schedule here. Working two days a month you'll be paid even more than you make now. We'll talk about it in a little while. Now, let's go for that surprise in Theresa's office."

While Robert contemplated to himself, wondering how he was to get out of it, John was appalled. Ted would reward this pedophile and put him in contact with children all because of misplaced admiration and some stupid sentimental chain. He looked at his watch more satisfied than ever that Robert's destruction was now in his hands and only a few minutes away.

FATE

A chauffeur dressed in a tux held open the door to a stretch limousine as Theresa approached.

"Where am I going?" she questioned as she got inside.

The man, having worked for Ted for years, knew how to answer without preparation. "Your destiny."

Before the car had moved, Theresa was rummaging through the bar.

"Is there anything other than water?"

The driver didn't answer and instead closed the partition between them to end any further questioning.

The restaurant was surprisingly close. She had passed it many times with her husband, but never dared to venture in given the prices.

"I need a minute," she said as the car idled in front. "Dear God, you have no reason to show me any mercy, but please don't give up on me. I admit I have a sickness, and I will do anything, absolutely anything, to get better."

Ted was excited as they filed into Theresa's office surprising the others by the overturned garbage pail on her desk.

“Wait until you see what is under here,” he gloated. “I’ve looked forward to unveiling this all day.”

Ted loved the metaphorical drum roll. This version of power.

CURTAINS

The sign in the window said, "Closed for private party." Theresa knew she was the party. She was one door away from selling yet another piece of her soul, just like she used to in the past. She questioned if perhaps death was a preferable alternative as she made up her mind and entered.

"Ah, Theresa?" the maître d' exclaimed, expecting her.

"Yes," she replied, wishing she wasn't.

"Signora, come."

The main dining room was dimly lit. All the tables were finely set but unoccupied. It seemed as though ghosts were sitting throughout, patiently waiting to be served.

"We have a special room set just for you in the back."

The words made her shudder. She could hardly begin to imagine what sick fantasy a man like Ted had preplanned. It was then she came to a fateful decision. As she passed one of the tables, she grabbed a steak knife and slipped it into her purse. There was one thing she could still control. She would take her life before he got there.

She was shaking when the maître d' opened the door. Without thinking, she stepped forward. The sight that greeted her nearly made her pass out.

DECEPTION

Gathered in the office, Ted lifted the pail. Underneath was a Waterford crystal candy dish.

"This was the closest I could find that looked like the dish that was on Mr. Maze's desk. I know it may not seem like much, but I'm thrilled to put it here."

At the restaurant, "Mommy!" Theresa's youngest daughter exclaimed. Standing to her left was her other daughter and then her husband. Joining them was her mother and several close friends.

Unable to comprehend, she didn't notice the tall stranger standing to her right.

"My name is Frank," he began, holding out his hand. "I have spent the last week getting to know everyone here, and I can tell you one thing for sure. They all love you like crazy, but, Theresa, things must change. Sit down beside your husband. Everyone has something they need to say. I think you know what this is."

THEORIES

Ted took his place in Theresa's chair and rolled the short distance to her bookshelf.

"My heart leaped when I saw she had this book." He pulled out *Addiction in Modern Society*. "Did you see who wrote this? It is our own Karen who stands before us. You won't find my name anywhere, but we wrote this together. All of what's in here, I learned in this school. Most of it from Mr. Maze."

"One of my passions is rehabilitation. I set up institutions that apply the methods in this book. One of the ones I founded is the Mathew Maze Center for Rehabilitation. We harness things like the most primal instinct, fear of death, to get people to change. It becomes a driver when they realize they must change or die. Most important is confronting feelings. Facing them head on, and learning to accept yourself along with them. Our success rate is as high as it gets.

"The program is otherwise free to anyone who reaches out for help but it does come with a catch. Any person entering the program must come in fully accepting their sickness and willing to do anything to get better. Without that, it's a waste of time.

"I'm sending Theresa there to study it. And I meant to thank you, Robert, for giving her the next three months off to do so."

"Paid? No notice?"

"Of course, who is going to mind?"

"The trustees for one. I can't give her that time off."

"Oh, but you did. When you signed the papers today, there was a clause that school employees are to be permitted time off for training as I see fit. Well, I see fit. If anyone gives you a problem, have them call me directly. I guarantee they will never bring it up again."

Ted took a breath to provide a momentary pause.

"And now, Karen, please leave the folders with me. I'd like to ask everyone except Sister Margaret to leave the room. We have a private matter to discuss."

VERDICT

Sister Margaret prayed as they exited. She knew in her heart this day would come. She had hoped she could just grow old and fade away. Now it was all over. She had hastily prepared a resignation letter.

"You know, don't you?" Sister Margaret stated more than inquiring, as he shut the door. "You know I'm Harriet."

"Yes, you were. The embezzlement, prison, your child, the stolen identity. Do I have it all?"

"You left out drug addict. But I think you are missing the most important part. I was a terrible person years ago, but I've changed. You believe people can change, don't you?"

"Have you been listening to anything I've been saying all day? But to truly change, the very first step is you must be able to end any and all lies you may tell yourself and others."

"Take this," she stated, extending her hand holding her resignation. "I assume you think I can't be trusted and that I stole the school's money. I need you to believe only one truth. I would never do anything to hurt the children. You can do anything you will to me. This is in God's hands."

"No, this is in my hands. The hands God gave me. When I came in this morning, I wasn't sure what happened. I didn't have time to thoroughly review the financials, but I didn't need to. I knew you would make a mistake that would reveal the answer and you did."

"What mistake? What could I have done?"

"First, let's take care of this nonsense," he said as he began to tear the resignation. "At two minutes after nine this morning I had one million dollars wired into the school's operating account. You knew money was coming in at some point today, yet by 1:42 p.m. you hadn't even checked."

"You must think I'm incompetent."

"Not sure that's what I would conclude, but one thing is for sure, that is not the behavior of a thief. You didn't bankrupt this school, you saved it."

"You saved it, Ted."

"No, I came in and gave money that I already have too much of. You worked here and struggled to keep it going every day. The way you dedicated your life and your sacrifices is how you saved it. And I have a few things here to recognize it. As you probably suspect, it involves these two folders in my hand. It comes with a catch of course."

He handed her the first.

"I'm afraid to open it."

"Well, *Margaret,* for over two decades you have been living under an assumed name. I can't imagine the pressure that must have put on you. Wondering every day if your world were to fall apart."

"And what is this?" she said, waving the folder.

"Your identity. That folder contains certified documents under your assumed name. It says you had your name legally changed twenty-eight years ago. There is a passport and a social security card with the number you have been using. These are all official court issued. None of these are fake. And that old warrant for your arrest was terminated as of an hour ago."

"I'm at a loss, I don't understand how—"

"I'll give you the short version. I do favors for the people who run the witness protection program all the time. Bluntly, they owe me. When I approached them for this, they went all-out."

"I can't believe this. I have to let it sink in before I can even thank you. This is truly real?" she asked upon opening the cover to find a photo of herself on the passport. "How did you get this photo?"

"As I said, I gave you the short version. Remember though, I did say there was a catch, and that leads me to folder number two."

REBIRTH

Her hands were shaking as she took the folder from him. Before she could open the cover a picture of a young boy fell from it to the floor.

"Sorry, let me get that," she said as she plucked it up. "Who is this?"

"Someone special," Ted responded.

"Is he *your* grandson?"

"No, his name is Ian, and he is your grandson. There is a picture of your granddaughter in there as well. Everything in there is information related to your daughter."

"My daughter?" She looked and felt as though she would faint.

Ted moved up and put an arm under her shoulder and guided her to a chair. Finally, flabbergasted, she was able to say something.

"Every day, every single day I wondered if she was okay."

"She's better than okay. She's an attorney working in Chicago, married, two children. There's a lot in that folder. Schools, friends, her adoptive family.

"I knew you would be shocked, but that look on your face, *wow*. However, would you like to discuss the catch?"

Sister Margaret remained too stunned to respond.

"All right, I guess I'll just go first. The condition I place on you is that you call her. You must do it today, now."

"I'm in shock, Ted."

"As she will be. You'll be on equal footing. If you put it off today, you will again tomorrow, and the day after, I'm standing here now. You will do it now, that is my price."

"I appreciate this, I really do. I'm going to recite special prayers for you, but I can't do what you ask. I can't call her."

"She's at her office. That was verified a few minutes ago. If all goes well, I want you to fly out to see her. I'll let you use my private jet. It's the one with the big sunflower on the side."

"No," she shook her head, "I can't, Ted, I abandoned her. I never saw her take her first steps or hear her speak her first word. I was not there when she was sick or frightened or had a broken heart. I was never there to make it all better."

"But you can be a part of her life now."

"She must hate me, and she has every right to. You wouldn't understand."

"I do understand!" He retorted forcefully. "You forget I have experience with this sort of thing. You asked me earlier what I thought of my mother. I told you it wasn't time. Now it is time.

"I don't know what was going on in my mother's life the day I was born, but she decided to give me up. Having had children of my own I could not imagine anything more painful on that day than knowing I would never see my own child again. It would break me apart, as I am sure it did you."

She could no longer maintain her composure. Grabbing a tissue, she spoke between sobs. "You have no idea. Maybe you do. I never even got to hold her," she spoke quivering.

"You can put your arms around her now. You can hold your grandchildren. But that still didn't answer your question as to my feelings toward my mother.

"They say the greatest love a man can have is to give his life for another. I think there is one greater. It is the love that must exist for a mother to give away something so precious as her own child because she wants them to have a life better than she can provide. That is what I think of my mother."

Overcome with emotion, tears rolled liberally down Sister Margaret's face. Ted sat patiently in silence before she looked to the phone.

"What would I possibly say to her?"

It appeared Ted was transfixed in thought. "I've got it. Tell her you have loved her every day of her life even though the last time you saw her was the day she was born. She'll instinctively understand."

The intention was to remain to provide any comfort she might want and leave when she was ready to dial the number. The plan was interrupted by a knock on the door.

"Not now!" he yelled.

"It's an emergency!" Karen shouted through the door.

Karen was not one for drama. Whatever it might be, was significant.

"My apologies. Apparently, I must leave. Make the call."

STANDOFF

Ted entered the school office to find a stalemate among Devon, John, and Robert.

"I was right in the middle—"

"You'd better sit, Ted," Devon instructed.

Now it was Karen *and* Devon. Against his instinct, he did as Devon suggested.

"All right, now I'm seated. What is going on?"

"Devon, would you?" asked Karen.

"John has accused Robert of being a pedophile."

Robert sat stone faced and closed his eyes, then dropped his face into his hands.

Ted showed the worst possible, most deeply concerning reaction, none at all. If there was ever a time to fear this man, this was it.

"And where did you get a notion like that?" he asked, his calmness like that of the eye of a hurricane.

"In those papers. It was there. I saw it. Beatings! Rape! Outright torture! How do you do that to kids? Five-year-olds! I hope you die a miserable death! And you, Ted, are even worse. You go ahead and reward this man all over some stupid chain you gave to some fat ass years ago."

"Are you done?"

John had expected more. The silence was only broken by Robert's sobbing.

Ted's hands were clenched and shaking. The stare he gave, had it been aimed at Medusa, would have turned her into stone.

"Okay, let's get something straight here. Those court documents you may have seen were all part of a trial. There were several children involved, unfortunately. Most unfortunately. The suffering that went on there is not something I can or want to describe. Cigarettes crushed out on their back, hair pulled out, beatings and as you might guess, sexual abuse of a level so depraved, I couldn't sleep for two days after reading it."

"There were several Jane Does cited, but only one child was mentioned by name. It was the one who bravely fought back. The one who put an end to the abuse and put those sick bastards away for life."

"When Robert gave me the chain, because of the connection, I realized one of the Jane Does must have been Anna. As for Robert, everyone in this room needs to know the truth."

Robert lifted his head. "Please, Ted, for the love of God don't."

"From the bottom of my heart, Robert, I am sorry, but this needs to be said. Robert is no pedophile. He was one of the unfortunate victims, and he was also the one who fought back."

"Holy God!" Devon exclaimed, then moved to Ted to place his hands on his shoulders so he wouldn't be able to get up. "You need to know something."

"Don't treat me like a child."

"I'm just going to say it but control yourself. John sent out a press release telling the world this school is being run by a pedophile."

"What!" Ted yelled and slammed his fist so hard onto the desk in front of him, the pictures on the wall shook.

Had Devon not been there he would have sprung across the room and beaten him to death in front of three witnesses.

"I hope he followed it with his obituary!" Ted yelled.

Robert interjected. "No, Ted, that is where you are wrong. I am what John called me. If you read those papers, you know. You know that I participated in her abuse. It's a sin I can never forgive myself for."

"I know what you did. It was all there. You were forced, Robert. They made you do it. Remember: sin isn't an action. It is a choice to do wrong. You didn't have a choice."

"I should have done something, told someone at school."

"Robert, you were what? Nine, ten, twelve years old?"

"It was during that time, but I did nothing."

"You are judging the actions of a child using the standards of an adult. You can't do that. And you are leaving something out. You did try to stop them. And when you did what happened? They hit you so hard they broke your ribs and had to take you to the hospital. That's when it all came crashing down and you told. You didn't abuse Anna, you saved her."

"I don't see it that way."

"That is not Anna's perspective. She recommended you for this job. Perception, Robert. I've spent the whole day trying to get you to realize that."

Robert buried his head onto his folded hands on his desk and wailed uncontrollably. John stood stone faced.

"All right, we have to fix this. What do we do? Think, think," Ted said, half to himself and paced the office several times before muttering, "I know how to do this."

He took a seat and began breathing deeply. Serenity, a peace moved over him.

He moved his thumb and first finger of each hand together. Other than the sound of Robert sobbing the room was quiet, and continued this way, nearly frozen, for several minutes. Calmly, he opened his eyes and stood. He knew what to do.

"We need a bigger controversy. Devon, get the office on the phone, top priority. We need to get a list of all the schools within fifty miles of here and the names of the principals. We are going to put out the exact same press release but change the name and school. We will release hundreds of them. Then we say our computers suffered a cyberattack and all those releases have to be ignored."

"Do you know the legal liability you are opening yourself up to?" Devon interrupted.

"It doesn't matter. This is my mess. I have to fix it."

"You mean it's John's mess."

"Devon, it may not be my fault, but it is my responsibility. Get a retraction out now and then get IT on the phone. We probably have a half hour to get this done."

"Wait!" Robert declared. "Ted, when you had that fight in the parking lot, how old did you say you were?"

"Twelve."

"And the girl was five. He broke your ribs too." He looked up, the revelation taking him by surprise. "It never happened, all of this. Everything you have been telling us today, all the stories. You made them up. You have been teaching us to face our demons."

"Nicely done, Robert, but that is only partially correct. There are lessons in these events I needed to make sure each of you knew. I admit to taking some artistic liberties with a few of the facts to make them fit better, but just about all of it happened."

"Which parts did you modify?"

"That does not matter. Whatever you believe to be true is true. The impact remains the same. I'm glad these things all happened to me the way they did. I am happy with who I am today. Had anything been different in the past, that might not be the case."

Robert took a huge breath and let go a deep sigh.

"I'm going to face it. What you said, it's time to let go of my fear. Don't send out that press release, just do the retraction. I'll deal with whatever the fallout might be."

"I know how much you suffered Robert, but just look at who it turned you into. Steel is forged in fire. Just look at how your troubled past has shaped you into the incredible person you are today. It has been an honor and privilege to be able to spend this day with you."

"Now I have one thing left to take care of," he said, turning to John. "Do I even need to go through the formality of firing you?"

The pale look on his face was still present, but his eyes rose as though he had something righteous to add.

"I wouldn't be that smug if I were you. We need to speak in the office. Alone."

"Okay, let's do it then. I can only imagine."

"Not him, he stays outside," John said, pointing to Devon as he went to follow Ted inside.

"John, the last thing you want is to be in a room alone with me right now."

"Fine, whatever, he should probably hear it anyway."

They entered the room and closed the door. Ted took a seat behind the desk, Devon stood by his side and John remained standing facing them both.

"You want to go first?" Ted stated to John.

"I do. Today, while you were busy being autistic, I was getting another job. I was just hired by someone I think you know. Does the name Benjamin James Arlington mean anything to you?"

"Now why would you want to be associated with a man like him?"

"Why? Because Ben is smarter than you, wealthier, more powerful, and far more dangerous."

"I wouldn't assume any of those things but continue. Why should I be concerned?"

"Because I have something of yours. As smart as you and everyone around you think you are, you are stupid when it comes to cybersecurity."

Ted's mouth dropped, speechless.

"That's right. It's all there, all your operations. Everyone you have had murdered. Horrible stuff."

"John, I'm going to give you one chance. Don't do this. Do you have any idea how completely I can destroy you?"

"I think what you mean to say is how completely I can destroy you. So, here's the deal. I gave Mr. Arlington a hard drive with everything on it. All he needs is the password. Should anything happen to me, I have it set to go to him in an email tomorrow at exactly twelve noon. Now, I'll stop this whole thing for the right price."

"And exactly how much do you think that is?" Ted calmly asked.

"Whatever your life is worth to you. I know what Ben will do to you. So, I'll let you decide, but whatever number it is, it better have at least seven zeros behind it."

"Are you crazy?"

"We'll see. You have my number," he said holding up his cell phone. "Good day to both of you." He gave the middle finger rather than a handshake as he left.

Ted put his face into his hands and rubbed his forehead before looking up.

"Devon, that was fascinating. He is every bit as stupid as you said."

"No, wait, you want to see stupid. Come to the window, Ted. I want you to see this."

"Don't do this to me, Devon."

"No, come here. Look, there he goes. Driving off in the Mercedes you bought for him. I told you when you hired him not to give him that as a sign-on bonus."

"Yeah, yeah, I know. I thought kids only treated their parents like this."

"Ted, I have to tell you. I almost lost it when he was going through that whole it-better-be-eight-figures thing. I guess he never heard you say the first line of defense against a thief is to make them believe they have something valuable."

John had not considered many items that were out of place. The fact Ben had not already destroyed Ted. The concern over the yearbook that morning.

Ben and Ted acted as though mortal enemies. What we think, because perception is manipulated to make us believe, is often in direct conflict with reality. The truth was, the two were closely tied. Way back, Ted had taught Ben how to buy stocks. Subsequently, Ben showed Ted how to buy entire companies.

The two became wealthy independently, but it all accelerated on a fateful day when Ben, unable to do two deals at once, sent his other deal over to Ted, making him a modest fortune. Having the abrasive nature he was known for, Ben couldn't leave it alone and endlessly rubbed the gesture in Ted's face.

Not to be outdone, Ted sent a bigger deal Ben's way, then exceeded him in the after-gloat. The money aspect no longer mattered. It became a war for bragging rights that went on to this day with the two secretly throwing deals at each other, each trying to gain the upper hand. Currently, Ted was winning.

Ben was not amused. Scheming and plotting, he looked forward to that glorious day he would send the FedEx declaring himself the winner.

"So, Devon, did you take care of Robert as we discussed?"

"His mortgage? Yes, it's gone. We also found six maxed out credit cards and an auto loan and knocked those out too."

"Good, how about the brokerage account?"

"Yes. One million transferred into his name. Everything has been recorded as a sign-on bonus, so we took care of the taxes as well."

"Excellent, you always anticipate."

"I'm confused about one thing. I thought as a rule you never gave out money to solve people's problems."

"I don't. I still believe money is the simplest and least effective way to solve a problem. This is different. Robert saved my dear friend. I want to make sure he knows that's how I view it."

"Today he came here flat broke. Are you going to tell him he's leaving a millionaire?" Devon inquired.

"No. I hate that whole scene where he has to thank me or try to give it back. He'll realize it when the account statements start coming in the mail. Odds are, after today, I will never encounter any of the three of them again. I'll just give him this note before I leave."

The note read, "Buy stock in companies whose product or service you like. Sell them when you stop liking the product or service they produce. Keep it simple. Follow this rule and you will do well."

FRIENDSHIPS

Ted went to open the office door, but quickly closed it.

"It appears Karen is giving Robert some advice. She has a wonderful touch with that stuff. Let's not interrupt. We'll hang back here for a while. So, what is on my agenda for next week?"

"Monday, just a couple of meetings. Tuesday the bank is coming to discuss the petroleum deal."

"No, Devon, the flowers?"

"Oh yes, of course. The files are waiting for you back at the office. It is set for Thursday. On the surface you are saving an animal shelter. For the main purpose you have four projects, all volunteer there. Shaniqua lost her daughter in a car accident two years ago and is battling severe depression. Larry is an ex con just diagnosed with terminal liver cancer. He found redemption and now regrets everything he has done with his life. They say he has six months. Caroline has two children. Her house burned down earlier this year, one of the kids has cystic fibrosis. She is one step away from being homeless. Finally, there is Samuel. He's a heck of a nice guy with a failing business who attempted to take his life two months ago."

"I'll work on it this weekend."

"Oh, Friday you have that obnoxious councilman who wants $50,000 to approve the building permits."

"Great, I get to wear my black hat with him."

"Speaking of black hats, what's the game plan for John?" Devon asked.

"He is going to be Ben's international liaison to Indonesia."

"Indonesia? Why there?"

"Ben has high-level connections within the government and the penalty for drug smuggling is death."

"I see. So you're going to have him killed?"

"That's a bit harsh. Don't you think? No, I'll swoop in at the last minute and save him. He is about to get one hell of an education, though. A few years from now, he will be changed, and a much better person."

"You need me for any of this?"

"Nah, Ben and I will work out the remaining details. We are getting together to play cards this weekend."

"By the way," Devon exclaimed, hitting Ted's arm, "you never told me you saved Ben Arlington's life."

"That's because I didn't. He's the one who always made a big deal of it."

"Do you realize what you did? You stepped in front of a loaded gun to save him."

"You say it as though I had a choice. Ben was my best friend, and I had made a vow that I was willing to give him my life."

"You made that vow in sixth grade. Most kids wouldn't take it seriously."

"I have a number of doctors who would say it's because of my Asperger's. Everything to me is literal. A deal is a deal, a vow a vow. I can't be indifferent. When I say I am going to change, I do it. My mind won't allow me to do otherwise. Ben proclaimed once that I am a better man than himself. If that is true it is my autism that made it so.

"Speaking of which," Devon inquired, "I know you don't leave loose ends. What did you do about the kid on the bicycle?"

"The one Theresa hit? Broke both legs. He's fine now. But talk full circle. I bought him a bike, the best they make, to replace the other one. He's going to find himself accepted to every college he applies to, and when he finishes, I'll make sure there is a good career opportunity open to him.

Just then Devon's cell phone rang. He listened for a minute then said, "Thank you," and hung up.

"That was Frank at the restaurant. He said she became so emotional they almost needed a spatula to scrape her off the floor. She had a specific message she wants relayed to you."

"Yes?"

"She said to tell you she wholeheartedly accepts your deal. She also wanted to say that this morning she thought you were the devil, but now realizes you are an angel."

"They are not one and the same, and she was right about me both times, yet I didn't change at all. I wonder how many people could solve that brain teaser!"

It appeared Karen was done counseling Robert, so they entered the office. Robert questioned, "I assume you fired John? He left in quite a huff."

"Not exactly, I have plans for him."

Just then Sister Margaret entered. Tear streaks were evident on her face, but her smile said it all.

"I prayed for this day. What can I say to you? What can I do for you?"

"If it was prayer that kept this school open, you can pray for me anytime. How did you leave it with her?"

"She wants to meet me. She said to come out as soon as I can."

"Good. Take the week off. Take two. My office can handle the stuff around here. And let me give you this," he said handing her a credit card.

"We will put you on the account. This has no real credit limit, use it while you are away. Be good to yourself. You deserve it after the stress you have been under. If that card doesn't come back buried into six digits, I'm going to be very disappointed."

An already-stunned Sister Margaret became more so. "I don't know what to say. You would give this to a thief?" She whispered into his ear.

"I would never do such a thing. In fact, I have an idea. Let everything settle after your reunion. In a few months I'll let you borrow the jet again. Take your new family and go to the Vatican, see Rome. I will have you blessed personally by the pope."

Looking at the clock he held up his hand. "It's time for my speech. I'm going to do this one alone. Everyone will be more relaxed if it's just me anyway."

He straightened his tie yet again, then pulled from his pocket and affixed that bull-and-bear tie clip from long ago.

Glancing at his watch, he exclaimed, "Karen, you never fixed that clock! It's still twenty-three seconds slow. Now I'm going to be late."

GARDENING

Knowing exactly where to go, he snaked his way through the halls to the church.

Rather than enter logically through the side door, he instead entered from the back. While many prefer a grand entrance, Ted prided himself on his ability to enter a venue unnoticed. He had developed a perfected slither so that even with shoes against marble floors, barely lifting his feet, if at all, he slinked in from the back to an audience of greater than ninety souls who did not sense his presence until he was upon them.

The chatter as he coiled in from the back was ever present. He knew how to get their attention. The execution was perfect.

He pulled an envelope from his jacket containing $10,000 in hundred-dollar bills. It had been brought in the event of some emergency requiring cash, but had become, at least in his mind, superfluous, given it was the end of the day. He divided the bills between his hands and spread out his arms, gently sprinkling them over the aisle as he slinked by the students, corralled in the first few rows.

"These are all hundred-dollar bills," he stated with an innocent casualness.

"They are! Hundreds!" one observant student excitedly exclaimed. That brought everyone's attention along with silence.

Two steps up and set off to the side was a podium with three empty chairs on each side. He recalled a different location to the front of the altar where the acoustics were perfect for being heard without the aid of a microphone. There he sat on the floor with his legs straight out resting on his palms. Without gray hair, he would have resembled an eight-year-old boy.

Without hesitation, he began while the kids were still captivated by the money and surprised by where and how he sat.

"Fellow classmates, decades apart. I'm not going to bother telling you my name. It has no relevance, and you will forget it anyway. Suffice to say, I am a nobody, but when you consider it, that makes me just about everybody."

"Your principal and the other administrators will not be joining us today. Take note of the empty seats over there. I'll tell you what it means. You can plan all you like but you never know where life will take you."

"The bills you see scattered on the floor, each of you will leave with one today. It is my graduation gift to you. First, though, you'll have to listen to me. I have a message that may be the most important of your entire lives, or it could be meaningless. It all depends on how well you listen and the extent to which you apply the advice I am about to give you."

"The pearl of wisdom that I share was given to me by my fifth-grade teacher in this school. At that age I had big dreams and ambitions. I thought I knew the key to happiness. I wanted to be rich and famous, I wanted to be a great success. I wanted to change the world. Alas, I had such minimal talent to bring me there."

"Young friends before me, it was my teacher who told me how. She shared the secret with me. If I wanted all those things, she said to find happiness, be a success, change the world, all I had to do was plant a flower. I was baffled by its simplicity. Plant a flower, she said, and watch it grow. Watch how it provides so much, beauty, shelter, and nourishment for all around. In time, the seeds will spread to grow more flowers and the cycle continues on and on. In a thousand years the world will be changed because of that one flower. Now, she said, close your eyes and imagine this. Imagine a world where you planted flowers every day."

"To the naive child I was, those inspirational words meant nothing. Thankfully, she wrote it down and insisted I put it in a special place. I placed it on this empty shelf I had in my bedroom. I called it my trophy shelf, although it never saw any trophies. Years later, I came across that paper and by that time I understood its grand eloquence."

"What she said made me realize that people's lives are like gardens. I'll provide some examples of how that is. You will experience challenges. There will be difficult times. You might want only sunny days, but every garden requires rain. You should come to understand you cannot experience life without it."

"Another thing you will face is change. Change is the fertilizer of life. It often stinks but it is necessary for growth."

"And just like any garden, you need to be careful of what and how you plant. You will need to spend time and nurture this garden. There is no such thing as gardening from afar. You must be involved. It is not enough to just write a check. You must get your hands dirty."

"Like every garden, you have to keep the weeds out. Things like the obsessive pursuit of fame, fortune and power. Characteristics you find in the seven deadly sins, lust, gluttony, sloth, greed, wrath, envy, and pride. All are terribly destructive weeds. Never allow them to take hold."

"Like it or not, you can refer to yourself as a doctor, lawyer, businessperson, parent, police officer, politician, or scoundrel. You are all gardeners. To do it well requires diligence, humility, intelligence, and most important of all, self-sacrifice. These are not easy and are why so many people prefer to look for the things they believe will bring them happiness elsewhere."

"Now, should you find yourself blessed with fortune or cursed with fame, there is nothing wrong with these, but my advice is to use them as tools to help you with your planting."

"Many years ago, as an altar boy, I served a wedding mass in this church and received a hundred-dollar bill as a tip. The same that each of you will receive today. I don't know what you will do with yours, but I planted mine, and from that a most beautiful flower grew."

"The meaning of life comes down to the effect you have on others. I am addressing you today because I want to help you succeed, but not in a way success is often perceived. The best way I know to do that is to help you realize how important it is to master gardening."

"I've said what I needed to say and as much as you needed to hear. You either got it or you didn't. My best to each of you. With your lives ahead of you, I wish upon you the cultivation of the loveliest flowers."

That was it. He got up and was out the door so quickly there was hardly time for polite obligatory applause. When he arrived at the office, Robert asked if he thought he got through to them.

"You really think I'll change their lives with a five-minute speech? All I was there to do was plant the seed. They looked at me like I had three heads. I'm still as different now as I was back then, and I pray that it never changes. Well, it's been a good day, much accomplished."

"Thank you for saving the school."

"Yes, that too. So, my work here is done. Time to get home."

They assumed he was eager to return to his life of luxury. Truth was it was his turn to do the laundry. One might have expected him to live in a mansion filled with servants, but nothing could be further from reality. He believed life is all about the everyday mundane. If you don't do them yourself and do them well, you ultimately miss out on everything. He lived a comfortable modest lifestyle, preferring a four-bedroom colonial to a mansion and a Toyota Corolla to a Rolls. He did own a private jet, but that was strictly for gardening, situations like flying Theresa to rehab, moving people away from disasters, angel flights. He had never been on it. He once saw it and that was from the outside. He wanted to get a look at the giant sunflower that he insisted be painted on its side.

He would never allow himself to fall into the materialistic trap Walter Burke had inflicted upon himself. Happily married with three children, he took off the entire months of July and December to spend with them. No email, phones or any way to contact him. It would be easier to spot the real Elvis than it was to find him during those months.

"But you didn't finish your story," Robert protested.

"I'd love to hear more," Sister Margaret interjected.

"I said everything I needed to say, and everything you needed to hear, you either got it or you didn't."

"But you left us on a cliffhanger. You said Tom was going to murder you. So, I need to know: Did Tom murder you?" Robert inquired.

Ted relented. "To spoil the ending, no, Tom did not murder me. However, the circumstances were surprising."

Caution

Spring 1980

At Tom's house, there were balloons tied to the mailbox. The front door was open with at least twenty people inside. Lightly knocking, still considering turning and running, Ted was met by a woman who introduced herself as Tom's aunt. Once ushered through, he became an instant VIP.

"Everyone, *this* is Ted," she proudly proclaimed.

The greetings from the room were warm and diverse. "What a wonderful young man," one exclaimed as others came to shake his hand.

He didn't know if he was frightened or relieved upon the sight of Tom, who suggested he come to his room and seemed to be going out of his way to be friendly. Human sacrifice. They must all be devil worshipers, and he was to be their offering. It was the only thing that made sense.

His eyes nervously scanned the doorframe to Tom's room, then the inside of the room, trying to spot some trapdoor or trip wires. All he noticed was just how much *Star Wars* memorabilia was packed everywhere. TIE fighters hung from the ceiling, *Star Wars* bedsheets, stormtrooper helmets on the shelves, posters of everything from Chewbacca to the *Millennium Falcon* adorned the walls. Apparently, Tom was insane for all things *Star Wars* in addition to just being flat-out insane.

"This is so awesome!" Ted gushed, not caring one iota about the crap but doing it to stay on Tom's good side. The act continued all through Tom's lengthy tour. Coming to his most prized possession, Lando Calrissian's cape, mounted on the wall like a jersey, he took it down so Ted could hold it.

"This was an extra on the set. I have a certificate of authenticity."

"How were you able to get anything this incredible?"

Ted had no idea what he was holding. For all he knew, a Lando Calrissian was the make of some new car model. *The Empire Strikes Back* had barely been out a week, and he had no interest in it.

"Got it at auction. You really like it?"

"Yeah, it's the coolest thing I have ever held in my hands." Ted laid it on thick before all his gushing backfired.

"You should take it."

"Huh? What?"

"Yeah, I want you to have it."

"Ah, this?" Mind still working on why this could be happening, he now figured Tom would accuse him of stealing it and use that as an excuse to kill him.

"I'll get the certificate that goes with it."

"No, no, no," Ted fired off in rapid succession. "Ah, how about…? You think maybe I could have one of those X-Wing fighters instead?"

There were about a dozen laying around.

"Seriously? You sure?"

"Those fighters are pretty neat."

"You want two?"

"No, one is plenty."

Just then Mr. Maze poked his head into the room.

"Hey, Ted, they told me you'd be in here."

"Oh, thank God!" Ted exclaimed, now not caring if he insulted Tom.

"I was expecting Rod Serling to jump out of a closet and *The Twilight Zone* music, do do do do, Do do do do, to come on at any moment," he added as they walked back to the main gathering.

"Did anybody tell you what this is?"

"I have no idea."

"They asked me to have a talk with you. Why don't we go out in the backyard for a minute?"

Happy to get out, they walked from the house to a quiet spot.

"This party and everything, it has to do with Tom's mother," Mr. Maze began. "I believe you know Mrs. Chenko has a problem?"

"Yeah, she's a drunk."

"Actually, the term we use is alcoholic. You see, when someone stops drinking, we call that sobriety. Do you know what an intervention is?"

Ted tried to guess but missed. Mr. Maze continued.

"It's not important. The fact is that she has not had a drink, an alcoholic drink that is, in six months. This is a sobriety party. It's a big deal for someone who is an alcoholic. The reason she got help is because Tom came to see me and that was because of you. That's why you are here. This is all because of you."

Suddenly, Ted looked distressed. He put one hand up to his face and groaned.

"Oh no, please don't do this to me. How embarrassing."

Mr. Maze could have easily countered with an instinctual "Don't feel that way," but he was a master.

"You can feel that way, and I understand why you might but try something. Later today, stand in front of a mirror. Pretend the reflection is someone else who did what you did. Then go over with that reflection all of the positive things that have come about because of those actions. Then tell that person how they should feel about it.

"On Monday during lunch, stop in and see me. I have something I want to show you."

Ted agreed, left the yard, and planted himself on a couch in the living room, explicitly chosen because no one else was there. His solitude was broken soon after. There he appeared, like a bear, a mountain, an asteroid, it was Mr. Chenko. He came into the room and sat on the opposite end of the couch. This left just one cushion between them with Ted feeling very uncomfortable.

He thought of switching to a different chair, but his legs were too frozen in fear to execute the maneuver. He diverted his gaze, moving it to the ceiling as though something up there was fascinating.

"I don't know why I'm here," Ted proclaimed almost apologetically and clearly nervous.

"I wanted you here." Mr. Chenko began. "So, how is school?"

"Fine," Ted replied with his all but patented answer.

"So, a lot going on. You know which high school you'll be going to?"

"Yeah, I managed to get into the one my friends are going to, All Saints Academy. I got accepted everywhere I applied. I don't know how that happened."

"I do, you're a smart kid."

"Well, we both know it wasn't on a baseball scholarship."

With that comment the temperature in the room must have dropped twenty degrees. The giant man suddenly seemed out of place in his own home. He rubbed his forehead then swept his hand over his bald head, bringing it to rest on the back of his neck. He turned toward Ted and said his next words with a never imagined softness.

"I never should have treated you the way I did."

"That's all right, it's okay."

"No!" the man snapped. "There is nothing okay about what I did, nothing at all. I was having problems in my own life, and I reacted by beating up on a ten-year old."

Ted sat still. His eyes moved everywhere but toward Mr. Chenko. "I was eleven," he whispered, as if it made a difference.

Mr. Chenko intended the conversation to wind its way into an apology, but a lump formed in his throat. Consumed by shame, his face reddened as he crossed his arms over his chest, eyes closed, and he took several deep breaths before getting up. Unable to take the conversation where he had intended, he only spoke as he left the room.

"If you ever need a letter of recommendation or anything, well, I suppose you already got into the school you wanted. I'm glad to hear it. All Saints Academy is quite an impressive school. They're lucky to have you."

If he wasn't already feeling out of place, those words topped it off. He wasn't about to sit there and be insulted. He glanced at the X-Wing fighter in his hand. It was time to tuck it away on his special shelf. He lifted it to the level of his eyes and in his mind strapped himself in and throttled the warp drive to full power.

Extending his arm as though it were pulling him, he got up and traveled home at light speed.

Leadership

"You left the party," Mr. Maze commented when Ted stuck his head through his office door that Monday. "We looked all over for you. They had a speech prepared and everything."

"Now I'm especially glad I left," Ted responded.

"Why? They wanted to acknowledge what you did."

"Oh yeah? Then why did Mr. Chenko start making fun of me?"

That left Mr. Maze dumbstruck. "I could not imagine that. What did he say?"

"It was the high school I'm going to. He said they were lucky to have me."

"And what's wrong with that?"

"You know what he's implying? That somehow the school's standards aren't up to ME. That academy? Only the smartest kids apply and eighty percent of them can't get in. Can you imagine?"

"Yes Ted, that is what he is implying and I assure you he was being serious. He credits you for what's taking place with his family. He holds you in very high regard. Trust me on that."

"He wasn't making fun of me?"

"I'm positive."

Ted stood staring blankly, thinking, contemplating.

"Really? I was miffed about it all weekend. You know something Mr. Maze? I'm going to tell you something I've never admitted to anyone. You ready for this? There is something wrong with me, I don't know what it is, but I never see things the way others do."

"Why do you think that is wrong?"

"How could it not be? The world sees something one way and nothing little me sees it differently?"

Mr. Maze thought, then spoke.

"Albert Einstein. Ever hear of him?" he said with a smile.

"Of course, who hasn't?"

"Think about him for a moment. There was a day he thought up the theory of relativity. It was one of the greatest discoveries of all mankind. On that day he was the only person on earth who saw what he saw. I'm sure many of the world's great minds would have said he was wrong on that day. But he knew differently. Sound familiar?"

Ted didn't answer and Mr. Maze leaned forward as if sharing a secret.

"I want you to consider something, maybe when that happens, it's actually your true genius shining through."

Ted thought about that. "I don't know, it gets me into such trouble. I never know the right thing to say or do, it's all so confusing."

It was just two sentences, but Mr. Maze's next words would forever uncomplicate his world.

"Ted, when your head is confused and you don't know what to do, recognize that. Then put your thoughts aside and do what your heart tells you. I don't think you should worry about it so much. I've gotten to know you pretty well, and I have to tell you that you seem to have the most special unique gift I have ever seen in a person."

"God gave me nothing to work with."

"You tuck this away, Ted, because I'm going to tell you what it is. I don't know how you do it, but you seem to have an almost supernatural ability to set things right. Now please, I asked you to come in today to show you something."

Ted sat patiently while he opened a box and set up a line of dominoes.

"Watch this." He then pushed the lead one over and in sync, one after the other, they all came down. He picked up the first domino and handed it to Ted.

"Do you know why this one is special?"

Ted looked at it curiously. Rolling it in his hand, inspecting the dots, the corners.

"Should I?"

"Here, let me have it back." He then set them up again, placing the domino Ted had been holding at the front of the line and repeated the exercise.

"How about now? Did you see it this time?"

Ted shook his head. He once again took that first domino and handed it to him.

"Let me tell you why that one is special. It's because it was the first. It made everything happen. Without it, nothing changes. What you did might have been the smallest of gestures, but it started everything rolling to restore a number of people's lives. Does that help you to understand why you were the featured guest at the Chenko celebration?

"I want you to keep it. Put it someplace where it won't get lost. Someday when needed, I want you to hold that domino in your hand. Think about why it is special and how much it represents you."

Mr. Maze knew he didn't understand, but that wasn't the purpose. Even if he had, he wasn't ready to accept it. The hope was to plant a seed that would blossom on some day when he needed it. Ted went home that day still not comprehending its meaning but at least had the good sense to place it on his trophy shelf.

EMULATION

Present Day

"In the symphony that is life, it is necessary for so many aspects—every instrument, if you will—to be finely tuned to create beauty. I never met with him again. I didn't know at the time, but that was to be my last concert attendance conducted by that master maestro. Things got busy with graduation and all. He died of a stroke a few years later. I never even thanked him," Ted commented, trying and failing to suppress deep emotion contained within his voice and spinning a domino between his fingers. Everyone assumed, correctly, it was the one Mr. Maze had given him.

"We take and take when we are young, and it becomes our responsibility, our duty, to give and give as we get old. The greatest gift we can give back is to live our lives in a way that makes those who supported us, loved us, proud of us. It is a gift that transcends time and the one thing that can be given to someone even after they die."

"Robert, hold out your hand." As he did, Ted placed the domino onto his palm, then forced his fingers to close around it.

"This domino means a lot to me. I want you to have it. Take it along with the advice Mr. Maze gave me."

“He gave that to you. I can’t accept it.”

“No, it is time to pass it along to someone more deserving than myself. I don’t think you understand how grateful I am for all you did for Anna.”

Speed

Spring 1980

For a young teen, a bicycle isn't just a mode of transportation—it is a social necessity. Friends would meet and ride off wherever. Having had his stolen, Ted was left out of his already small circle of friends. His top priority was to buy a replacement, but his funds were low, and he refused to let his parents help. Instead, he went around to his neighbors, willing to do anything, cleaning, weeding, errands, to try to earn a few dollars, but found no takers.

He was getting tired of hearing about his friends' trip to the mall on Saturday mornings. He liked malls, especially ones that had water fountains and the one they were going to, four miles away, had recently added a new wing that had three.

Since he wasn't going with them, there was full justification for sleeping late. That was the plan at least until his mother knocked on his bedroom door.

"Ted, get up. Someone is here."

"What? Who?"

There was no reply. He knew he had to get dressed first. He wouldn't be caught dead in the pajamas he was wearing. They had pictures of little dinosaurs scattered on the bottoms and a big T-Rex head on the shirt. He was way too old to be wearing something so juvenile, but they came in his size and were exceptionally comfortable.

By the time he was ready, his impromptu guest had left. His mom was walking back inside the house, having been outside.

"Who is it? Who's here?

"It was that guy Walter. You should have seen his car."

"Mr. Burke! Mr. Burke was here? At our house? Why didn't you scream it was an emergency?"

"He asked me not to bother you. We needed to talk about something. Then he had to go, but he left you a gift."

"I'm awake, right? You said Mr. Burke was here?"

"Go outside. Look in the driveway."

There to the side was a ten-speed bike adorned with a yellow bow. It was a brand Ted didn't recognize, extremely light, and it looked like it was built for speed.

This meant the return of his freedom, his friends, his social circle. It was nothing short of readmission to a club whose membership had been suspended. The entrance ticket was sitting right there in his driveway with enough time to get to Chuck's house and join them at the mall. Those weren't his plans.

He ran into the house, scribbled a note onto a piece of paper, tucked it into an envelope, then out to mount his new, fantastic ride. While it was far, he was determined to ride to the Burke mansion.

On his old bike he would have turned back. This ride was so smooth, effortless. The miles passed like nothing, and he made the trip in under two hours. He stared at the buzzer outside the closed iron gates for the better part of ten minutes trying to decide if he should ring the buzzer or just leave the note. With a difficulty those without some level of autism would have trouble understanding, he finally pressed it. Following a brief exchange on an intercom the gate swung open.

He rode the long driveway past the line of tall pine trees that blocked the view of the mansion until it took a sharp right turn then rode the several hundred feet up to the front door. He received a warm greeting from Vince, who was apparently serving today as doorman and butler.

"You rode all the way here from your home?" he said with surprise.

"Yeah, I have something for Mr. Burke. Is he here?"

"That had to be forty miles. Sorry to tell you the family is out for the day but come in."

"I can't. I don't have a lock for my bike."

"No one is going to take it."

"I can't leave it. Mr. Burke just gave it to me this morning."

"Walter gave you that?" Vince's eyes perked as he made a closer inspection, realizing Ted was on a bike that cost more than some cars.

"Yeah, I won't leave it out here. Could I bring it in the house?"

The entire grounds were encircled by a ten-foot-high wrought iron fence, but Vince figured he wouldn't stop worrying no matter what he said.

"Sure, we'll find a spot."

Once inside, Vince led him to a large table in the kitchen and poured a glass of fruit punch for his guest.

"What can I make you for lunch?"

"Oh, no, thanks, I'm just here to drop something off. It's this envelope. Would you give it to him?"

"I absolutely will. Anything you want me to say with it?"

"I wish I knew what to say. He's always so good to me. He asked me a while ago if I had any stocks I liked. Well, I think I found one. It's this grocery store chain. They bought this shoe company, so they are going to sell groceries and shoes."

"Sounds kind of strange."

"Yeah, right, that's what I thought. Papers thought the same thing. Then I asked myself why would they do that? You see it's a different idea and that's what I like. They got a lot of money, and they are growing fast. I think this is the start of a broader strategy."

"Think about it. Why do people go to a supermarket? 'Cause they have everything. Department store? Because they have everything. So, what if you put the two together? Shoes are only the start. They add more and more stuff like TVs, furniture, clothes, plants. Maybe even new cars someday. You get everything, absolutely everything in one place. The groceries bring you in each week and the convenience sells you the rest."

Vince had been quiet up until now. "Incredible."

"Yeah, that's what I said. It's a great investment. I wrote down the name in the envelope."

"No, by incredible I mean I can understand why Walter is so impressed with you."

"He said that?"

"Not in so many words. But trust me on it. What's the name of the company if you don't mind my asking?"

"Not at all but I doubt you have heard of it. It's called Walmart. They already have a bunch of stores in the South, and my bet is they expand all over."

"I'll check it out. Sure I can't make you something?"

"Yeah positive, I got to be getting back."

"I have a suggestion. How about we put your bike in one of the cars and I drive you home?"

"That's okay. This bike rides like a magic carpet. Just please give Mr. Burke the envelope."

With that, Ted left to go home to interrogate his mom about her conversation with Walter. She played it off that it was all about the bike, making no mention of the gift he had left for graduation day. In the envelope was a card and a brokerage account in Ted's name, funded with more than enough for him to start investing in his own recommendations.

Yearbook

As the school year was winding to its final few days, the teacher sent a question around the room. asking what each of them were doing for summer vacation.

The answers were diverse and initially Anna's was like the others.

"I'm going to camp."

"That's great, Anna," her head indicated the next student should go but Anna continued.

"I've always wanted to go. This year I saved up the money and I get to go for three weeks. It's a sleepaway camp."

Suddenly paying more attention, the teacher clarified with amazement.

"You're paying for it yourself?"

"Yeah, I've been selling pictures and doing makeup," she said with such humility she made it sound like nothing.

The teacher was about to make the biggest deal about that, but Anna provided one more thing.

"It's a fat camp," she said to everyone's stunned expression. "All the kids there are heavy. They teach you about nutrition and how to eat right. I really need to be doing something about my weight."

Cheers started. "You can do it, Anna!" "Show them how it's done!" These were among the many shouts of encouragement amidst what became a cacophony of applause.

Yearbooks were passed out the next day and the order of business was getting them signed.

Almost the entire class wrote something in Ted's, but one stood out as the most meaningful and that was from Anna:

If anyone I know is going to make it big in this world, it will be you,

You gave me so much more than a gold chain.

I will cherish you forever.

—Love always, Anna

Annabelle

Held on a warm day in late May in the vast cathedral, even with all the students, friends, relatives, teachers, and administrators, the church remained barely half full. Of course, the graduation ceremony had to be turned into a mass. One final dose of Catholic before they set off into the world.

Everyone knew when to rise, sit, and kneel. It had been drilled into them over the past eight years like an endless session of boot camp. The extended mass, mostly ignored, mainly served to build anticipation. It ended with the familiar words "Thanks be to God." Before the echo had settled into oblivion, the obligatory speeches started the run-up to the calling of student names and handing out diplomas.

Anyone who has attended such an event knows a surge of applause accompanies the first graduate called. It quickly lessens to a trickle as the realization comes that it would require twenty straight minutes of clapping if it were to continue.

This is not to say some didn't receive more fanfare than others. Ciro had a notable upsurge of cheers thanks to his loudmouthed family. Not surprisingly, Ashton Burke was given above-average recognition despite the absence of his father. He was away on business taking care of seemingly more important things.

There was one, though, who received an ovation so grand it likely held the record for the longest and loudest of any student graduating from that school past, present, or future. Unusual, certainly out of alignment with standard protocol, when this name was called, it was not just the audience who clapped, but also every member of the student body. All of them, down to the last, rose from their seats as well. The applause became virulently contagious and deafening as Anna approached the podium to receive her diploma.

There were whispers in the audience of "She's so talented," and "That's the girl who was doing those sketches at the fair," "She's amazing," "She's incredible." If only they understood how right they were. No one could comprehend after all she had suffered just how great a miracle, a stunning victory, what it took for her to simply be standing there.

Usually allergic to the spotlight, she wore the warmth of the displayed sentiment like a favorite blanket. It was not for herself that this made her so happy, but rather that her nana, who came two hours early to ensure a place in the first row, was witness to it all.

It may have been that some of her peers were reaching for a final shot at redemption. But at its core, down to its heart, what that thunderous applause really turned out to be was a unified apology from the entire class.

Revelation

Concluding with those in the office, Ted had deliberately skipped over an event that had taken place several days before the graduation ceremony. The memory so special, the point so important, he wanted to close with it.

It involved the senior graduation dance. Ted was assigned to help and was given a simple task, but it would never be completed. He was to go to the principal's office to pick up a box of decorations for that night. Principal Bethany and Sister Howard were lamenting about the class that would be leaving. Ted couldn't help but pick up on it.

"I'm sure you'll be glad to be rid of me," he said.

"Why would you say that?" Sister Bethany inquired.

"I know I've been a big pain"—he was going to complete it with "in the ass," but after eight years in the school, knew better.

"You don't see it correctly. This is a difficult time of year for us," Sister Bethany explained.

"It never gets any easier," Sister Howard chimed in.

"All of you are like our children. We've watched you grow up right before our eyes. We are happy you are moving on, but it's still sad to see you go."

"We will definitely miss you," Sister Howard added.

Even though they had come to peace, Ted never liked that old nun and, as usual, spoke without applying a filter.

"You sure? I thought you referred to me as a bastard."

There was a slight gasp from both. Sister Howard quickly brought her hand to her lips.

"I would never say such a thing."

Sister Bethany could not help but shoot her a look.

"Well, if I did, then may God forgive me," Sister Howard responded, "and may you forgive me too."

"Not a problem," Ted replied. "This bastard forgives you."

So inappropriate yet amusing, Sister Bethany would have scolded him had the need to suppress a laugh not been so high. She collected herself and decided to keep it positive.

"I remember the first day you walked in here in your little jacket. I told Sister Howard you were different. Do you remember that?" she called over to Sister Howard.

"Yes, I do. You did say this one is different."

"Different. Yeah, but is that good or bad?" Ted asked.

"Different, Ted? Different isn't good or bad. Different is wonderful. Different is a miracle, a gift from God. Without different there would be no color in this world. No discoveries, no science, no art, nothing at all. Calling you different is a great compliment. You, Ted, truly are a miracle."

"You know I almost didn't make it here," Ted said, now reflecting on his past.

"You remember in third grade when we didn't have any money. I was almost thrown out."

"I remember it well. I prayed for you. I prayed for a miracle and the Lord saw to it."

"Yeah, well, it wasn't the Lord. It was my mother."

"How do you mean?" Sister Bethany replied curiously.

"Not my mother here. You know, my birth mother in Canada. She was the one who paid for it. She saved me."

"No," Sister Howard blurted mindlessly, "it was a wealthy parishioner."

"Loraine!" Sister Bethany snapped at the senile nun.

"Does that wealthy parishioner have a son in my class?" Ted inquired, face now a shade of alabaster.

"You know I can't tell you that," Sister Bethany responded.

Ted knew that meant yes. Becoming dizzy, he felt as though he'd been shot in the head realizing the world is always skewed the way people want to see it. He had committed this mortal mistake.

Memories flashed and pieces fell together. That was the reason Walter Burke knew his name at Ashton's birthday party when he was ten. It suddenly made sense as to why he had been invited at all. Walter Burke probably wanted to get a look at him. Then there was the car ride from the stock exchange. What a strange thing he had said about how sometimes a good deed comes back 850-fold. About two million, the money Walter had made on the stock, divided by 850. The result was roughly, he figured, the cost of a half year of tuition.

Hope and happiness, present just moments before, fled from his body. Heartbroken, he realized there was no one special secretly looking over him. And he would never know her. His birthmother would never be part of his life. There, right in that office he was transported to a funeral that represented a relationship that would never be.

In a feat few could have pulled off, he put a half smile on his face. With a dagger in his heart he turned, and as though a zombie, made his way out the door. The emotion could be held off a few minutes, but not longer.

"Are you okay?" Sister Bethany called from behind her desk.

"I'm fine," Ted replied as he juggled his emotions, trying to make it to the cafeteria before it all fell apart.

A handful of his classmates were putting up decorations at the far end, enabling him to enter unnoticed. He grabbed a folding chair and opened it in the opposite corner of the room. There he sat with his head between his knees, hands clutching the back of his neck. A collection of tears began to gather on the floor beneath his face.

All he wanted was to be alone in misery, but that wish was not granted.

Footsteps revealed the approach of someone. He didn't dare look up, deathly afraid to show the emotion written across his face.

"We need to talk," Anna commanded.

"Now is not a good time," he whispered back.

Seeing there was a crisis, Anna knew this type of situation all too well. She knelt to one knee and placed a hand on his shoulder and began rubbing.

"Are you all right?" she asked, concerned.

"Yeah, I just got some bad news, that's all."

She leaned forward and put her arms around him in a tight embrace. Despite a slight struggle to release him she held it unbroken for some time. She just hugged and let the warmth and the silence speak for itself.

"Is there anything I can do to help? Would you like a tissue?" she finally said softly.

"No, it's okay. I have this," he said, pulling a cloth handkerchief from his pocket and blowing his nose before dabbing his eyes.

"Do you want to talk?"

"No, and please, you saw none of this," he said to Anna as he wiped his eyes.

"Of course not. Sorry to have to do this. I know you're upset, but we still need to talk."

"Can it wait?"

"No, it can't."

Ted sighed. "All right, what is so important?"

"You going to the dance tonight?"

"Ugh. That, I suppose."

"Well, you have to go."

"And why is that?"

"Because you have to ask June to dance."

"Why?"

"Why? Are you serious? You've never noticed how June looks at you? I said when you asked me out there was someone else."

"No, you didn't."

"I said there is someone else who might like to go out with you. You didn't take the hint. Why do you think I said no?"

"I thought you thought I was gross or something."

"Ted, turning you down was one of the hardest things I ever had to do. I'd love to go out with you, but I couldn't do that to my best friend."

"So, you think June likes me?"

"Likes you! Like? Ted, you are using the wrong word."

"June? I don't believe it. If she felt that way, why didn't she ask me out?"

"Did you ever think, Ted, you're the one who's supposed to do that?"

"Well, she could ask me to dance tonight if she wants."

"Ugh," she grunted. "You know, you guys spend so much time trying to get girls, but you're all a bunch of idiots. You have to promise me you'll ask her to dance tonight."

Ted wiped his eyes clean.

"All right, I'll ask her."

"Great! Do it early. Don't wait for half the night to go by. Oh, and this is important. Don't tell her I told you. She'd never speak to me again. Swear you won't."

"I swear I won't say anything."

Candeo

The oversize sports jacket Walter Burke had bought for him years before fit perfectly. Looking sharp, Ted added a red tie peppered with black diamonds and took time to style his hair. He affixed his bull-and-bear tie clip, not to show off, but solely in honor of the man who had saved him those years ago. A splash of cologne topped it off.

Ted waited outside the cafeteria, now transformed into a dance hall, staring at his watch, waiting for it to strike exactly 8:00 p.m. so he could go in. Decorations in place, music yet to start, Itch and Chuck had already taken their places at the far end of the room.

Boys slowly filed in as the minutes passed, but most of the girls preferred to arrive fashionably late. Ashley was earlier than most but only to hold court with her friends outside and shoot condescending looks at the other girls as they entered. All that was set aside as Ashton arrived, this night, chauffeured in his father's Rolls-Royce.

He emerged and pulled his jacket tight onto his frame. Smiling as he passed Ashley and company, he made eye contact with none of them. Every girl had her eye on him, and all wondered who among them would get to be his partner for the first dance. In the pecking order of that evening, it was clear he was highest on the food chain.

The music started, but Ashton was in no rush, clearly enjoying his desirability. He hung with the guys, making small talk, acting as though the girls were invisible. He briefly paused his conversation. All did, when Ashley, dressed in a stunning low-cut obnoxiously tight pink evening gown entered to take all the attention. A few of the girls had already made a bet that if she sneezed, at least one of her boobs would come bursting out of it.

None of the guys were dancing, but a few girls, knowing they stood no chance with Ashton, took themselves out of the running, paired off and danced with each other.

Next it was June, who walked in with Anna and Dorothy. A beautiful blue strapless evening gown, a white rose implanted in her finely styled hair, stiletto heels, perfectly applied makeup, even the girls did a double take.

"Holy smokes! Is that June?" Chuck blurted.

"Ashley's got competition tonight," Itch added. "What do you think, Ted?"

Ted stared like a mute statue, wrestling with what he was seeing against what he had been told and found himself unable to reconcile the two.

Music was playing, and a thin line formed around the dance floor. Eyes were on Ashton, who was still playing it cool, chatting with the guys and pretending to pay no attention at all to the girls.

"Maybe I'll ask June to dance," Ted responded to the previous question, having paused so long they had forgotten it was still out there.

"Dude, you would have more of a chance getting me to dance with you," Itch retorted.

"Yeah," Ted croaked in a sigh, then resumed his position holding up the wall behind them. Anna was in no mood for his hesitation.

"Well? There she is. Go get her!"

"Nah, see, I can't dance to this stuff. I need a slow dance. I'll ask her when the right song comes on. How about that?"

"That has to be the silliest excuse. Get going and ask her. I told you how she feels."

"Yeah, I know but Anna, come on. Look at her and look at me. I can't ask her. Just forget it, I'm not going to do this. Seriously, I can't."

Anna put both hands on his shoulders. "I was given advice one time by someone very great, and it changed my whole life. Do you want to know what it was?"

"Tell me!" Ted responded. The opportunity to behold such a nugget of wisdom was the type of thing he lived for.

"He told me I could never accomplish anything great until I let go of my fear."

The surest way to impress Ted was to twist his own words against him. Hit by his own grenade, he headed for June, who was standing beside Dorothy and gazing out over the dance floor.

A few paces away, he stopped to gather his nerve. June glanced over and saw him approach but pretended not to notice. She turned her head back to the dance floor, only to find herself eye to eye with Ashton. Ted watched helplessly as his hopes crashed to the floor.

"May I have the honor of first dance with you tonight?" he inquired, elegantly holding his hand out toward her.

June smiled while she fished for an appropriate response.

"I'm very flattered, I really am, but there's someone else I'm hoping is going to ask me."

Confused, Ashton needed a second for it to sink in. He was convinced there was not one girl who would consider turning him down. Ever the gentleman, though, he quickly recovered.

"Well, I hope he realizes what a lucky guy he is. How about you? Would you like to dance?" he said almost reflexively to the girl behind June, attempting to stabilize his pride.

Not needing to be asked twice, she nearly knocked June over in her rush to take him up on it.

With the two now away, June gave a hard, deliberate stare at Ted, then replaced it with an aloof look as she turned away. A romantic slow dance began to play. Ted's knees were wobbling, but he stepped the few feet up to her and rubbed his sweaty palms against his jacket. June looked at him, giving an inviting but reserved smile.

Swallowing, then taking a breath, he wanted to look away but didn't. If he was going to get shot down, she would have to say it to his face.

"Um, June," he began, "Anna told me you wanted me to ask you to dance."

The smile left June's face. She turned and leaned in toward him, her eyes now fixed on his.

"Well, Ted, why don't you find out if Anna is correct?"

Such a beautiful mind and then to add her golden-blond hair, gorgeous face, magnificent blue eyes, taking him in, no less. Wishing he could run for the door or just pass out, he reluctantly continued.

"June, would you like to dance? Dance with me, that is?"

Barely allowing him to finish, "I'd love to," she replied.

Before she moved toward Ted, she looked at Dorothy, who tapped her elbow and gave a coy smile.

"See, I told you he would ask," she whispered.

"Thanks for everything," June shot back before turning to Ted trying to contain an excitement that otherwise would have been embarrassing.

"There's one problem. I don't know how to dance," Ted confessed.

"That's no problem. I'll show you."

She grabbed his hand and yanked him so hard toward the center of the floor that it nearly gave him whiplash. Hauling him to the very center, Ted reasoned, could only mean one thing—she intended to humiliate him. There could be no other possibility.

June did have a motive too simple for Ted to grasp. She wanted everyone to see that she was the chosen one dancing with him.

As clueless to dancing as most other things, he stood before her like a deer in the headlights. She took one hand and began guiding him along. He responded by reaching out and gingerly placing his fingertips under the bottom of her ribcage, afraid to touch her in any way she might find offensive.

"You can hold me if you want to," she said in response to his hesitation.

With the invitation, he slid his arm behind her back, which put them in contact.

"Wow!" he blurted from the incredible sensation of having a girl in his arms for the first time. He cringed, embarrassed, wishing he hadn't verbalized the feeling. June didn't mind it at all. Although unsaid, she had thought the same.

Halfway before they had even started, the song soon ended. He felt June's arm stiffen against his back like a steel bar, making it clear he was going nowhere. A second slow song came on, which Ted thought a lucky coincidence until he saw Anna talking with the DJ. On the mostly empty floor, the only other guy he had to share it with was Ashton, who, already on his third partner, proved to be a skilled dancer. This raised a question.

"Why didn't you want to dance with Ashton?" he whispered into June's ear.

The song played on, and as the pause for her answer grew, he became convinced that she wished she'd accepted. How long he wondered before she would walk off and lament to her friends about the whole thing. She ended his wondering when she gently pulled his earlobe down toward her so she could whisper directly into his ear.

"Because he's not you."

Unable to comprehend, he could not resist. "First dance with him? You know you blew the opportunity of a lifetime."

"Not at all, I want to spend tonight with you more than anyone."

It rattled through his head. His brow furrowed. "Why!" he exclaimed.

June let go and took several steps back, grabbing everyone's attention.

Conversations stopped, drinks motionless, contrasting the blaring music was otherwise silence. All thought the same. What had Ted done to screw this up?

June looked to the floor in frustration, but when her gaze returned to Ted, her heart melted all over again.

"Well, it's not because you are romantic," she replied, then softened. "Listen, you're a really smart guy. I'm sure, if you take a good look at yourself, you'll figure it out."

June could see the expression on all faces as they gazed at Ted with amused ridicule. That was unacceptable. How dare they! With all eyes upon them, and specifically because all eyes were upon them, she stepped up, stood on her toes, wrapped her arms around his neck, and placed a kiss so solidly on his lips he could feel his heart beating three feet outside his chest.

That was the moment any care of what anyone else thought disappeared. The night continued, and one song melted into the next. Ted never comprehended how much it thrilled her to be the one in his arms, nor the jealousy heaped on her by so many of the other girls.

Following a slow start, Ted turned out to be pretty good on the dance floor and confidently took the lead. June relaxed, taking opportunities to look into his eyes and admiringly run her fingers over the well-defined muscles in his arms.

Guys approached, thinking they might cut in, but the scowl Ted gave kept them from asking. The girls, having no such barrier, made it through. While many asked for a dance, Ted responded politely that he was already taken. That was until Ashley.

"My turn," she said with a confidence as though she were owed some obligation.

"Take a number," Ted responded abruptly.

"I hate her so much. She's so into herself. She always has to ruin it for everyone else," June whispered into Ted's ear once she had turned away.

Having never experienced something so foreign as rejection, Ashley figured Ted would change his mind if given a minute.

"Come on, what's one dance?" she bargained upon her return.

Ted broke from June so his reply would be clear. For an instant, she thought he was releasing her to accept the invitation. In one eye was confidence, the other doubt, but he quickly put her fears to rest.

"Ashley, unless you're blind, you can see how beautiful she is. And we all know how smart she is. But I learned something tonight for myself, and that is just how sweet she is. So, no, I'm not letting her go. Not even for one single dance."

When we put someone on a pedestal, all too often the image turns out unjustified. As Ted brushed Ashley away, June thought to herself with delight that perhaps the pedestal she had placed him on had not been high enough. She sighed in relief and let her head melt into his shoulder where it remained for most of the night.

On the last song, Ted ended the evening by delivering a kiss that made the one she had given him earlier seem like a peck on the cheek, prompting a throat clearing from a nearby nun. While the evening was wondrous, something much greater had occurred.

* * *

Ted concluded his story to those in the office.

"It was while I was dancing with June that I realized the trophy shelf I had, despite being devoid of trophies, had through the years filled to such an extent there was room for not one thing more. The greatest miracles in our lives are a result of an innumerable number of the smallest. That night I attained something I wish everyone to achieve. A lesson I never let go. I found satisfaction, true happiness, in the knowledge that I was nothing more, and not one bit less, than just me."

www.ingramcontent.com/pod-product-compliance
Lightning Source LLC
LaVergne TN
LVHW010625110826
845149LV00014B/2780